D0840643

The Complete Book of Christian Prayer

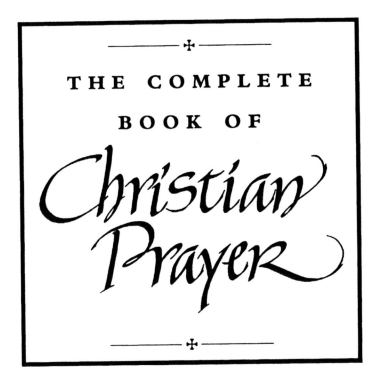

THE COMPLETE

BOOK OF

Christian Prayer

CONTINUUM

NEW YORK · LONDON

2000
The Continuum International Publishing Group Inc
370 Lexington Avenue, New York, N.Y. 10017

Selection, arrangement and indexing of this anthology
Copyright © SPCK 1995

All rights reserved. No part of this book may be reproduced,
stored in a retrieval system, or transmitted, in any form or by any means,
electronic, mechanical, photocopying, recording, or otherwise, without
the written permission of The Continuum Publishing Company

Printed in the United States of America

ISBN 0–8264–1269–6 (pbk)

Library of Congress Catalog Card Number
95–70331

CONTENTS

CONTENTS

PREFACE

Continuum is publishing this new anthology of prayers in the hope that it will prove to be a useful resource both for personal reference and for all who are called to lead others in worship – whether in church, in school, or in the home. With that in mind, our overriding concern in selecting the prayers has been that they should readily lend themselves to being prayed by Christians today, and that nothing should be included that is now of little more than antiquarian interest.

Another major concern has been to include prayers from a wide variety of traditions, places, and times, while also representing some of the best material from prayer writers of the present. Over a third of the 1,200 prayers gathered here are by 20th-century authors, and many are by authors still writing today. Altogether there are over 560 different sources represented – more, we believe, than in any other collection of prayers to have been published.

Where the information is available, years of birth and death are given after the names of authors, except for those born in the current century.

Although initially we had hoped to include verses from favourite hymns, space has permitted only those that are known to have begun their life as prayers, whether as poetry or prose, before being set to music.

To assist the reader, the entire collection is thoroughly indexed, both by theme and author. For ease of reference the prayers are arranged in alphabetical order of author within each section – preceded, where appropriate, by biblical prayers and by those designated 'source unknown'. (Occasionally this rule has been broken in order to contain as many complete prayers as possible on a page.)

In addition to those authors and publishers listed in the Acknowledgements at the back of the book, we wish to express our thanks to the following authors and advisors for their help in suggesting, and in some cases writing, prayers that appear in this anthology:

David Adam, John Barton, Nicholas Beddow, Fiona Bowie, Lavinia Byrne IBVM, Frank Colquhoun, Oliver Davies, Ruth Etchells, Monica

Furlong, Kathy Galloway, Tracy Hansen, Richard Harries, Richard Holloway, Martin Israel, Gordon Jeff, Christopher Lamb, Henry Morgan, Janet Morley, Gordon Mursell, Lesslie Newbigin, Peter Nott, Michael Perham, John Polkinghorne, Brother Ramon SSF, Stephen Smalley, Frazer Smith, David Stancliffe, R. S. Sugirtharajah, Angela Tilby, Catherine Wakeling.

Special thanks are due to Robert Backhouse for his work on the initial draft of the anthology, and to Margaret Pawley and Jennifer Wild for their help and advice in editing subsequent drafts.

The Complete Book of Christian Prayer

---✠---

INTRODUCTION

APPROACHES TO PRAYER

---✠---

Draw near to God, and God

will draw near to you.

James 4.8

INTRODUCTION

APPROACHES TO PRAYER

Beginning to pray

We all come to prayer with a tangled mass of motives – altruistic and selfish, merciful and hateful, loving and bitter. Frankly, this side of eternity we will never unravel the good from the bad, the loving and bitter. But what I have come to see is that God is big enough to receive us with all our mixture. We do not have to be bright, or pure, or filled with faith, or anything. That is what grace means, and not only are we saved by grace, we live by it as well. And we pray by it. . . .

We will never have pure enough motives, or be good enough, or know enough in order to pray rightly. We simply must set all these things aside and begin praying. In fact, it is in the very act of prayer itself – the intimate, ongoing interaction with God – that these matters are cared for in due time.[1]

Richard Foster

Being yourself

The crucial and liberating truth to grasp is that it is actually me-as-I-am that God is wanting to meet when I pray. The incredible fact is GOD WANTS TO MEET ME! What a wonderful truth! But how rarely it sinks in. It is because of this that we may have the freedom in prayer to be just who we are, and how we are, with no super-spiritual act, no pretence.

It is because God has reconciled us to himself that we are able to meet him in prayer – not because of how we are or the way we feel. This means, then, that I don't have to wait until I'm feeling 'good enough' or 'spiritual enough' to pray.[2]

Paul Wallis

To pray is to live

Praying is no easy matter. It demands a relationship in which you allow the other to enter into the very centre of your person, to speak there, to touch the sensitive core of your being, and allow the other to see so much that you would rather leave in darkness. And when do you really want to do that? Perhaps you would let the other come across the threshold to say something, to touch something, but to allow the other into that place where your life gets its form, that is dangerous and calls for defence.

The resistance to praying is like the resistance of tightly clenched fists. This image shows the tension, the desire to cling tightly to yourself, a greediness which betrays fear. . . . When you dare to let go and surrender one of those many fears, your hand relaxes and your palms spread out in a gesture of receiving. You must have patience, of course, before your hands are completely open and their muscles relaxed. . . .

Then you feel a bit of new freedom, and praying becomes a joy, a spontaneous reaction to the world and the people around you. Praying becomes effortless, inspired, and lively or peaceful and quiet. Then you recognize the festive and the modest as moments of prayer. You begin to suspect that to pray is to live.[3]

Henri Nouwen

With God in the darkness

I am quite sure that there will always be moments of inner peace and joy as a result of spending time in prayer for those of us who do not regard ourselves as greatly advanced in the spiritual life. Nevertheless, the experience of many of us is that prayer can be very hard work indeed. Quite often prayer is unrewarding and there is not much joy in the doing of it. It is at moments like these that we can be tempted to give it up. That would be the fatal mistake. We have to keep going. One reason is this: we are learning that an important part of prayer is to please God. We want to please, so that is why we pray. Carrying on when we seem to be getting nowhere is a proof of our faithfulness to God, and it shows that we are selfless and generous in our service of him. We are prepared to do the right thing for his sake, and not for ours.

From time to time our motives must be purified and so must our hearts. We shall be asked, perhaps, to experience only darkness in our prayer life. We find ourselves without any support. Nothing is of any avail. Spiritual books, fine thoughts, great sermons – they leave us cold and unresponsive. That can all be very disappointing when we can honestly say that we have done our best to be faithful to prayer. There is a reason for this too. Our faith is being purified. This means that we are being led to trust less and less in ourselves, in our own ideas about God, and more in God himself, and in God alone. We have to go through these periods of darkness in order to be able to receive his light. And when faith is purified (and it can be a painful process) charity increases. We love more.[4]

Basil Hume

The language of love

When we pray we know two things about God. One is that he is very near to us, and is our friend, our brother, sister, father and mother. He is very close to us indeed. However, we also know that he is so different that words fail us. All we can do is use poetry – that is, words which don't just mean what they say, but which try to point beyond.

'Glory to you, our mighty Prime Minister' would sound bombastic and far from the humility which expresses true service. But 'Glory to you, Eternal Father, Almighty God' doesn't mean what it says: it is poetry which attempts to say the unsayable. It is not the language of bombast, but the language of love, where nothing can say too much about the one who is loved. To speak such words as these is not to grovel or flatter – it is a special language, the language of thanksgiving, praise and love. It is saying a poem to someone who deserves poems. If we simply take the words at face value we have missed the point. Poetry plays a very important role in our conversation with God.[5]

George Guiver

Praying by heart

There is a need for some sort of prayer which is not spontaneous but which is truly rooted in conviction. To find this you can draw from a great many existing prayers. We already have a rich panoply of prayers which were wrought in the throes of faith, by the Holy Spirit. For example, we have the Psalms, we have so many short and long prayers in the liturgical wealth of all the Churches from which we can draw. What matters is that you should learn and know enough of such prayers so that at the right moment you are able to find the right prayers. It is a question of learning by heart enough meaningful passages, from the Psalms or from the prayers of the saints. Each of us is sensitive to certain particular passages. Mark these passages that go deep into your heart, that move you deeply, that make sense, that express something which is already within your experience, either of sin, or of bliss in God, or of struggle. Learn those passages, because one day when you are so completely low, so profoundly desperate that you cannot call out of your soul any spontaneous expression, any spontaneous wording, you will discover that these words come up and offer themselves to you as a gift of God, as a gift of the Church, as a gift of holiness, helping our simple lack of strength. And then you really need the prayers you have learnt and made a part of yourself.[6]

Anthony Bloom

Becoming still

Christian tradition recognizes that it is difficult for busy and active people to be still, and that is why many traditional methods of prayer are very repetitive, the repetition being designed to still the mind. If the repetition is also rhythmic, either in time with our step if we are walking, or with our breathing if we are physically still, it can be even more effective. The repetition may be of a single word, or of a simple phrase, like the famous pilgrim prayer, 'Lord Jesus Christ have mercy on me', or of a longer prayer, for example, the Our Father, each syllable being repeated in time with our step if we are walking, or with our breath if physically still. Many traditional forms of prayer began as pilgrim prayers. When walking it is more difficult to concentrate the mind than when we are still, but the constant repetition of a word or phrase in time with our step can induce an inner stillness of mind. In such a stillness, the rhythmic repetition may cease. If this happens, let it happen and do not continue with the rhythmic repetition. In general, follow your own inner promptings in prayer rather than be slavishly obedient to some prescribed method.[7]

Gerard Hughes

Loving God

If prayer works, the human personality always increases. It never diminishes. The self that emerges this way comes forth unshackled, scoured, clean, uncovered because anchored in God. Yoked to a true centre, one finds everything personal rearranged. This is the leaving of the world that the saints did literally in their retirement to the wilderness or a remote hermitage, which those who pray sincerely today do symbolically. The inner movement, however, remains what it always was – detachment from peripheral concerns as one is drawn toward the heart of things. We seek, now, first things above all else, seeing the goal of life as praising and glorifying God in numerous ways, thoughts, words, deeds, some open and obvious, some subtle, even sly. This is what is meant by loving God with all our heart, strength, mind, and soul. This is a love so full it spills over to change all our dealings with each other, with our neighbours, with our own selves, as the Spirit invades psyche and soul and enlists us in its service.[8]

Ann and Barry Ulanov

Loving humanity

The God of Christian prayer is an involved God, a social God. Involvement and society are among the essential marks of Christian prayer because this prayer is actually a participation in God. God is involved in humanity, and so prayer is an involvement in humanity. God is social and not isolated, and so prayer is a social, not an isolated, activity. There is a fundamental solidarity about prayer which is central to the Christian understanding. The taking of manhood into God embraces spirituality and politics, the inner and outer worlds, in one process. . . . The quest for union with God and the quest for the unity of mankind is one quest. Prayer needs always to be seen within this social context, for there is no such thing as *private* prayer. The word private comes from the Latin *privatio* which means robbery. To the Christian, nothing is private, least of all prayer. God is not private, but personal and social, Being-in-relationship. That is the meaning of the symbol of the Trinity: that in God there is social life, community, sharing. To share in God is to share in that life.[9]

Kenneth Leech

Discerning God's will

Part of the Spirit's gift is discernment. If we are to pray for ourselves and others according to the mind of Christ we need to be led by the Spirit to know what to pray for and how and when. Jesus too had to pray for discernment; his mind was subjected to the Spirit not automatically but through prayer. He needed to soak himself in the Father's presence and sensitize himself to the Father's will. . . .

In conforming our minds to the mind of Christ the Spirit also gives us the attitudes the Lord demanded if prayer is to be acceptable: total forgivingness, a spirit of repentance and unconditional trust. If we come before God to ask for healing for others, whether physical, mental or moral, whether individual or social, we must be prepared for the work to begin on ourselves: 'Heal my wife/husband, but change me first'; 'Heal that apparently impossible situation, but begin by clearing the blocks in me that prevent me from being an open channel for your power.' In attuning us to himself the Lord deepens our loving awareness of one another; when our relationships are right he can use us as channels for what he wants to give infinitely more than we can want to receive it.[10]

Maria Boulding

Prayer makes a difference

All events are controlled into being what they are – a stone falling, a person dying, a baby being born – by a vast network of constraints: some may be passive, as frequently the laws of motion are; others are active, belonging maybe to the agency of human will (itself constrained). All of these are sustained and held in being by the constantly creative action of the Holy Spirit. But what prayer for others does is to bring the *particular* constraint of God to bear, in a deliberate relation to this person, or this moment, or this event. This will not cancel the other, existing constraints. Some things are as impossible to God in the conditions of his own creation as they are to us: God cannot walk uphill and downhill at the same time any more than we can. . . .

But does that mean that prayer for others is impotent and that it cannot make a difference? Does it mean that the prayer of faith is never anything more than a coincidence in relation to what was going to happen anyway? The answer to those questions is, No: absolutely and certainly not so. Prayer always makes a difference; and the difference may be dramatic in terms of healing. But why, then, is the difference not always dramatic and obvious? The answer is, because prayer does not cancel or suspend the particular network of constraint which is bringing this event or outcome into being. Prayer is the means through which the specific action of God works in and through that network, bringing the event into what will always be a different outcome from what it would otherwise have been.[11]

John Bowker

Prayer never ends

Prayer is the sum of our relationship with God.

We are what we pray.

The degree of our faith is the degree of our prayer. The strength of our hope is the strength of our prayer. The warmth of our charity is the warmth of our prayer. No more nor less.

Our prayer has had a beginning because we have had a beginning. But it will have no end. It will accompany us into eternity and will be completed in our contemplation of God, when we join in the harmony of heaven and are 'filled with the flood of God's delights'. The story of our earthly-heavenly life will be the story of our prayer.[12]

Carlo Carretto

REFERENCES

[1] Richard Foster: *Prayer* (HarperCollins San Francisco/Hodder & Stoughton 1992)

[2] Paul Wallis: *Rough Ways in Prayer* (Triangle/SPCK 1991)

[3] Henri Nouwen: *Springs of Hope* (Bantam Books/Darton, Longman & Todd 1989)

[4] Basil Hume: *To Be a Pilgrim* (SPCK/St Paul Publications 1984)

[5] George Guiver: *Everyday God* (Triangle/SPCK 1994)

[6] Anthony Bloom: *School for Prayer* (Darton, Longman & Todd 1970)

[7] Gerard Hughes: *God of Surprises* (Darton, Longman & Todd/Cowley Publications 1985)

[8] Ann and Barry Ulanov, in Jones, Wainwright & Yarnold (eds): *The Study of Spirituality* (SPCK/OUP New York 1986)

[9] Kenneth Leech: *True Prayer* (SPCK/HarperCollins San Francisco 1980)

[10] Maria Boulding: *Marked for Life* (Triangle/SPCK 1979/85)

[11] John Bowker: *A Year to Live* (SPCK 1991)

[12] Carlo Carretto: *Letters from the Desert* (Orbis Books 1972)

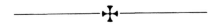

THE SPIRIT OF PRAYER

Be still and know that I am God.

Psalm 46.10

SEEKING GOD'S PRESENCE

Father, my Father! 1
Send the Spirit of your Son into my heart.

Galatians 4.6 (Good News Bible, adapted)

God be in my head, and in my understanding; 2
God be in mine eyes, and in my looking;
God be in my mouth, and in my speaking;
God be in my heart, and in my thinking;
God be at mine end, and at my departing.

Source unknown (found in Pynson's Horae, 1514)

O Lord my God, 3
    teach my heart where and how to seek you,
    where and how to find you.
    Lord, if you are not here but absent,
        where shall I seek you?
    But you are everywhere, so you must be here,
        why then do I not seek you? . . .
Lord, I am not trying to make my way to your height,
for my understanding is in no way equal to that,
but I do desire to understand a little of your truth
    which my heart already believes and loves.
I do not seek to understand so that I may believe,
    but I believe so that I may understand;
        and what is more,
I believe that unless I do believe I shall not understand.

Anselm, 1033–1109

4

O supreme and unapproachable light!
O whole and blessed truth!
How far thou art from me, who am so near to thee!
How far art thou removed from my vision,
though I am so near to thine!
Everywhere thou art wholly present,
and I see thee not.
In thee I move, and in thee I have my being,
and cannot come to thee;
thou art within me, and about me,
and I feel thee not.

Anselm, 1033–1109

5

Look upon us, O Lord,
and let all the darkness of our souls vanish
before the beams of thy brightness.
Fill us with holy love,
and open to us the treasures of thy wisdom.
All our desire is known unto thee,
therefore perfect what thou hast begun,
and what thy Spirit has awakened us to ask in prayer.
We seek thy face,
turn thy face unto us and show us thy glory.
Then shall our longing be satisfied,
and our peace shall be perfect.

Augustine, 354–430

6 Lord Jesus Christ, pierce my soul with thy love so that I may always long for thee alone, who art the bread of angels and the fulfilment of the soul's deepest desires. May my heart always hunger and feed upon thee, so that my soul may be filled with the sweetness of thy presence. May my soul thirst for thee, who art the source of life, wisdom, knowledge, light and all the riches of God our Father. May I always seek and find thee, think upon thee, speak to thee and do all things for the honour and glory of thy holy name. Be always my only hope, my peace, my refuge and my help in whom my heart is rooted so that I may never be separated from thee.

Bonaventure, 1217–74

Come, Lord, work upon us, set us on fire and clasp us close, be 7
fragrant to us, draw us to thy love, let us run to thee.

Augustine, 354–430

My God, I love thee above all else and thee I desire as my last end. 8
Always and in all things, with my whole heart, and strength I seek
thee. If thou give not thyself to me, thou givest nothing; if I find thee
not, I find nothing. Grant to me, therefore, most loving God, that I
may ever love thee for thyself above all things, and seek thee in all
things in this life present, so that at last I may find thee and keep thee
for ever in the world to come.

Thomas Bradwardine, c.1290–1349

God of surprises, 9
when I think you are not present in my life,
you reveal yourself in the love of friends and family
and nurture me in your never-ending affection.

God of surprises,
when we think you are not present in our community,
you labour to make us of one heart
and cause us to share gladly and generously.

God of surprises,
when people think you are not present in our world,
you bring hope out of despair
and create growth out of difficulty.

God of surprises,
you are ever with us.

When the days go by and our vision fades,
keep surprising us.
When our hope dims and our patience wears thin,
keep coming to us.
Teach us to keep our lamps lit
and to be prepared,
that we may see your loving presence among us.

Francis Brienen

10   My God, my God, let me for once look on thee
As though nought else existed, we alone!
And as creation crumbles, my soul's spark
Expands till I can say – Even for myself
I need thee and I feel thee and I love thee.

Robert Browning, 1812–89

11   May your Spirit guide my mind,
Which is so often dull and empty.
Let my thoughts always be on you,
And let me see you in all things.

May your Spirit quicken my soul,
Which is so often listless and lethargic.
Let my soul be awake to your presence,
And let me know you in all things.

May your Spirit melt my heart,
Which is so often cold and indifferent.
Let my heart be warmed by your love,
And let me feel you in all things.

Johann Freylinghausen, 1670–1739

12 Lord, thou art in me and shalt never be lost out of me, but I am not near thee till I have found thee. Nowhere need I run to seek thee, but within me where already thou art. Thou art the treasure hidden within me: draw me therefore to thee that I may find thee and serve and possess thee for ever.

Walter Hilton, 14th century (adapted)

13   God, of thy goodness, give me thyself,
for thou art sufficient for me.
I may not ask for anything less
than what befits my full worship of thee.
If I were to ask anything less I should always be in want,
for in thee alone do I have all.

Julian of Norwich, 1342–c.1416

Grant, O Lord, that I may be so ravished in the wonder of thy love   *14*
that I may forget myself and all things; may feel neither prosperity
nor adversity; may not fear to suffer all the pain in the world rather
than be parted from thee.

O let me find thee more inwardly and verily present with me than I
am with myself; and make me most circumspect how I do use myself
in the presence of thee, my holy Lord.

Robert Leighton, 1611–84

Lord, make me see thy glory in every place.   *15*

Michelangelo, 1475–1564

My Lord and my God, take me from all that keeps me from thee.   *16*
My Lord and my God, grant me all that leads me to thee.
My Lord and my God, take me from myself and give me completely
   to thee.

Nicholas of Flue, 1417–87

Lift up our souls, O Lord, to the pure, serene light of thy presence;   *17*
that there we may breathe freely, there repose in thy love, there may
be at rest from ourselves, and from thence return, arrayed in thy
peace, to do and bear what shall please thee; for thy holy name's sake.

Edward Bouverie Pusey, 1800–82

Lord, come to me, my door is open.   *18*

Michel Quoist

O God of peace, who hast taught us that in returning and in rest we   *19*
shall be saved, and in quietness and in confidence shall be our
strength: by the might of thy Spirit lift us, we pray thee, to thy presence, where we may be still and know that thou art God; through
Jesus Christ our Lord.

J. W. Suter, 1890–

20 Come, true light.
Come, life eternal.
Come, hidden mystery.
Come, treasure without name.
Come, reality beyond all words.
Come, person beyond all understanding.
Come, rejoicing without end.
Come, light that knows no evening.
Come, unfailing expectation of the saved.
Come, raising of the fallen.
Come, resurrection of the dead.
Come, all-powerful, for unceasingly you create, refashion and
    change all things by your will alone.
Come, invisible whom none may touch and handle.
Come, for you continue always unmoved, yet at every instant you are
    wholly in movement; you draw near to us who lie in hell, yet you
    remain higher than the heavens.
Come, for your name fills our hearts with longing and is ever on our
    lips; yet who you are and what you nature is, we cannot say or
    know.
Come, Alone to the alone.
Come, for you are yourself the desire that is within me.
Come, the consolation of my humble soul.
Come, my joy, my endless delight.

Symeon the New Theologian, 949–1022

21 When the heart is hard and parched up, come upon me with a shower
    of mercy.
When grace is lost from life, come with a burst of song.
When tumultuous work raises its din on all sides shutting me out
    from beyond, come to me, my Lord of silence, with thy peace and
    rest.
When my beggarly heart sits crouched, shut up in a corner, break
    open the door, my king, and come with the ceremony of a king.
When desire blinds the mind with delusion and dust, O thou holy
    One, thou wakeful, come with thy light and thunder.

Rabindranath Tagore, 1861–1941

Lord, enfold me in the depths of your heart; and there hold me, refine, 22
purge, and set me on fire, raise me aloft, until my own self knows
utter annihilation.

Pierre Teilhard de Chardin, 1881–1955

Lord Jesus, I am not an eagle. All I have are the eyes and the heart of 23
one. In spite of my littleness, I dare to gaze at the sun of love, and long
to fly toward it. I want to imitate the eagles, but all I can do is flap my
small wings. What shall I do? With cheerful confidence I shall stay
gazing at the sun till I die. Nothing will frighten me, neither wind nor
rain. O my beloved sun, I delight in feeling small and helpless in your
presence; and my heart is at peace.

Thérèse of Lisieux, 1873–97

Wilt thou not visit me? 24
The plant beside me feels thy gentle dew,
And every blade of grass I see
From thy deep earth its quickening moisture drew.

Wilt thou not visit me?
Thy morning calls on me with cheering tone;
And every hill and tree
Lend but one voice – the voice of thee alone.

Come, for I need thy love,
More than the flower the dew or grass the rain;
Come, gently as thy holy dove;
And let me in thy sight rejoice to live again.

I will not hide from them
When thy storms come, though fierce may be their wrath,
But bow with leafy stem,
And strengthened follow on thy chosen path.

Yes, thou wilt visit me:
Nor plant nor tree thine eye delights so well,
As, when from sin set free,
My spirit loves with thine in peace to dwell.

Jones Very, 1813–80

25 Bless us in all we think and do, seeking to know the light of thy truth and to taste of thy love. The world is too much with us: help us to get nearer to thee and to the things and thoughts that die not, evermore. Thou hast promised that thou wilt hear and answer the prayer of thy children in their needs. Save us from ourselves at all times, O our God, and keep us for thy kingdom.

Lauchlan Maclean Watt, 1867–1957

26 O Lord God, in whom we live and move and have our being, open our eyes that we may behold thy fatherly presence ever with us. Draw our hearts to thee with the power of thy love. Teach us to be anxious for nothing, and when we have done what thou givest us to do, help us, O God our Saviour, to leave the issue to thy wisdom. Take from us all doubt and mistrust. Lift our hearts up to thee in heaven, and make us to know that all things are possible to us through thy Son our Redeemer.

Brooke Foss Westcott, 1825–1901

PREPARING TO PRAY

27 Holy Spirit, help me, weak as I am; I do not know how I ought to pray. See into my heart, and plead for me in groans that words cannot express.

Romans 8.26–7 (Good News Bible, adapted)

28 O Lord, the Scripture says, 'There is a time for silence and a time for speech.' Saviour, teach me the silence of humility, the silence of wisdom, the silence of love, the silence of perfection, the silence that speaks without words, the silence of faith. Lord teach me to silence my own heart that I may listen to the gentle movement of the Holy Spirit within me and sense the depths which are of God.

Source unknown, 16th century

Give us grace, almighty Father, to address thee with all our hearts as   29
well as with our lips. Thou art everywhere present: from thee no secrets can be hidden. Teach us to fix our thoughts on thee, reverently and with love, so that our prayers are not in vain, but are acceptable to thee, now and always; through Jesus Christ our Lord.

Jane Austen, 1775–1817

Grant us grace, almighty Father, so to pray as to deserve to be heard.   30

Jane Austen, 1775–1817

Lord God,   31
teach me
the precious insignificance of prayer.

Teach me the value
of its hiddenness in my public life;
    its wastefulness in the world's eyes;
    its disregard for eloquence
    if my spirit can only groan.

Let my prayer be filled
with the enjoyment of you
for your name's sake
    and for none other.

John Bell (Iona Community)

O God, early in the morning I cry to you. Help me to pray and to con-   32
centrate my thoughts on you; I cannot do this alone.

    In me there is darkness, but with you there is light; I am lonely, but you do not leave me; I am feeble in heart, but with you there is help; I am restless, but with you there is peace.

    In me there is bitterness, but with you there is patience; I do not understand your ways, but you know the way for me.

Dietrich Bonhoeffer

33 Almighty God, from whom every good prayer cometh, deliver us, when we draw nigh to thee, from coldness of heart and wanderings of mind, that with steadfast thought and kindled desire we may worship thee in the faith and spirit of Jesus Christ our Lord.

William Bright, 1824–1901

34 Give me a candle of the Spirit, O God, as I go down into the deeps of my being. Show me the hidden things, the creatures of my dreams, the storehouse of forgotten memories and hurts. Take me down to the spring of my life, and tell me my nature and my name. Give me freedom to grow, so that I may become that self, the seed of which you planted in me at my making. Out of the deep I cry to you, O God.

Jim Cotter (based on a prayer by George Appleton)

35 Teach me to pray, pray thou thyself in me.

François Fénelon, 1651–1715

36   In silence
To be there before you Lord, that's all.
To shut the eyes of my body,
To shut the eyes of my soul,
And to be still and silent,
To expose myself to you who are there, exposed to me.

To be there before you, the Eternal Presence.
I am willing to feel nothing, Lord,
    to see nothing,
    to hear nothing.

Empty of all ideas,
    of all images,
In the darkness.
Here I am, simply
To meet you without obstacles,
In the silence of faith,
Before you, Lord.

Michel Quoist

O Lord, hear our prayers, not according to the poverty of our asking 37
but according to the richness of your grace, so that our lives may conform to those desires which accord with your will; through Jesus
Christ our Lord.

Reinhold Niebuhr, 1892–1971

Our heavenly Father, who through thy Son Jesus Christ hast said that 38
men ought always to pray and not to faint, we beseech thee, teach us
to pray. Our spirit is willing but our flesh is weak. Give us grace each
day to approach thy throne and seek thy face; to be concerned as
much for thy glory as for our need; and in everything by prayer and
supplication with thanksgiving to make our requests known to thee,
until all our lives be gathered up into thy presence and every breath is
prayer, through Jesus Christ thy Son, our ransom and mediator.

John R. W. Stott

Holy Jesus, give me the gift and spirit of prayer; and do thou by thy 39
gracious intercession supply my ignorance, and passionate desires,
and imperfect choices; procuring and giving me such returns of
favour which may support my needs, and serve the ends of religion
and the Spirit, which thy wisdom chooses, and thy passion hath
purchased, and thy grace loves to bestow upon all thy saints and
servants.

Jeremy Taylor, 1613–67

Teach us to pray often, that we may pray oftener. 40

Jeremy Taylor, 1613–67

41 Enable me, O God, to collect and compose my thoughts before an immediate approach to you in prayer. May I be careful to have my mind in order when I take upon myself the honour to speak to the Sovereign Lord of the universe, remembering that upon the temper of my soul depends, in very great measure, my success.

You are infinitely too great to be trifled with, too wise to be imposed on by a mock devotion, and abhor a sacrifice without a heart. Help me to entertain an habitual sense of your perfections, as an admirable help against cold and formal performances.

Save me from engaging in rash and precipitate prayers and from abrupt breaking away to follow business or pleasure as though I had never prayed.

Susanna Wesley, 1669–1742

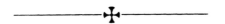

PRAISE AND THANKSGIVING

Praise the Lord!

O give thanks to the Lord, for he is good;

for his steadfast love endures for ever.

Psalm 106.1

GOD'S GREATNESS AND GOODNESS

I thank you, Father, that you listen to me. 42

John 11.41 (Good News Bible)

O thou good omnipotent, 43
who so carest for every one of us,
as if thou caredst for him alone;
and so for all,
as if all were but one!
Blessed is the man who loveth thee,
and his friend in thee, and his enemy for thee;
For he only loses none dear to him,
to whom all are dear in him who cannot be lost.
And who is that but our God,
the God that made heaven and earth, and filleth them,
even by filling them and creating them.
And thy law is truth,
and truth is thyself.
I behold how some things pass away
that others may replace them,
but thou dost never depart, O God,
my Father supremely good,
Beauty of all things beautiful.
To thee will I entrust
whatsoever I have received from thee,
so shall I lose nothing.
Thou madest me for thyself
and my heart is restless until it repose in thee.

Augustine, 354–430

44 Almighty Father, thy love is like a great sea that girdles the earth. Out of the deep we come to float a while upon its surface. We cannot sound its depth nor tell its greatness, only we know it never faileth. The winds that blow over us are the breathing of thy Spirit; the sun that lights and warms us is thy truth. Now thou dost suffer us to sail calm seas; now thou dost buffet us with storms of trouble; on the crest of waves and sorrow thou dost raise us, but it is thy love that bears us up; in the trough of desolation thou dost sink us that we may see nought but thy love on every side. And when we pass into the deep again the waters of thy love encompass and enfold us. The foolish call them the waters of misery and death; those who have heard the whisper of thy Spirit know them for the boundless ocean of eternal life and love.

Source unknown

45   O thou whose reason guides the universe,
    Maker of earth and heaven,
    Who from eternity dost send forth time
    And thyself motionless
    Giv'st all things power to move.
    No cause outside thyself prevailed on thee
    To fashion floating matter to a world,
    But an instinctive pattern in thy mind.
    Utterly good, and with no taint of malice
    Thou didst fashion all things in that heavenly mould.
    Thou the supreme beauty, carrying
    A world of beauty in thy mind, didst shape
    A perfect whole and made it then release
    Its perfect parts: numbered the elements,
    That cold might contain fire, and dryness water:
    Lest fire too pure might vanish into air,
    Or weight of water drag down flooded earth.
    O Father, give the spirit power to climb
    To the fountain of all light, and be purified.
    Break through the mists of earth, the weight of the clod,
    Shine forth in splendour, thou that art calm weather,
    And quiet resting place for faithful souls.
    To see thee is the end and the beginning,
    Thou carriest us, and thou dost go before,
    Thou art the journey, and the journey's end.

    Boethius, 480–c.524

No coward soul is mine,   46
No trembler in the world's storm-tossed sphere:
I see heaven's glories shine,
And faith shines equal, arming me from fear.

O God within my breast,
Almighty, ever-present Deity!
Life – that in me has rest,
As I – undying Life – have power in thee!

Vain are the thousand creeds
That move men's hearts: unutterably vain;
Worthless as withered weeds,
Or idlest froth amid the boundless main,

To waken doubt in one
Holding so fast by thine infinity;
So surely anchored on
The steadfast rock of immortality.

With wide-embracing love
Thy spirit animates eternal years,
Pervades and broods above,
Changes, sustains, dissolves, creates, and rears.

Though earth and man were gone,
And suns and universes ceased to be,
And thou were left alone,
Every existence would exist in thee.

There is not room for Death,
Nor atom that his might could render void:
Thou – THOU art Being and Breath,
And what THOU art may never be destroyed.

Emily Brontë, 1818–48

19

47 O Lord, thou hast me searched and known:
Thou know'st my sitting down
And rising up. Yea all my thoughts
Afar to thee are known.

My soul, praise, praise the Lord!
O God, thou art great:
In fathomless works
Thyself thou dost hide.
Before thy dark wisdom
And power uncreate,
Man's mind, that dare praise thee,
In fear must abide.

Robert Bridges, 1844–1930 (based on Psalm 139)

48 My God and my all.

Francis of Assisi, 1181–1226

49 You are holy
You are holy, Lord, the only God and your deeds are wonderful.
You are strong, you are great.
You are the most high, you are almighty.
You, holy Father, are King of heaven and earth.
You are three and one, Lord God, all good.
You are good, all good, supreme good, Lord God, living and true.
You are love, you are wisdom
You are humility, you are endurance.
You are rest, you are peace.
You are joy and gladness, you are justice and moderation.
You are all riches, and you suffice for us.
You are beauty, you are gentleness.
You are our protector, you are our guardian and defender.
You are courage, you are our haven and our hope.
You are our faith, our great consolation.
You are our eternal life, great and wonderful Lord.
God almighty, merciful Saviour.

Francis of Assisi, 1181–1226

Now we must praise the ruler of heaven,   *50*
The might of the Lord and his purpose of mind,
The work of the glorious Father; for he,
God eternal, established each wonder,
He, holy creator, first fashioned the heavens
As a roof for the children of earth.
And then our guardian, the everlasting Lord,
Adorned this middle-earth for men.
Praise the almighty king of heaven.

Cædmon, 7th century

O Immanence, that knows nor far nor near, but as the air we breathe *51*
is with us here, our breath of life, O Lord, we worship thee.

Amy Carmichael, 1868–1951

You alone are unutterable,   *52*
from the time you created all things
   that can be spoken of.
You alone are unknowable,
from the time you created all things
   that can be known.
All things cry out about you;
those which speak,
   and those which cannot speak.
All things honour you;
those which think,
   and those which cannot think.
For there is one longing, one groaning,
   that all things have for you . . .

All things pray to you
that comprehend your plan
   and offer you a silent hymn.
In you, the One, all things abide,
and all things endlessly run to you
   who are the end of all.

Gregory of Nazianzus, 329–389

53 Lord, how much juice you can squeeze from a single grape.
How much water you can draw from a single well.
How great a fire you can kindle from a tiny spark.
How great a tree you can grow from a tiny seed.
My soul is so dry that by itself it cannot pray;
Yet you can squeeze from it the juice of a thousand prayers.
My soul is so parched that by itself it cannot love;
Yet you can draw from it boundless love for you and for my
      neighbour.
My soul is so cold that by itself it has no joy;
Yet you can light the fire of heavenly joy within me.
My soul is so feeble that by itself it has no faith;
Yet by your power my faith grows to a great height.
Thank you for prayer, for love, for joy, for faith;
Let me always be prayerful, loving, joyful, faithful.

Guigo the Carthusian, died 1188

54 Let all the world in every corner sing
      My God and King.
The heavens are not too high,
His praise may thither fly:
The earth is not too low,
His praises there may grow.
Let all the world in every corner sing
      My God and King.

Let all the world in every corner sing
      My God and King.
The Church with psalms must shout,
No door can keep them out:
But above all, the heart
Must bear the longest part.
Let all the world in every corner sing
      My God and King.

George Herbert, 1593–1633

I learned that love was our Lord's meaning.   55
And I saw for certain, both here and elsewhere,
that before ever he made us, God loved us;
and that his love has never slackened,
       nor ever shall.
In this love all his works have been done,
and in this love he has made everything serve us;
and in this love our life is everlasting.
Our beginning was when we were made,
but the love in which he made us
       never had beginning.
In it we have our beginning.
All this we shall see in God for ever.
May Jesus grant this.

Julian of Norwich, 1342–c.1416

Let our mouth be filled with thy praise, O Lord, that we may sing of   56
thy glory, for that thou hast counted us worthy to partake of thy holy,
divine, immortal and life-giving mysteries: preserve thou us in thy
holiness, that we may learn of thy righteousness all the day long.
Alleluia, Alleluia, Alleluia.

Liturgy of John Chrysostom and Basil the Great

Worthy of praise from every mouth,   57
of confession from every tongue,
of worship from every creature,
is thy glorious name, O Father, Son, and Holy Ghost:
who didst create the world in thy grace
       and by thy compassion didst save the world.
To thy majesty, O God, ten thousand times ten thousand
bow down and adore, singing and praising without ceasing
       and saying,
Holy, holy, holy, Lord God of hosts;
Heaven and earth are full of thy praises;
Hosanna in the highest.

Nestorian Liturgy, 5th century

58 Almighty Lord God, your glory cannot be approached, your compassion knows no bounds, and your love for all mankind is beyond human expression; in your mercy look on us and all your people: do not leave us to our sins but deal with us according to your goodness. Guide us to the haven of your will and make us truly obedient to your commandments, that we may not feel ashamed when we come before your Messiah's dread judgement seat.

For you, O God, are good and ever-loving, and we glorify you, Father, Son and Holy Spirit, now and for ever, to the ages of ages.

Orthodox Liturgy

59 What can I say to you, my God? Shall I collect together all the words that praise your holy Name? Shall I give you all the names of this world, you, the Unnameable? Shall I call you 'God of my life, meaning of my existence, hallowing of my acts, my journey's end, bitterness of my bitter hours, home of my loneliness, you my most treasured happiness'? Shall I say: Creator, Sustainer, Pardoner, Near One, Distant One, Incomprehensible One, God both of flowers and stars, God of the gentle wind and of terrible battles, Wisdom, Power, Loyalty and Truthfulness, Eternity and Infinity, you the All-merciful, you the Just One, you Love itself?

Karl Rahner

60 O Lord my God, most merciful, most secret, most present, most constant, yet changing all things, never new and never old, ever in action, yet ever quiet, creating, upholding, and perfecting all, who hath anything but thy gift? Or what can any man say when he speaketh of thee? Yet have mercy upon us, O Lord, that we may speak unto thee, and praise thy Name.

Jeremy Taylor, 1613–67 (based on Augustine, 354–430)

O Lord my God, thou art above all things   61
the best, the strongest and most high.
Thou alone most full and most sufficient,
thou alone the sweetest, full of consolation.
Thou alone most noble
and glorious beyond all things,
for in thee are gathered all good things.
Never may my heart find rest
unless it rests with theec.

Thou brightness of eternal glory,
thou comfort of the pilgrim soul,
with thee is my tongue without voice,
and my very silence speaketh unto thee.
Come, oh come,
for without thee I shall have not joyful day or hour;
for thou art my joy,
and without thee my table is empty.
Praise and glory be unto thee;
let my mouth,
    my soul,
    and all creatures together,
praise and bless thee.

Thomas a Kempis, c.1380–1471

God, I give you the praise for days well spent. But I am yet unsatisfied,   62
because I do not enjoy enough of you. I apprehend myself at too great
a distance from you. I would have my soul more closely united to you
by faith and love.

You know Lord that I would love you above all things. You made
me, you know my desires, my expectations. My joys all centre in you
and it is you that I desire. It is your favour, your acceptance, the
communications of your grace that I earnestly wish for more than
anything in the world.

I rejoice in your essential glory and blessedness. I rejoice in my relation to you, that you are my Father, my Lord and my God. I thank
you that you have brought me so far. I will beware of despairing of
your mercy for the time which is yet to come, and will give you the
glory of your free grace.

Susanna Wesley, 1669–1742

63 O Thou transcendent,
Nameless, the fibre and the breath,
Light of the light, shedding forth universes, thou centre of them,
Thou mightier centre of the true, the good, the loving,
Thou moral, spiritual fountain – affection's source – thou reservoir,
(O pensive soul of me – O thirst unsatisfied – waitest not there?
Waitest not haply for us somewhere there the Comrade perfect?)
Thou pulse – thou motive of the stars, suns, systems,
That, circling, move in order, safe, harmonious,
Athwart the shapeless vastnesses of space,
How should I think, how breathe a single breath, how speak, if, out
    of myself,
I could not launch, to those, superior universes?

Walt Whitman, 1819–1892 (from 'Passage to India' (Book XXVII))

THE BEAUTY OF CREATION

64 O thou who through the light of nature hast aroused in us a longing
for the light of grace, so that we may be raised in the light of thy
majesty, to thee, I give thanks, Creator and Lord, that thou allowest
me to rejoice in thy works. Praise the Lord ye heavenly harmonies,
and ye who know the revealed harmonies. For from him, through
him and in him, all is, which is perceptible as well as spiritual; that
which we know and that which we do not know, for there is still
much to learn.

Johann Kepler, 1571–1630

Creator Spirit, who broodest everlastingly over the lands and waters 65
of earth, enduing them with forms and colours which no human skill
can copy, give me today, I beseech thee, the mind and heart to rejoice
in thy creation.

John Baillie, 1886–1960

Dear God, there are times 66
when I hear your voice most clearly
in greenness: in the singing of sap,
the conversations of the leaves, the whisperings
of shoot and stem, root, sap and cell,
calling me back to creation
to feel again the freshness of you
running through everything
like a bright emerald current.

God of greenness, you know well my tendency
to fill my life with my own methods
of communication. Thank you
for constantly returning me
to the simplicity of yours.
Again I experience you in the rejoicing
of bare feet on a damp forest path,
in the wonder of light thrown against
a kaleidoscope of tree ferns,
in the myriad textures of leaves,
the embrace of moss-clad trees,
in the shining of you beneath every surface.

Beloved Creator, coming to your greenness
is always a coming home,
a time of peace and grace
as the unimportant in me falls away
and I know again that bright green shoot
of my own beginning
which comes from you
and is one with you,
bright and beautiful God.

Joy Cowley

67 God of the high and holy places
    where I catch a glimpse of your glory,
    above the low levels of life,
    above the evil and emptiness which drags me down,
    beyond the limits of my senses and imagination,
    you lift me up.

    In the splendour of a sunset,
    in the silence of the stars,
    in the grandeur of the mountains,
    in the vastness of the sea,
    you lift me up.

    In the majesty of music,
    in the mystery of art,
    in the freshness of the morning,
    in the fragrance of a single flower,
    you lift me up.

    Awe-inspiring God,
    when I am lost in wonder
    and lost for words,
    receive the homage of my silent worship
    but do not let me be content to bear your beauty and be still.
    Go with me to the places where I live and work.
    Lift the veil of reticence behind which I hide.
    Give me the courage to speak of the things which move me,
    with simple and unselfconscious delight.
    Help me to share my glimpses of glory
    until others are drawn to your light.

    Jean Mortimer

Pied Beauty 68

Glory be to God for dappled things –
for skies of couple-colour as a brinded cow;
For rose-moles all in stipple upon trout that swim;
Fresh-firecoal chestnut-falls; finches' wings;
Landscape plotted and pieced-fold, fallow, and plough;
And all trades, their gear and tackle and trim.

All things counter, original, spare, strange;
Whatever is fickle, freckled (who knows how?)
With swift, slow; sweet, sour; adazzle, dim;
He fathers-forth whose beauty is past change:
Praise him.

Gerard Manley Hopkins, 1844–89

Our God, God of all men, 69
God of heaven and earth, seas and rivers,
God of sun and moon, of all the stars,
God of high mountain and lowly valleys,
God over heaven, and in heaven, and under heaven.
He has a dwelling in heaven and earth and sea
    and in all things that are in them.
He inspires all things, he quickens all things.
He is over all things, he supports all things.

He makes the light of the sun to shine,
He surrounds the moon and the stars,
He has made wells in the arid earth,
Placed dry islands in the sea.
He has a Son co-eternal with himself . . .
And the Holy Spirit breathes in them;
Not separate are the Father and the Son and Holy Spirit.

Patrick, c.389–c.461

70 O God, we thank you for this earth, our home; for the wide sky and the blessed sun, for the salt sea and the running water, for the ever-lasting hills and the never-resting winds, for trees and the common grass underfoot.

We thank you for our senses by which we hear the songs of birds, and see the splendour of the summer fields, and taste of the autumn fruits, and rejoice in the feel of the snow, and smell the breath of the spring.

Grant us a heart wide open to all this beauty; and save our souls from being so blind that we pass unseeing when even the common thornbush is aflame with your glory, O God our creator, who lives and reigns for ever and ever.

Walter Rauschenbusch, 1861–1918

71 For all things bright and beautiful,
for all things dark and mysterious and lovely,
For all things green and growing and strong,
For all things weak and struggling to push life up through rocky earth,
For all human faces, hearts, minds, and hands which surround us,
And for all nonhuman minds and hearts, paws and claws, fins and wings,
For this Life and the life of this world,
For all that you have laid before us, O God,
We lay our thankful hearts before you. In Christ's name.

Gail A. Ricciuti

THE BLESSINGS OF LIFE

God our Creator, our centre, our friend,   72
we thank you for our good life,
for those who are dear to us,
for our dead,
and for all who have helped and influenced us.
We thank you for the measure of freedom we have,
and the extent to which we control our lives;
and most of all we thank you for the faith that is in us,
for our awareness of you and our hope in you.
Keep us, we pray you, thankful and hopeful
and useful until our lives shall end.

Anglican Church in Aotearoa, New Zealand and Polynesia.
A New Zealand Prayer Book

I praise thee for the life that stirs within me: 73
I praise thee for the bright and beautiful world into which I go:
I praise thee for earth and sea and sky, for scudding cloud and singing
    bird:
I praise thee for the work thou hast given me to do:
I praise thee for all that thou hast given me to fill my leisure hours:
I praise thee for my friends:
I praise thee for music and books and good company and all pure
    pleasures.

John Baillie, 1886–1960

O God, I thank thee for all the joy I have had in life.   74

Byrhtnoth, 10th century

75　　　I thank thee, O Lord, my Lord,
　　　　for my being,
　　　　　　my life,
　　　　　　my gift of reason;
　　　　for my nurture,
　　　　　　my preservation,
　　　　　　my guidance;
　　　　for my education,
　　　　　　my civil rights,
　　　　　　my religious privileges;
　　　　for thy gifts of grace,
　　　　　　of nature,
　　　　　　of this world;
　　　　for my redemption,
　　　　　　my regeneration,
　　　　　　my instruction in the Christian faith;
　　　　for my calling,
　　　　　　my recalling,
　　　　　　my manifold renewed recalling;
　　　　for thy forbearance and long-suffering,
　　　　　　thy prolonged forbearance, many a time,
　　　　　　　　and many a year;
　　　　for all the benefits I have received,
　　　　　　and all the undertakings wherein I have prospered;
　　　　for any good I may have done;
　　　　for the use of the blessings of this life;
　　　　for thy promise,
　　　　　　and my hope of the enjoyment of good things to come;
　　　　. . . for all these and also for all other mercies,
　　　　known and unknown,
　　　　open and secret,
　　　　remembered by me, or now forgotten,
　　　　kindnesses received by me willingly, or
　　　　　　even against my will,
　　　　I praise thee, I bless thee, I thank thee,
　　　　　　all the days of my life.

Lancelot Andrewes, 1555–1626

The milk-float,   76
the poor man begging,
the staircase and the lift,
the railway lines, the furrows of the sea,
the pedigree dog and the ownerless dog,
the pregnant woman,
the paper-boy,
the man who sweeps the streets,
the church, the school,
the office and the factory,
streets being widened,
hills being laid low,
the outward and the homeward road,
the key I used to open my front door;
whether sleeping or waking –
All, all, all
make me think of you.

What can I give to the Lord
for all he has given me?

Helder Camara

Glory to God for all things!   77

John Chrysostom, c.347–407

I thank thee for Pain,   78
the sister of Joy.
I thank thee for Sorrow,
the twin of Happiness.

Pain, Joy, Sorrow, Happiness.
Four angels at work on the Well of Love.

Pain and Sorrow dig it deep with aches.
Joy and Happiness fill it up with tears
that come with smiles.

For the seasons of emotion in my heart,
I thank thee, O Lord.

Chandran Devanasen

79   Lord of all blessing,
As we walk about your world,
Let us know ourselves blessed at every turn;
Blessed in the autumnal sun and leaves;
Blessed in the winter wind;
Blessed in rain and shafts of sunlight;
Blessed in the moving stars;
Blessed in the turning of the world beneath our feet;
Blessed in silence;
Blessed in sleep;
Blessed in our children, our parents and our friends;
Blessed in conversation and the human voice;
Blessed in waiting for the bus, or train, or traffic lights;
Blessed in music, blessed in singing voices,
Blessed in the song of birds;
Blessed in the cry that pierces the heart;
Blessed in the smile of strangers;
Blessed in the touch of love, blessed in laughter;
Blessed in pain, in darkness, in grief;
Blessed in the desert and the frost;
Blessed in waiting for the spring;
Blessed in waiting and waiting and waiting.
Lord of all blessing, we bless you.

Hugh Dickinson

80 O God our Father, we would thank thee for all the bright things of life. Help us to see them, and to count them, and to remember them, that our lives may flow in ceaseless praise; for the sake of Jesus Christ our Lord.

J. H. Jowett, 1846–1923

81 Is not sight a jewel? Is not hearing a treasure? Is not speech a glory? O my Lord, pardon my ingratitude and pity my dullness who am not sensible of these gifts. The freedom of thy bounty hath deceived me. These things were too near to be considered. Thou presented me with thy blessings, and I was not aware. But now I give thanks and adore and praise thee for thy inestimable favours.

Thomas Traherne, 1636–74

GOD'S LOVE AND MERCY
IN CHRIST

Thanks be to God who gives us the victory through our Lord Jesus   82
Christ!

1 Corinthians 15.57 (Good News Bible)

O Lord Jesus Christ, make me worthy to understand the profound   83
mystery of your holy incarnation, which you have worked for our
sake and for our salvation. Truly there is nothing so great and wonderful as this, that you, my God, who are the creator of all things,
should become a creature, so that we should become like God. You
have humbled yourself and made yourself small that we might be
made mighty. You have taken the form of a servant, so that you
might confer upon us a royal and divine beauty.

You, who are beyond our understanding, have made yourself
understandable to us in Jesus Christ. You, who are the uncreated
God, have made yourself a creature for us. You, who are the
untouchable One, have made yourself touchable to us. You, who are
most high, make us capable of understanding your amazing love and
the wonderful things you have done for us. Make us able to understand the mystery of your incarnation, the mystery of your life,
example and doctrine, the mystery of your cross and Passion, the
mystery of your resurrection and ascension.

Blessed are you, O Lord, for coming to earth as a man. You were
born that you might die, and in dying that you might procure our salvation. O marvellous and indescribable love! In you is all sweetness
and joy! To contemplate your love is to exalt the soul above the world
and to enable it to abide alone in joy and rest and tranquillity.

Angela of Foligno, 1248–1309

84   I am happy because you have accepted me, dear Lord.
Sometimes I do not know what to do with all my happiness.
I swim in your grace like a whale in the ocean.
The saying goes: 'An ocean never dries up',
but we know that your grace also never fails.
Dear Lord, your grace is our happiness. Hallelujah!

Source unknown (West Africa)

85 O Christ, my Lord, again and again I have said with Mary Magdalene, 'They have taken away my Lord and I know not where they have laid him.'

I have been desolate and alone.

And you have found me again, and I know that what has died is not you, my Lord, but only my idea of you, the image which I have made to preserve what I have found, and to be my security.

I shall make another image, O Lord, better than the last. That, too, must go, and all successive images, until I come to the blessed vision of yourself, O Christ, my Lord.

George Appleton

86   You keep us waiting.
You, the God of all time;
Want us to wait
For the right time in which to discover
Who we are, where we must go,
Who will be with us, and what we must do.

So, thank you . . . for the waiting time.

You keep us looking.
You, the God of all space,
Want us to look in the right and wrong places
For signs of hope,
For people who are hopeless,
For visions of a better world which will appear
Among the disappointments of the world we know.

So, thank you . . . for the looking time.

You keep us loving.
You, the God whose name is love,

Want us to be like you –
To love the loveless and the unlovely and the unlovable;
To love without jealousy or design or threat;
And, most difficult of all,
To love ourselves.

So, thank you . . . for the loving time.

And in all this,
You keep us.
Through hard questions with no easy answers;
Through failing where we hoped to succeed
    and making an impact when we felt we were useless;
Through the patience and the dreams and the love of others;
And through Jesus Christ and his Spirit,
You
Keep us.

So, thank you . . . for the keeping time.
                And for now,
                and for ever.

John Bell (Iona Community)

Jesus, preaching good tidings to the poor,   87
    proclaiming release to the captives,
    setting at liberty them that are bound,
        I adore thee.

Jesus, Friend of the poor,
    Feeder of the hungry,
    Healer of the sick,
        I adore thee.

Jesus, denouncing the oppressor,
    instructing the simple,
    going about doing good,
        I adore thee.

Jesus, Teacher of patience,
    Pattern of gentleness,
    Prophet of the kingdom of heaven,
        I adore thee.

A Book of Prayers for Students

88 Dear Lord, it seems that you are so madly in love with your creatures that you could not live without us. So you created us; and then, when we turned away from you, you redeemed us. Yet you are God, and so have no need of us. Your greatness is made no greater by our creation; your power is made no stronger by our redemption. You have no duty to care for us, no debt to repay us. It is love, and love alone, which moves you.

Catherine of Siena, 1347–80

89 Blessed be he who in his love stooped to redeem mankind! Blessed be the King who made himself poor to enrich the needy! Blessed be he who came to fulfil the types and emblems of the prophets! Blessed be he who made creation rejoice with the wealth and treasure of his Father! Blessed be he whose glory the dumb sang with hosannas! Blessed be he to whom little children sang new glory in hymns of praise! Blessed be the new King who came that new-born babes might glorify him! Blessed be he unto whom children brought faltering songs to praise him among his disciples!

Ephraem the Syrian, c.306–73

90
King of glory, King of peace,
    I will love thee;
And that love may never cease,
    I will move thee.

Thou hast granted my request,
    Thou hast heard me:
Thou didst note my working breast,
    Thou hast spared me.

Wherefore with my utmost art
    I will sing thee,
And the cream of all my heart
    I will bring thee.

Though my sins against me cried
    Thou didst clear me;
And alone, when they replied,
    Thou didst hear me.

Seven whole days, not one in seven,
 I will praise thee.
In my heart, though not in heaven,
 I can raise thee.

Thou grew'st soft and moist with tears,
 Thou relentedst:
And when Justice called for fears,
 Thou dissentedst.

Small it is in this poor sort
 To enrol thee:
Ev'n eternity is too short
 To extol thee.

George Herbert, 1593–1633

Although I am dust and ashes, Lord, I am tied to you by bonds of   91
love. Therefore I feel I can speak freely to you. Before I came to know
you, I was nothing. I did not know the meaning of life, and I had no
understanding of myself. I have no doubt that you had a purpose in
causing me to be born; yet you had no need of me, and on my own I
was of no use to you. But then you decided that I should hear the
words of your Son, Jesus Christ. And that as I heard his words, you
enabled his love to penetrate my heart. Now I am completely satu-
rated in his love and faith, and there is no remedy. Now, Lord, I cannot change my attitude to my faith; I can only die for it.

Hilary of Poitiers, c.310–67

We thank thee, O God, the Father of our Lord Jesus Christ, that thou   92
hast revealed thy Son to us, on whom we have believed, whom we
have loved, and whom we worship. O Lord Jesus Christ, we commend our souls to thee. O heavenly Father, we know that although
we shall in thine own good time be taken away from this life, we shall
live for ever with thee. 'God so loved the world, that he gave his only
begotten Son, that whosoever believeth in him should not perish, but
have everlasting life.' Father into thy hands we commend our spirits;
through Jesus Christ our Lord.

Martin Luther, 1483–1546

93   *O Deus Ego Amo Te*

O God, I love thee, I love thee –
Not out of hope of heaven for me
Nor fearing not to love and be
   In the everlasting burning.
Thou, thou, my Jesus, after me
   Didst reach thine arms out dying,
For my sake sufferedst nails and lance,
Mocked and marrèd countenance,
   Sorrows passing number,
   Sweat and care and cumber,
Yea and death, and this for me,
   And thou couldst see me sinning:
Then I, why should not I love thee,
Jesu, so much in love with me?
Not for heaven's sake; not to be
Out of hell by loving thee;
Not for any gains I see;
But just the way that thou didst me
I do love and I will love thee;
What must I love thee, Lord, for then?
For being my king and God. Amen.

Gerard Manley Hopkins, 1844–89

94   Almighty God in trinity
From all my heart be thanks to thee
For thy good deed, that thou me wrought,
And with thy precious blood me bought,
And for all good thou lendst to me,
O Lord God, blessed may thou be!
All honour, joy and all loving
Be to thy name without ending.

Richard Rolle, 1295–1349

Glory be to God on high, 95
and on earth peace,
peace among those of good will.
We praise you, we bless you,
we worship you, we glorify you,
we give you thanks for your great glory,
holy God, tender God, God our beloved creator.

Christ our desire,
only embodiment of God,
bone of our bone and flesh of our flesh,
foolishness of God, greater than human wisdom,
poverty of God, stronger than human pride,
emptiness of God, full of our redemption,
bearing away the sin of the world,
have mercy upon us.
Holy one, bearing away the sin of the world,
have mercy upon us.
Beloved one, bearing away the sin of the world,
receive our prayer.

For you alone are holy,
you alone our desire.
You alone, O Christ,
with the comforter of fire,
are radiant with the grace and glory of God most high.

Janet Morley

Though waves and storms go o'er my head, 96
Though strength and health and friends be gone,
Though joys be withered all, and dead,
Though every comfort be withdrawn,
On this my steadfast soul relies, –
Father! Thy mercy never dies.

Johann A. Rothe, 1799–1867

Thank you, Lord Jesus, that you will be our hiding place whatever 97
happens.

Corrie ten Boom, 1892–1983

98

Strong Son of God, immortal Love,
　　Whom we, that have not seen thy face,
　　By faith, and faith alone, embrace,
Believing where we cannot prove;

Thine are these orbs of light and shade;
　　Thou madest life in man and brute;
　　Thou madest death; and lo, thy foot
Is on the skull which thou hast made.

Thou wilt not leave us in the dust:
　　Thou madest man, he knows not why,
　　He thinks he was not made to die;
And thou hast made him: thou art just.

Thou seemest human and divine,
　　The highest, holiest manhood, thou:
　　Our wills are ours, we know not how;
Our wills are ours, to make them thine.

Our little systems have their day;
　　They have their day and cease to be:
　　They are but broken lights of thee,
And thou, O Lord, art more than they.

Alfred, Lord Tennyson, 1809–92 (from 'In Memoriam')

99　Father, we thank thee for our happiness: for thy great gift of life: for the wonder and bloom of the world. We bless thee that it takes a very little thing to make us happy, yet so great a thing to satisfy us that only thyself canst do it, for thou alone art greater than our hearts. We bless thee for thy calling which is so high that no man can perfectly attain unto it, and for thy grace which stoops so low that none of us can ever fall too low for it. Above all we bless thee that thou didst send thy Son, Jesus Christ our Lord, for having seen him we have seen thee, whose truth doth ever warm, and whose grace doth ever keep.

Helen Waddell, 1889–1965

My Jesus, from all eternity you were pleased to give yourself to us in   *100*
love. And you planted within us a deep spiritual desire that can only
be satisfied by yourself.

I may go from here to the other end of the world, from one country
to another, from riches to greater riches, from pleasure to pleasure,
and still I shall not be content. All the world cannot satisfy the
immortal soul. It would be like trying to feed a starving man with a
single grain of wheat.

We can only be satisfied by setting our hearts, imperfect as they are,
on you. We are made to love you; your created us as your lovers.

It sometimes happens that the more we know a neighbour, the less
we love him. But with you it is quite the opposite. The more we know
you, the more we love you. Knowledge of you kindles such a fire in
our souls that we have no energy left for worldly desires.

My Jesus, how good it is to love you. Let me be like your disciples
on Mount Tabor, seeing nothing else but you. Let us be like two
bosom friends, neither of whom can ever bear to offend the other.

Jean-Baptiste Marie Vianney, 1786–1859

O Lord Jesus, who can love as you do?   *101*
Through your deeds and labour I have become
As ripened fruit.
How blessed it is to share in your glory
Eternally in your providence.
I am your treasure,
Product of your arduous labour.

(Brother) Wong

102

My God, I love thee — not because
I hope for heaven thereby,
Nor yet because who love thee not
Are lost eternally.

Thou, O my Jesus, thou didst me
Upon the cross embrace;
For me didst bear the nails and spear,
And manifold disgrace;

And griefs and torments numberless,
And sweat of agony,
Yea, death itself — and all for one
Who was thine enemy.

Then why, O blessed Jesus Christ,
Should I not love thee well?
Not for the sake of winning heaven,
Or of escaping hell;

Not with the hope of gaining aught;
Not seeking a reward;
But as thyself hast loved me,
O ever-loving Lord.

E'en so I love thee, and will love,
And in thy praise will sing;
Solely because thou art my God
And my eternal King.

Francis Xavier, 1506–52

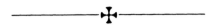

DEDICATION TO GOD'S WILL

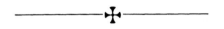

Be transformed by the renewing of your minds,

so that you may discern what is the will of God –

what is good and acceptable and perfect.

Romans 12.2

Father, not my will but your will be done. 103

Luke 22.42 (Good News Bible)

Give us grace, O Lord, not only to hear thy Word with our ears, but 104
also to receive it into our hearts and to show it forth in our lives; for
the glory of thy great name.

Source unknown

Oh Lord, I know not what to ask of thee. 105
Thou alone knowest what are my true needs.
Thou lovest me more than I know how to love myself.
Help me to see my real needs which are concealed from me.
I dare not ask either a cross or consolation,
I can only wait on thee.
My heart is open to thee;
visit and help me, for thy great mercy's sake;
strike me and heal me,
cast me down and raise me up.
I worship in silence thy holy will and inscrutable ways.
I offer myself as a sacrifice to thee.
I put all my trust in thee.
I have no other desire than to fulfil thy will.
Teach me how to pray.
Pray thou thyself in me.

Source unknown

My God, I am not my own but yours. 106
Take me for your own,
and help me in all things to do your holy will.
My God, I give myself to you,
    in joy and sorrow,
    in sickness and in health,
    in success and in failure,
    in life and in death,
    in time and for eternity.
Make me and keep me your own;
through Jesus Christ our Lord.

Source unknown

107   I am giving thee worship with my whole life,
I am giving thee assent with my whole power,
I am giving thee praise with my whole tongue,
I am giving thee honour with my whole utterance,
I am giving thee reverence with my whole understanding,
I am giving thee offering with my whole thought,
I am giving thee praise with my whole fervour,
I am giving thee humility in the blood of the Lamb.
I am giving thee love with my whole devotion,
I am giving thee kneeling with my whole desire,
I am giving thee love with my whole heart,
I am giving thee affection with my whole sense;
I am giving thee my existence with my whole mind,
I am giving thee my soul, O God of all gods.

Source unknown (Early Scottish)

108   O King of glory and Lord of valours, who hast said, 'Be of good cheer, I have overcome the world': be thou victorious in us thy servants, for without thee we can do nothing. Grant thy compassion to go before us, thy compassion to come behind us: before us in our undertakings, behind us in our ending. And what more shall we say but that thy will be done; for thy will is our salvation, our glory, and our joy.

Alcuin, 735–804

109   Lord God Almighty, Shaper and Ruler of all creatures, we pray thee for thy great mercy, that thou guide us better than we have done, towards thee. And guide us to thy will, to the need of our soul, better than we can ourselves. And steadfast our mind towards thy will and to our soul's need. And strengthen us against the temptations of the devil, and put far from us all lust, and every unrighteousness, and shield us against our foes, seen and unseen. And teach us to do thy will, that we may inwardly love thee before all things, with a pure mind. For thou art our Maker and our Redeemer, our Help, our Comfort, our Trust, our Hope; praise and glory be to thee now, ever and ever, world without end.

(King) Alfred, 849–901

Lord Jesus,   *110*
I give thee my hands to do thy work.
I give thee my feet to go thy way.
I give thee my eyes to see as thou seest.
I give thee my tongue to speak thy words.
I give thee my mind that thou mayest think in me.
I give thee my spirit that thou mayest pray in me.
Above all, I give thee my heart that thou mayest love in me
    thy Father, and all mankind.
I give thee my whole self that thou mayest grow in me, so that it is
    thee, Lord Jesus, who live and work and pray in me.
I hand over to thy care, Lord, my soul and body, my prayers and my
    hopes, my health and my work, my life and my death, my parents
    and my family, my friends and my neighbours, my country and all
    men. Today and always.

Adapted from Lancelot Andrewes, 1555–1626

In thee would we lose ourselves utterly; do in us what thou wilt.   *111*

Jakob Boehme, 1575–1624

      Thy way, not mine, O Lord,   *112*
      However dark it be;
      Lead me by thine own hand,
      Choose out the path for me.
      Smooth let it be or rough,
      It will be still the best;
      Winding or straight, it leads
      Right onward to thy rest.
      Choose thou for me my friends,
      My sickness or my health;
      Choose thou my cares for me,
      My poverty or wealth.
      Not mine, not mine the choice
      In things or great or small;
      Be thou my guide, my strength,
      My wisdom, and my all.

      Horatius Bonar, 1808–89

113 I am bending my knee
  In the eye of the Father who created me,
  In the eye of the Son who purchased me,
  In the eye of the Spirit who cleansed me,
   In friendship and affection.
  Through thine own Anointed One, O God,
  Bestow upon us fullness in our need,
   Love towards God,
   The affection of God,
   The smile of God,
   The wisdom of God,
   The grace of God,
   The fear of God,
   And the will of God
  To do on the world of the Three,
  As angels and saints
  Do in heaven;
   Each shade and light,
   Each day and night,
   Each time in kindness,
   Give thou us thy Spirit.

Carmina Gadelica

114 O Father, calm the turbulence of our passions; quiet the throbbing of our hopes; repress the waywardness of our wills; direct the motions of our affections; and sanctify the varieties of our lot. Be thou all in all to us; and may all things earthly, while we bend them to our growth in grace, and to the work of blessing, dwell lightly in our hearts, so that we may readily, or even joyfully, give up whatever thou dost ask for. May we seek first thy kingdom and righteousness; resting assured that then all things needful shall be added unto us.

 Father, pardon our past ingratitude and disobedience; and purify us, whether by thy gentler or thy sterner dealings, till we have done thy will on earth, and thou removest us to thine own presence with the redeemed in heaven.

Mary Carpenter

Lord, I make you a present of myself. I do not know what to do with *115*
myself. So let me make this exchange: I will place myself entirely in
your hands, if you will cover my ugliness with your beauty, and tame
my unruliness with your love. Put out the flames of false passion in
my heart, since these flames destroy all that is true within me. Make
me always busy in your service.

Lord, I want no special signs from you, nor am I looking for intense
emotions in response to your love. I would rather be free of all emotion, than to run the danger of falling victim once again to false passion. Let my love for you be naked, without any emotional clothing.

Catherine of Genoa, 1447–1510

Lord, teach us to number our days, that we may apply our hearts *116*
unto wisdom. Lighten, if it be thy will, the pressures of this world's
cares. Above all, reconcile us to thy will, and give us a peace which the
world cannot take away; through Jesus Christ our Lord.

Thomas Chalmers, 1780–1847

Be thou a light unto my eyes, music to mine ears, sweetness to my *117*
taste, and full contentment to my heart. Be thou my sunshine in the
day, my food at table, my repose in the night, my clothing in nakedness, and my succour in all necessities. Lord Jesu, I give thee my body,
my soul, my substance, my fame, my friends, my liberty and my life.
Dispose of me and all that is mine as it may seem best to thee and to
the glory of thy blessed name.

John Cosin, 1594–1672

O Lord Jesu, who art the only health of all men living, and the ever- *118*
lasting life of those who die in thy faith: I give myself wholly unto thy
will, being sure that the thing cannot perish which is committed unto
thy mercy.

Thomas Cromwell, c.1485–1540 (Part of a prayer he repeated before his execution)

119   My Father, I abandon myself to you. Do with me as you will. Whatever you may do with me I thank you. I am prepared for anything. I accept everything, provided your will is fulfilled in me and in all creatures. I ask for nothing more, my God. I place my soul in your hands. I give it to you, my God, with all the love of my heart, because I love you. And for me it is a necessity of love, this gift of myself, this placing of myself in your hands without reserve in boundless confidence, because you are my Father.

Charles de Foucauld, 1858–1916

120   O God, the true and only life, in whom and from whom and by whom are all good things that are good indeed; from whom to be turned is to fall, to whom to turn is to rise again; in whom to abide is to dwell for ever, from whom to depart is to die; to whom to come again is to revive, and in whom to lodge is to live: take away from me whatsoever thou wilt, so that thou give me only thyself.

Thomas Dekker, c.1570–1632

121   Cleanse our minds, O Lord, we beseech thee, of all anxious thoughts for ourselves, that we may learn not to trust in the abundance of what we have, save as tokens of thy goodness and grace, but that we may commit ourselves in faith to thy keeping, and devote all our energy of soul, mind and body to the work of thy kingdom and the furthering of the purposes of thy divine righteousness; through Jesus Christ our Lord.

Euchologium Anglicanum

122   Most High and glorious God, enlighten the darkness of our hearts and give us a true faith, a certain hope and a perfect love. Give us a sense of the divine and knowledge of yourself, so that we may do everything in fulfilment of your holy will; through Jesus Christ our Lord.

Francis of Assisi, 1182–1226

123   God almighty, eternal, righteous, and merciful, give to us poor sinners to do for thy sake all that we know of thy will, and to will always what pleases thee, so that inwardly purified, enlightened, and kindled by the fire of the Holy Spirit, we may follow in the footprints of thy well-beloved Son, our Lord Jesus Christ.

Francis of Assisi, 1182–1226

O Father, I will trust thee: for all the known and all the unknown   124
good that I have ever had has come from thee. Sweet Saviour, I will
trust thee: thy grace is all-sufficient for my soul, as mighty as thy
power and as matchless as thy love. Blest Spirit, I will trust thee: how
can I ever dare to trust myself, to think, or speak, or act apart from
thee? O God, my God, my hope and stay, who knowest and orderest
all that is best, I know not what to will or do aright; then make me
ever love to choose and do thy will.

Walter Howard Frere, 1863–1938

Thou who art over us,   125
Thou who art one of us,
Thou who art also within us,
May all see thee in me also,
May I prepare the way for thee,
May I thank thee for all that shall fall to my lot,
May I also not forget the needs of others,
Keep me in thy love
As thou wouldest that all should be kept in mine.
May everything in this my being be directed to thy glory
And may I never despair.
For I am under thy hand,
And in thee is all power and goodness.

Give me a pure heart – that I may see thee,
A humble heart – that I may hear thee,
A heart of love – that I may serve thee,
A heart of faith – that I may abide in thee.
To love life and men as God loves them – for the sake of their infinite
    possibilities,
        to wait like him
        to judge like him
        without passing judgment,
        to obey the order when it is given
        and never look back –
    then he can use you – then, perhaps, he will use you.
And if he doesn't use you – what matter. In his hand,
    every moment has its meaning, its greatness, its glory,
    its peace, its co-inherence.

Dag Hammarskjold

126 A wreathed garland of deserved praise,
Of praise deserved, unto thee I give,
I give to thee, who knowest all my ways,
My crooked winding ways, wherein I live,
Wherein I die, not live: for life is straight,
Straight as a line, and ever tends to thee,
To thee, who art more far above deceit,
Than deceit seems above simplicity.
Give me simplicity, that I may live,
So live and like, that I may know thy ways,
Know them and practise them: then shall I give
For this poor wreath, give thee a crown of praise.

George Herbert, 1593–1633

127 O come, Holy Spirit, inflame my heart, set it on fire with love. Burn
away my self-centredness so that I can love unselfishly. Breathe your
life-giving breath into my soul so that I can live freely and joyously,
unrestricted by self-consciousness, and may be ready to go wherever
you may send me. Come like a gentle breeze and give me your still
peace so that I may be quiet and know the wonder of your presence,
and help diffuse it in the world. Never let me shut you out; never let
me try to limit you to my capacity; act freely in me and through me,
never leave me, O Lord and giver of life!

Michael Hollings and Etta Gullick

128 Take, Lord, and receive all my liberty, my memory, my understanding, and all my will, all that I have and possess. Thou hast given them
to me; to thee, O Lord, I restore them; all things are thine, dispose of
them according to thy will. Give me thy love and thy grace, for this is
enough for me.

Ignatius Loyola, 1491–1556

129 Let the healing grace of your love, O Lord, so transform me that I
may play my part in the transfiguration of the world from a place of
suffering, death and corruption to a realm of infinite light, joy and
love. Make me so obedient to your Spirit that my life may become a
living prayer, and a witness to your unfailing presence.

Martin Israel

Dearest Lord, teach me to be generous; 130
Teach me to serve thee as thou deservest;
To give and not to count the cost,
To fight and not to heed the wounds,
To toil and not to seek for rest,
To labour and not to seek reward,
Save that of knowing that I do thy will.

*Ignatius Loyola, 1491–1556 (This prayer is sometimes
combined with the next one to form a single prayer)*

Fill us, we pray thee, with thy light and life, that we may show forth 131
thy wondrous glory. Grant that thy love may so fill our lives that we
may count nothing too small to do for thee, nothing too much to give
and nothing too hard to bear.

Ignatius Loyola, 1491–1556

Father, I abandon myself into your hands; do with me what you will. 132
Whatever you may do, I thank you; I am ready for all, I accept all. Let
only your will be done in me, and in all your creatures – I wish no
more than this, O Lord. Into your hands I commend my soul; I offer
it to you with all the love of my heart, for I love you Lord, and so need
to give myself, to surrender myself into your hands, without reserve,
and with boundless confidence, for you are my Father.

Jesus Caritas

Lord, thou knowest what I want, 133
if it be thy will that I have it,
and if it be not thy will,
good Lord, do not be displeased,
for I want nothing which you do not want.

Julian of Norwich, 1342–c.1416

Lord, I give and offer up unto thee myself and all that is mine, actions 134
and words, repose and silence; only do thou preserve and guide me,
and direct my hand and mind and tongue to things that are acceptable to thee, and withdraw me from anything from which it were better to abstain, by and for the sake of Jesus Christ our Lord.

William Laud, 1573–1645

135 Stir us up to offer thee, O Lord, our bodies, our souls, our spirits, in all we love and all we learn, in all we plan and all we do, to offer our labours, our pleasures, our sorrows to thee; to work through them for thy kingdom, to live as those who are not their own, but bought with thy blood, fed with thy body; thine from our birth-hour, thine now, and thine for ever and ever.

Charles Kingsley, 1819–75

136 O Jesus, fill me with thy love now, and I beseech thee, accept me, and use me a little for thy glory. O do, do, I beseech thee, accept me and my service, and take thou all the glory.

David Livingstone, 1813–73

137 Use me, then, my Saviour, for whatever purpose, and in whatever way, thou may require. Here is my poor heart, an empty vessel; fill it with thy grace. Here is my sinful and troubled soul; quicken it and refresh it with thy love. Take my heart for thine abode; my mouth to spread abroad the glory of thy name; my love and all my powers, for the advancement of your believing people; and never suffer the stead-fastness and confidence of my faith to abate; so that at all times I may be enabled from the heart to say, 'Jesus needs me, and I am his.'

Dwight L. Moody, 1837–99

138 Dear Jesus, help us to spread your fragrance everywhere we go. Flood our souls with your spirit and life. Penetrate and possess our whole being so utterly that our lives may only be a radiance of yours. Shine through us, and be so in us, that every soul we come in contact with may feel your presence in our soul. Let them look up and see no longer us but only Jesus! Stay with us, and then we shall begin to shine as you shine; so to share as to be a light to others; the light, O Jesus, will be all from you, none of it will be ours; it will be you, shin-ing on others through us. Let us preach you without preaching, not by words but by our example, by the catching force, the sympathetic influence of what we do, the evident fullness of the love our hearts bear to you.

Cardinal Newman, 1801–90 (Prayed daily by Mother Teresa's Missionaries of Charity)

O our God, we believe in thee, we hope in thee, and we love thee, 139
because thou hast created us, redeemed us, and dost sanctify us.
Increase our faith, strengthen our hope, and deepen our love, that
giving up ourselves wholly to thy will, we may serve thee faithfully all
the rest of our life; through Jesus Christ our Lord.

The Narrow Way, 1869

Dear Lord, help me keep my eyes on you. You are the incarnation of 140
divine love, you are the expression of God's infinite compassion, you
are the visible manifestation of the Father's holiness. You are beauty,
goodness, gentleness, forgiveness, and mercy. In you all can be found.
Outside of you nothing can be found. Why should I look elsewhere or
go elsewhere? You have the words of eternal life, you are food and
drink, you are the Way, the Truth, and the Life. You are the light that
shines in the darkness, the lamp on the lampstand, the house on the
hilltop. You are the perfect icon of God. In and through you I can see
and find my way to the Heavenly Father. O Holy One, Beautiful One,
Glorious One, be my Lord, my Saviour, my Redeemer, my Guide, my
Consoler, my Comforter, my Hope, my Joy, and my Peace. To you I
want to give all that I am. Let me be generous, not stingy or hesitant.
Let me give you all – all I have, think, do, and feel. It is yours, O Lord.
Please accept it and make it fully your own.

Henri Nouwen

O Lord, let me not henceforth desire health or life except to spend 141
them for thee and with thee. Thou alone knowest what is good for
me; do therefore what seemeth thee best. Give to me or take from me;
conform my will to thine; and grant that, with humble and perfect
submission, and in holy confidence, I may receive the orders of thine
eternal providence; and may equally adore all that comes to me from
thee, through Jesus Christ our Lord.

Blaise Pascal, 1623–62

To thee, O Jesu, I direct my eyes; to thee my hands, to thee my humble 142
knees; to thee my heart shall offer sacrifice; to thee my thoughts, who
my thoughts only sees; to thee my self – my self and all I give; to thee
I die; to thee I only live.

(Sir) Walter Raleigh, 1552–1618 (attributed)

143   All gifts are thine, O God, and of thine own have we given thee. By the leading of thy Spirit may we render to thee that which thou most desirest, even our whole heart and mind and will, in loving and grateful service.

The Rodborough Bede Book

144   Govern all by thy wisdom, O Lord, so that my soul may always be serving thee as thou dost will, and not as I may choose. Do not punish me, I beseech thee, by granting that which I wish or ask, if it offends thy love, which would always live in me. Let me die to myself that so I may serve thee; let me live to thee, who in thyself art the true life.

Teresa of Avila, 1515–82

145   Deliver me, O God, from a slothful mind, from all lukewarmness, and all dejection of spirit. I know these cannot but deaden my love to thee; mercifully free my heart from them, and give me a lively, zealous, active, and cheerful spirit; that I may vigorously perform whatever thou commandest, thankfully suffer whatever thou choosest for me, and be ever ardent to obey in all things thy holy love.

John Wesley, 1703–91

146   O Lord, my God! the amazing horrors of darkness were gathered round me, and covered me all over, and I saw no way to go forth; I felt the depth and extent of the misery of my fellow-creatures separated from the divine harmony, and it was heavier than I could bear, and I was crushed down under it; I lifted up my hand, I stretched out my arm, but there was none to help me; I looked round about, and was amazed.

In the depths of misery, O Lord, I remembered that thou art omnipotent; that I had called thee Father; and I felt that I loved thee, and I was made quiet in my will, and I waited for deliverance from thee. Thou hadst pity upon me, when no man could help me; I saw that meekness under suffering was showed to us in the most affecting example of thy Son, and thou taughtest me to follow him, and I said: 'Thy will, O Father, be done!'

John Woolman, 1720–72

Lord, may your will be done wherever two or three are gathered in   147
your name: may we witness to your saving love through telling the
good news, caring for those in pain, and working for the justice of
your kingdom on earth, as in heaven; through Jesus Christ our
Redeemer.

World Council of Churches

FOR THE LOVE OF GOD

Kindle, O Lord, in our hearts, we pray,   148
the flame of that love which never ceases,
that it may burn in us and give light to others.
May we shine for ever in your temple,
set on fire with that eternal light of yours
which puts to flight the darkness of this world;
in the name of Jesus Christ your Son our Lord.

Source unknown

Set our hearts on fire with love of thee, O Christ our God, that in that   149
flame we may love thee with all our heart, with all our mind, with all
our soul, and with all our strength, and our neighbours as ourselves;
so that, keeping thy commandments, we may glorify thee, the giver of
all good gifts.

Source unknown (Eastern Orthodox)

150 O God, we have known and believed the love that you have for us. May we, by dwelling in love, dwell in you, and you in us. Teach us, O heavenly Father, the love wherewith you have loved us; fashion us, O blessed Lord, after your own example of love; shed abroad, O you Holy Spirit of love, the love of God and man in our hearts. For your name's sake.

Henry Alford, 1810–71

151 We love thee, O our God; and we desire to love thee more and more. Grant to us that we may love thee as much as we desire, and as much as we ought. O dearest friend, who hast so loved and saved us, the thought of whom is so sweet and always growing sweeter, come with Christ and dwell in our hearts; then thou wilt keep a watch over our lips, our steps, our deeds, and we shall not need to be anxious either for our souls or our bodies. Give us love, sweetest of all gifts, which knows no enemy. Give us in our hearts pure love, born of thy love to us, that we may love others as thou lovest us. O most loving Father of Jesus Christ, from whom floweth all love, let our hearts, frozen in sin, cold to thee and cold to others, be warmed by this divine fire. So help and bless us in thy Son.

Anselm, 1033–1109

152 Lord, because you have made me, I owe you the whole of my love; because you have redeemed me, I owe you the whole of myself; because you have promised so much, I owe you all my being. Moreover, I owe you as much more love than myself as you are greater than I, for whom you gave yourself and to whom you promised yourself. I pray you, Lord, make me taste by love what I taste by knowledge; let me know by love what I know by understanding. I owe you more than my whole self, but I have no more, and by myself I cannot render the whole of it to you. Draw me to you, Lord, in the fullness of love. I am wholly yours by creation; make me all yours, too, in love.

Anselm, 1033–1109

Lord, give us hearts never to forget thy love; but to dwell therein   *153*
whatever we do, whether we sleep or wake, live or die, or rise again to
the life that is to come. For thy love is eternal life and everlasting rest;
for this is life eternal to know thee and thy infinite goodness. O let its
flame never be quenched in our hearts; let it grow and brighten, till
our whole souls are glowing and shining with its light and warmth.
Be thou our joy our hope, our strength and life, our shield and
shepherd, our portion for ever. For happy are we if we continue in the
love wherewith thou hast loved us; holy are we when we love thee
steadfastly. Therefore, O thou, whose name and essence is love,
enkindle our hearts, enlighten our understanding, sanctify our wills,
and fill all the thoughts of our hearts, for Jesus Christ's sake.

Johann Arndt, 1555–1621

We implore thee, by the memory of thy cross's hallowed and most   *154*
bitter anguish, make us fear thee, make us love thee, O Christ.

Bridget, 453–523

> Lord: *155*
> How do I love thee? Let me count the ways.
> I love thee to the depth and breadth and height
> my soul can reach, when feeling out of sight
> for the ends of being and of ideal grace.
> I love thee to the level of every day's
> most quiet need, by sun and candlelight.
> I love thee freely, as men strive for right;
> I love thee purely, as they turn from praise.
> I love thee with a passion put to use
> in my old griefs, and with my childhood faith.
> I love thee with a love I seemed to lose
> with my lost saints – I love thee with the breath,
> smiles, tears, of all my life!
> And, God, if thou dost choose
> I shall love thee better after death.
>
> *Elizabeth Browning, 1806–1861 (adapted)*

156   Father, forgive the cold love of the years,
       While here in the silence we bow,
       Perish our cowardice! Perish our fears!
       Kindle us, kindle us now.

       Lord, we believe, we accept, we adore,
       Less than the least though we be.
       Fire of love, burn in us, burn evermore
       Till we burn out for thee.

       Amy Carmichael, 1868–1951

157 Grant me, I beseech thee, my God, in the name of Jesus Christ thy
Son, the charity which never fails, that my light may shine, warming
my own heart and enlightening others.

Columbanus, c.550–615

158 O Lord Jesus Christ, draw thou our hearts unto thee; join them
together in inseparable love, that we may abide in thee and thou in us,
and that the everlasting covenant between us may stand sure for ever.
Let the fiery darts of thy love pierce through all our slothful members
and inward powers, that we, being happily wounded, may so become
whole and sound. Let us have no lover but thyself alone; let us seek no
joy nor comfort except in thee.

Miles Coverdale, 1488–1568

159   Hark, my soul! it is the Lord;
       'Tis thy Saviour, hear his word;
       Jesus speaks, and speaks to thee:
       'Say, poor sinner, lov'st thou me?'

       Lord, it is my chief complaint
       That my love is weak and faint;
       Yet I love thee and adore,
       Oh for grace to love thee more!

       William Cowper, 1731–1800

Batter my heart, three person'd God; for, you 160
As yet but knocke, breathe, shine, and seeke to mend;
That I may rise, and stand, o'erthrow mee, and bend
Your force, to breake, blowe, burn and make me new.
I, like an usurpt towne, to another due,
Labour to admit you, but Oh, to no end,
Reason your viceroy in mee, mee should defend,
But is captiv'd, and proves weake or untrue.
Yet dearely I love you, and would be loved faine,
But am betroth'd unto your enemie:
Divorce me, untie, or breake that knot againe,
Take mee to you, imprison mee, for I,
Except you enthrall mee, never shall be free,
Nor ever chaste, except you ravish mee.

John Donne, 1573–1631

May the power of your love, Lord Christ, fiery and sweet as honey, so 161
absorb our hearts as to withdraw them from all that is under heaven.
Grant that we may be ready to die for love of your love, as you died
for love of our love.

Francis of Assisi, 1182–1226

My God, I desire to love thee perfectly: with all my heart which thou 162
madest for thyself, with all my mind which only thou canst satisfy,
with all my soul which fain would soar to thee, with all my strength,
my feeble strength, which shrinks before so great a task, and yet can
choose naught else but spend itself in loving thee. Claim thou my
heart, fill thou my mind, uplift my soul, and reinforce my strength,
that where I fail thou mayest succeed in me, and make me love thee
perfectly.

Walter Howard Frere, 1863–1938

Eternal God, the light of the minds that know thee, the joy of the 163
hearts that love thee, the strength of the wills that serve thee; grant us
so to know thee that we may truly love thee, so to love thee that we
may freely serve thee, to the glory of thy holy name.

Gelasian Sacramentary, 5th century

164   O Love, O God, who created me, in your love recreate me.
O Love, who redeemed me, fill up and redeem for yourself in me
whatever part of your love has fallen into neglect within me.
O Love, O God, who, to make me yours, in the blood of your Christ
purchased me, in your truth sanctify me.
O Love, O God, who adopted me as a daughter, after your own heart
fashion and foster me.
O Love, who as yours and not another's chose me, grant that I may
cleave to you with my whole being.
O Love, O God, who first loved me, grant that with my whole heart,
and with my whole soul, and with my whole strength, I may love
you.

O Love, O God almighty, in your love confirm me.
O Love most wise, give me wisdom in the love of you.
O Love most sweet, give me sweetness in the taste of you.
O Love most dear, grant that I may live for you alone.
O Love most faithful, in all my tribulations comfort and succour me.
O Love who is ever with me, work all my works in me.
O Love most victorious, grant that I may persevere to the end in you.

Gertrude of Thuringen, 1256–c.1303

165   Move our hearts with the calm, smooth flow of your grace. Let the
river of your love run through our souls. May my soul be carried by
the current of your love, towards the wide, infinite ocean of heaven.
    Stretch out my heart with your strength, as you stretch out the sky
above the earth. Smooth out any wrinkles of hatred or resentment,
Enlarge my soul that it may know more fully your truth.

Gilbert of Hoyland, died 1170

166   Grant, O Lord, that your love may so fill our lives that we may count
nothing too small to do for you, nothing too much to give, and nothing too hard to bear, for Jesus Christ's sake.

Ignatius Loyola, 1491–1556

167   Ah, blessed Lord, I wish I knew how I might best love you and please
you, and that my love were as sweet to you as your love is to me.

Margery Kempe, c.1373–c.1432

Set my heart on fire with the love of thee, most loving Father, and   *168*
then to do thy will, and to obey thy commandments, will not be grievous to me. For to him that loveth, nothing is difficult, nothing is
impossible; because love is stronger than death. Oh, may love fill and
rule my heart. For then there will spring up and be cherished between
thee and me a likeness of character, and union of will, so that I may
choose and refuse what thou dost. May thy will be done in me and by
me forever.

Jacobus Horstius Merlo, 1597–1664

O my God, let me walk in the way of love which knoweth not how to   *169*
seek self in anything whatsoever. Let me love thee for thyself, and
nothing else but in and for thee. Let me love nothing instead of thee,
for to give all for love is a most sweet bargain. Let thy love work in me
and by me, and let me love thee as thou wouldst be loved by me.

Gertrude More, 1606–1633

O my sweet Saviour Christ, which in thine undeserved love towards   *170*
mankind so kindly wouldst suffer the painful death of the cross, suffer me not to be cold nor lukewarm in love again towards thee.

(Sir) Thomas More, 1478–1535

O my God, give me thy grace so that the things of this earth and   *171*
things more naturally pleasing to me, may not be as close as thou art
to me. Keep thou my eyes, my ears, my heart from clinging to the
things of this world. Break my bonds, raise my heart. Keep my whole
being fixed on thee. Let me never lose sight of thee; and while I gaze
on thee, let my love of thee grow more and more every day.

John Henry Newman, 1801–90

Most loving Lord, give me a childlike love of thee, which shall cast   *172*
out all fear.

Edward Bouverie Pusey, 1800–82

173   O God, whose love is without measure: out of the depths of my own creatureliness and yearning I call to you. Out of your own immense depths of power and mystery you call to me. Enable me to enter into the beginnings of the secrets of your love, and let the poor stream of my life flow into the immensity of your being.

(Brother) Ramon

174   Thanks be to thee,
O Lord Christ,
for all the benefits which thou hast given us;
for all the pains and insults which thou hast borne for us.

O most merciful redeemer,
friend
and brother,
may we know thee more clearly,
love thee more dearly,
and follow thee more nearly;
for thine own sake.

Richard of Chichester, 1197–1253

175   O God, the author of peace and lover of concord, grant unto us to be so firmly established in the love of thyself, that no trials whatsoever may be able to part us from thee.

Roman Breviary

176   O most loving Jesu, pattern of charity, who makest all the commandments of the law to consist in love towards God and towards man, grant to us so to love thee with all our heart, with all our mind, and all our soul, and our neighbour for thy sake; that the grace of charity and brotherly love may dwell in us, and all envy, harshness, and ill-will may die in us; and fill our hearts with feelings of love, kindness, and compassion, so that by constantly rejoicing in the happiness and good success of others, by sympathizing with them in their sorrows, and putting away all harsh judgments and envious thoughts, we may follow thee, who art thyself the true and perfect love.

Treasury of Devotion, 1869

O blessed Jesus, who knowest the impurity of our affection, the nar- *177*
rowness of our sympathy, and the coldness of our love, take possession of our souls and fill our minds with the image of thyself; break
the stubbornness of our selfish wills and mould us in the likeness of
thine unchanging love, O thou who only could, our Saviour, our
Lord and our God.

William Temple, 1881–1944

My God, my Love: thou art all mine, and I am all thine. Enlarge me in *178*
love; that with the inner mouth of my heart I may taste how sweet it
is to love. Let me love thee more than myself, and myself only for
thee, and in thee all that love thee truly: as the law of love comman-
deth shining forth from thee.

Thomas a Kempis, c.1380–1471

O God, the God of all goodness and of all grace, who art worthy of a *179*
greater love than we can either give or understand: fill our hearts, we
beseech thee, with such love toward thee that nothing may seem too
hard for us to do or to suffer in obedience to thy will; and grant that
loving thee, we may become daily more like thee, and finally obtain
the crown of life which thou hast promised to those that love thee;
through Jesus Christ our Lord.

Brooke Foss Westcott, 1825–1901

FOR THE LOVE OF HUMANITY

180 O God, who of thy great love to man didst reconcile earth to heaven through thine only-begotten Son: grant that we who by the darkness of our sins are turned aside from brotherly love, may be filled with his Spirit shed abroad within us, and embrace our friends in thee and our enemies for thy sake; through Jesus Christ our Lord.

Mozarabic Liturgy, 7th century

181 O Holy and ever-blessed Lord, teach us, we beseech thee, to love one another, to exercise forbearance and forgiveness towards our enemies; to recompense no man evil for evil, but to be merciful even as thou, our Father in heaven, art merciful: that so we may continually follow after thee in all our doings, and be more and more conformed to thine image and likeness.

New Church Book of Worship, 1876

182 Lord, thou art the living flame, burning ceaselessly with love for man. Enter into me and inflame me with thy fire so that I might be like thee.

John Henry Newman, 1801–90

183 O God, who has bound us together in this bundle of life, give us grace to understand how our lives depend on the industry, the honesty and integrity of our fellow men; that we may be mindful of their needs, grateful for their faithfulness, and faithful in our responsibilities to them; through Jesus Christ our Lord.

Reinhold Niebuhr, 1892–1971

O God, fountain of love, pour thy love into our souls, that we may 184
love those whom thou lovest with the love thou givest us, and think
and speak with the love thou givest us, and think and speak of them
tenderly, meekly, lovingly; and so loving our brethren and sisters for
thy sake, may grow in thy love, and dwelling in thy love may dwell in
thee, for Jesus Christ's sake.

Edward Bouverie Pusey, 1800–82

O God almighty, by whom and before whom we all are brethren: 185
grant us so truly to love one another, that evidently and beyond all
doubt we may love thee; through Jesus Christ thy Son, our Lord and
brother.

Christina Rossetti, 1830–94

Pour on us, O Lord, the spirit of love and brotherly-kindness; so that, 186
sprinkled by the dew of they benediction, we may be made glad by
thy glory and grace; through Jesus Christ our Lord.

Sarum Breviary

Like your disciples on the road to Emmaus, we are so often incapable 187
of seeing that you, O Christ, are our companion on the way. But
when our eyes are opened we realize that you were speaking to us
even though perhaps we had forgotten you. Then the sign of our trust
in you is that, in our turn, we try to love, to forgive with you. Independent of our doubts or even our faith, O Christ, you are always there:
your love burns in our heart of hearts.

(Brother) Roger Schutz

Grant me to recognize in other men, Lord God, 188
the radiance of your own face.

Pierre Teilhard de Chardin, 1881–1955

Go-between God: 189
inweave the fabric of our common life,
that the many-coloured beauty of your love
may find expression in all our exchanges.

Jennifer Wild

190   O God of love, we pray thee to give us love:
Love in our thinking, love in our speaking,
Love in our doing, and love in the hidden places of our souls;
Love of our neighbours near and far;
Love of our friends, old and new;
Love of those with whom we find it hard to bear,
And love of those who find it hard to bear with us;
Love of those with whom we work,
And love of those with whom we take our ease;
Love in joy, love in sorrow;
Love in life and love in death;
That so at length we may be worthy to dwell with thee,
Who art eternal love.

William Temple, 1881–1944

191   I love you, O God,
my Love,
my Warmth,
my Solace,
my Fulfilment.
All that I am,
all that I do
finds meaning and purpose in you.
Fill me with the full force
of your Love
and its passionate splendour,
so that I might hold
and heal all those who are crying out for love.
Love through me
all the unreconciled
whose homes and hearts
are broken,
and let them know
I am able to love
because you have first loved me.

Miriam Therese Winter

---✠---

PRAYERS FOR FAMILIES

AND FRIENDS

---✠---

**Be subject to one another out of
reverence for Christ.**

Ephesians 5.21

HOMES AND FAMILIES

We are a broken, divided family 192
of lonely individuals,
each alone;
truly, we're not a family.
Communication with each other
seems impossible,
and love vanishes into the void.
Yet both are what we desperately need.
We all need and want
each other,
but we're too proud to admit it,
or to confess
that we're each to blame
for our separation,
loneliness, and pain.
We add brick upon brick
to the wall that divides
and isolates us.

You alone are our hope,
O God of our salvation.
Your love breaks down
walls that isolate and divide us.
Your love heals, forgives,
and makes us whole again.
Restore us, O God of our salvation.
Reconcile us,
that we may be a family,
and live.

Vienna Cobb Anderson

193   Father of all mankind, make the roof of my house wide enough for all opinions, oil the door of my house so it opens easily to friend and stranger and set such a table in my house that my whole family may speak kindly and freely around it.

Source unknown (Hawaii)

194   Let us ask God to bless our home.
Jesus, King of love, you shared in the life of your earthly home at Nazareth with Mary and Joseph. Bless, we pray, our new home and our life here, that we may help each other and those who visit us to grow more and more in your love. We ask this in your name and for your sake.

Anglican Church of Canada. Alternative Service Book

195   Eternal Spirit, Earth-maker, Pain-bearer, Life-giver,
Source of all that is and shall be,
Father and Mother of us all,
Loving God, in whom is heaven,
enfold this family with your grace.
May their home be a place of your presence,
your forgiveness and your freedom.
May your will be done in them and through them
this day and for ever.

Anglican Church in Aotearoa, New Zealand and Polynesia.
A New Zealand Prayer Book

196   Most gracious Father,
this is our home;
let your peace rest upon it.
   Let love abide here,
   love of one another,
   love of mankind,
   love of life itself,
   and love of God.
Let us remember that
as many hands build a house,
so many hearts make a home.

Hugh Blackburne

O heavenly Father, shed forth thy blessed Spirit richly on all members   *197*
of this household. Make each one of us an instrument in thy hands for
good. Purify our hearts, strengthen our minds and bodies, fill us with
mutual love. Let no pride, no self-conceit, no rivalry, no dispute, ever
spring up among us. Make us earnest and true, wise and prudent, giving no just cause for offence; and may thy holy peace rest upon us this
and every day, sweetening our trials, cheering us in our work, and
keeping us faithful to the end; through Jesus Christ, our Lord.

Church Guild, 19th century

Dear Lord and Father, please help the members of my family who do   *198*
not seek your love. As you look after your family, please help me to
look after mine, and help them to open their hearts and minds to you.
I want to share my faith and joy, but they do not listen.

I ask this in the name of your Son, Jesus Christ, who died to save us
all.

Joy Edwards

Dear Jesus, see the unmarried mother.   *199*

Bless her. Love her. She feels alone in deep decision. She feels the
dilemma of determining whether she is capable of raising her child
alone or whether she should let others accept this opportunity for
her.

She gets discouraged knowing the subtle and flagrant judgment of
other persons, needing the sound advice of those who are objective
and wise waiting, waiting . . . unsure.

She lives in stark reality. The past is truly past for her. Today and
the unknown tomorrow are her life now. The movement of a small
one constantly reminds her of the irrevocable decision she must
make.

Please, Jesus, love her. Help her to know what is best and to live
with her resolution. Soothe her in moments of despair and fear and in
her hours of labour and delivery. Give her warm friends and loved
ones who care, people to be with her now and in the days to come.
Give her dignity. She is a human being in need of tenderness and
respect.

I pray for the unmarried mother – that she may be loved and understood and blessed.

Judith Mattison

200 Self-giving God, calling us to tread the path of suffering,
yet standing by us in every place of sacrifice,
we praise you for the courage and faithfulness
of unknown, unrecognized, unexceptional people
who exercise a ministry of extraordinary care.

Hear our prayers for . . .
single parents struggling to make ends meet on low wages or
inadequate benefits, with no time or money for themselves,
stretched to breaking point by trying to fulfil two roles;
unmarried sons and daughters, who have lost their youth and middle
years in looking after demanding parents, whose own chance of
retirement may be darkened by the shadow of senility;
parents exhausted and grown old before their time from the daily
strain of caring for a child with special emotional or physical
needs;
the families of people who suffer from manic depression,
schizophrenia, or other mental illness, whose own happiness is
defined by dramatic mood swings or rationed by unpredictable
behaviour.

Watch with them when they get no sleep.
Calm them when their patience snaps
and they lash out with hand or tongue.
Strengthen them when they feel that they can't carry on.
Empower them to claim the resources and respect they deserve.

Self-giving God, calling us to tread the path of suffering,
yet standing by us in every place of sacrifice,
by these prayers and the actions which flow from them
may we begin to share the cost of their caring
and celebrate their selfless offering of love.

Jean Mortimer

201 O God, our Father, we thank thee for our home and family;
for love and forbearance, for friends and foes,
for laughter enjoyed and sorrow shared, for the daily bread of thy
bounty in good times and bad. Help us to be mindful of thy gifts and
glad to show forth thy praise; through Jesus Christ our Lord.

R. N. Rodenmayer

Give, we pray thee, to all children grace reverently to love their 202
parents, and lovingly to obey them. Teach us all that filial duty never
ends or lessens: and bless all parents in their children, and all children
in their parents. O thou in whom the fatherless find mercy, make all
orphans, we beseech thee, loving and dutiful unto thee, their true
Father. Be thy will their law, thy house their home, thy love their
inheritance. And we earnestly pray thee, comfort those who have lost
their children, giving mothers grace to be comforted though they are
not; and grant us all faith to yield our dearest treasures unto thee with
joy and thanksgiving, that where with thee our treasure is, there our
hearts may be also. Thus may we look for and hasten unto the day of
union with thee, and of reunion.

Christina Rossetti, 1830–94

God you have shown yourself as a welcoming father and a tender 203
mother. I have yearned to have my own parent be like you. I feel
wounded, disappointed in the behaviour that I have experienced.
There is constant struggle and pain in this relationship. Deep down
inside I yearn to have him/her meet my needs and expectations for
love and acceptance. It is difficult to love my father/mother because
of the human weaknesses and flaws which I so easily see. I have a mixture of feelings tumbling in me – anger, guilt, discouragement, love,
self-doubts, concern.

You are a God who heals the wounded. You bless the pain in us
when we are overcome with the hurts of life. You promise us a future
full of hope. See here in my spirit all the hurt of the past. Heal me of
my disillusionment, the distress of differences, the heartaches and
tensions over past problems. I beg of you to help me to forgive my
parent for his/her faults. I also beg assistance in lowering my expectations of all I want my parent to be for me. Help me to see the strengths
and the goodness which are also there. Most of all, draw me to a deep
love which accepts this parent as he/she is.

Joyce Rupp

Visit we beseech thee most gracious Father, this family and house- 204
hold with thy protection. Let thy blessing descend and rest on all who
belong to it. Guide us here, and hereafter bring us to thy glory;
through Jesus Christ our Lord.

John Charles Ryle, 1816–1900

205 Heavenly Father, we beseech thee to look in thy mercy upon this household. Grant that every member of it may be taught and guided of thee. Bless the relations and friends of each of us: thou knowest their several necessities; and prosper our efforts to advance thy kingdom at home and abroad; for our Lord Jesus Christ's sake.

Archibald Campbell Tait, 1811–82

206 O eternal God, our most merciful Lord and gracious Father, thou art my guide, the light of mine eyes, the joy of my heart, the author of my hope, and the object of my love and worshippings, thou relievest all my needs, and determinest all my doubts, and art an eternal fountain of blessing, open to all thirsty and weary souls that come and cry to thee for mercy and refreshment. Have mercy upon thy servant, and relieve my fears and sorrows, and the great necessities of my family; for thou alone, O Lord, canst do it.

Jeremy Taylor, 1613–67

COUPLES

207 Creator Spirit,
we thank you for your gift of sexual love,
by which husband and wife
may express their delight in each other,
find refreshment,
and share with you the joy of creating new life.
By your grace may — and — remain lovers,
rejoicing in your goodness.

Anglican Church of Aotearoa, New Zealand and Polynesia.
A New Zealand Prayer Book

To be honest, Lord,   208
Yes, I do like him.
And he likes me.
He hasn't actually said so
But I can tell.
He's really nice, Lord.
You'd like him!
He's kind, and helpful,
And intelligent and sporty,
and good at art –
And simply terrific at the guitar.
In fact you could say
He was re-a-lly dishy, Lord!
What do you say, Lord!
You do like him?
Oh great . . .
But does he like you?
Well I don't think
I mentioned that earlier, did I?
No . . .
One thing he did say, I forgot.
No, Lord,
He doesn't like you.
Thank you for reminding me.
Loving you is the most important
Quality that my partner must have.

Halcyon Backhouse

Heavenly Father, we pray for those whose marriage is losing the love   209
and joy that once was theirs.

Awaken in them the desire to overcome the problems and difficulties that face them.

And grant that through the grace of the Lord Jesus Christ they may
rediscover their love for one another and grow together again,
through Jesus Christ our Lord.

Frank Colquhoun

210 We remember before you, Lord, those whose marriages are at risk or have broken down.

You alone know the story behind each unhappy and broken marriage.

We remember especially just now — and —.

Make them willing to recognize where they may be at fault; give them a sincere desire to put things right; and teach them in their desperate need to turn to you, whose love is unfailing and whose power can make all things new, in Jesus our Lord.

Llewellyn Cumings

211 Lord Jesus Christ, who by your presence and power brought joy to the wedding at Cana: bless those engaged to be married, that there may be truth at the beginning of their lives together, unselfishness all the way, and perseverance to the end.

May their hopes be realized and their love for each other deepen and grow, that through them your name may be glorified.

Mothers' Union

212   Eternal God, author of harmony and happiness,
        we thank you for the gift of marriage
        in which men and women may seek and find
            the consummation of bodily union,
            the satisfaction of life-long companionship,
            and the fulfilment of creative and responsible parenthood.
        Give patience to those who look forward to marriage;
        give courage to those who face trials within their marriage;
        give comfort to those whose marriage has broken;
        and to those whose marriages are successful and fruitful
            give gratitude and understanding,
            that they may be examples to all of your great love.
        Through Jesus our Lord.

Michael Saward

CHILDREN

Heavenly Father, 213
from whom all parenthood comes,
teach us so to understand our children
that they may grow in your wisdom and love
according to your holy will.

Fill us with sensitive respect
for the great gift of human life
which you have committed
to our care;
help us to listen with patience
to their worries and problems,
and give us the tolerance
to allow them to develop
as individuals.

For your name's sake.
Michael Buckley

Almighty God and heavenly Father, we thank thee for the children 214
which thou hast given us: give us also grace to train them in thy faith,
fear and love; that as they advance in years they may grow in grace,
and may hereafter be found in the number of thine elect children;
through Jesus Christ our Lord.
John Cosin, 1594–1672

Almighty God, heavenly Father, you have blessed us with the joy and 215
care of children: give us calm strength and patient wisdom as we
bring them up, that we may teach them to love whatever is just and
true and good, following the example of our Saviour Jesus Christ.
Episcopal Church of the United States of America. Book of Common Prayer

216 God our Father, we pray for our young people growing up in an unstable and confusing world.

Show them that your ways give more meaning to life than the ways of the world, and that following you is better than chasing after selfish goals.

Help them to take failure not as a measure of their worth but as a chance for a new start.

Give them strength to hold their faith in you, and to keep alive their joy in your creation; through Jesus Christ our Lord.

Episcopal Church of the United States of America. Book of Common Prayer

217 O God of love and mercy, help us to understand our children as they grow in years and in knowledge of your world. Make us compassionate for their temptations and failures and encouraging in their seeking after truth and value for their lives. Stir in us appreciation of their ideals and sympathy for their frustrations; that with them we may look for a better world than either we or they have known, through Jesus Christ, our common Lord and Master.

Massey Hamilton Shepherd, Jnr.

218 O God, it might seem odd to some to pray for someone not yet born – but not to you and not to me. In these nine months of womanly patience, I have learned more than ever to marvel at your creative plans – and our part in them. I rejoice that the fashioning of a baby, and the founding of a family, requires the gifts of body, mind and spirit you have given to each of us. Bless these days of waiting, of preparation, of tender hope.

Let only things and thoughts that are clean and strong and glad be about us. I give you thanks that from childhood till this experience of maturity, you have made it both beautiful and natural for me to give love and to receive it. In this newest experience, hold us each safe, relaxed, and full of eager hope – even as you count each life in your presence, precious.

Rita Snowden

O Lord my God, shed the light of your love on my child. Keep him   *219*
safe from all illness and all injury. Enter his tiny soul, and comfort
him with your peace and joy. He is too young to speak to me, and to
my ears his cries and gurgles are meaningless nonsense. But to your
ears they are prayers. His cries are cries for your blessing. His gurgles
are gurgles of delight at your grace. Let him as a child learn the way of
your commandments. As an adult let him live the full span of life,
serving your kingdom on earth. And finally in his old age, let him die
in the sure and certain knowledge of your salvation. I do not ask that
he be wealthy, powerful or famous. Rather I ask that he be poor in
spirit, humble in action, and devout in worship. Dear Lord, smile
upon him.

Johann Starck, 1680–1756

Bless our children with healthful bodies, with good understandings,   *220*
with the graces and gifts of thy Spirit, with sweet dispositions and
holy habits; and sanctify them throughout in their bodies, souls and
spirits, and keep them unblamable to the coming of our Lord Jesus
Christ.

Jeremy Taylor, 1613–67

NEIGHBOURS AND FRIENDS

221 O God, our heavenly Father, who hast commanded us to love one another as thy children, and hast ordained the highest friendship in the bond of thy Spirit, we beseech thee to maintain and preserve us always in the same bond, to thy glory, and our mutual comfort, with all those to whom we are bound by any special tie, either of nature or of choice; that we may be perfected together in that love which is from above, and which never faileth when all other things shall fail. Send down the dew of thy heavenly grace upon us, that we may have joy in each other that passeth not away; and, having lived together in love here, according to thy commandment, may live for ever together with them, being made one in thee, in thy glorious kingdom hereafter, through Jesus Christ our Lord.

John Austin, 1613–69

222
        Dear God,
        Lover of us all,
        do not let me go down into the grave
        with old broken friendships unresolved.
        Give to us and to all with whom
        we have shared our lives
        and deepest selves
        along the Way,
        the courage not only to express anger
        when we feel let down,
        but your more generous love
        which always seeks to reconcile
        and so to build a more enduring love
        between those we have held dear
        as friends.

        Kathy Keay

Heavenly Father,   223
look in love on all our friends and neighbours.
Keep them from harm,
deepen our friendship with them
and may we grow in love of you,
our Saviour and friend.

Michael Botting

Let us pray for our friends,   224
that they may lead happy and useful lives;
Let us pray for any friends
    with whom we have quarrelled,
that we may have the chance to be reconciled;
Let us pray for those who are living in new surroundings
    and lack friends.
Let us pray for those who have lost their friends
    by the way they live;
Let us pray for those who befriend the friendless.
God our Father,
make us true and loyal friends.
Grant that all our friends
    may lead us nearer you.

Caryl Micklem

O heavenly Father,   225
who has bestowed on us
the comfort of earthly friends:
look in love upon those dear to us
from whom we are separated.
Protect them and keep them from harm;
prosper and bless them in all good things;
suffer them never to be desolate or afraid,
and let no shadow come between them and us
    to divide our hearts;
but in your own good time
may we renew the comfort of sight and sound;
    through Jesus Christ our Lord.

New Every Morning

226 May the God of love who is the source of all our affection for each other formed here on earth take our friendships into his keeping, that they may continue and increase throughout life and beyond it, in Jesus Christ our Lord.

William Temple, 1881–1944

227 O God, who art present to thy people in every place, mercifully hear our prayers for those we love who are now parted from us: watch over them, we beseech thee, and protect them from anxiety, danger and temptation; and assure both them and us that thou art always near, and that we are one in thee for ever; through Jesus Christ our Lord.

Brooke Foss Westcott, 1825–1901

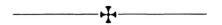

PRAYERS FOR PEOPLE

IN SPECIAL NEED

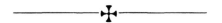

You have been a refuge to the poor,

a refuge to the needy in their distress,

a shelter from the rainstorm

and a shade from the heat.

Isaiah 25.4

THE ABUSED

You gave us to each other, Lord,
In love to live and grow,
One flesh created, giving life,
Delight and trust to know.

228

With grace for joy and constancy
You bless each human soul,
To mirror your self-giving love,
Make mind and body whole.

But anguished cries now rise to you
From hearts betrayed and shamed,
By lashing tongue and thrusting fist,
And touch unasked, unnamed.

The hands you made for tender care,
Love's openness to tell,
Strip self-esteem, wreak fear and death,
Make home a hidden hell.

Stretch out your nail-marked hands in love,
Make violence to cease;
Heal those whose cruel acts and words
Destroy their loved ones' peace.

Restore the homes deprived of joy,
Deliver those in pain,
Bring justice, liberty from fear,
And hope to live again.

Anna Briggs

229

You chose, O loving God,
to enter this world
quietly, humbly, and as an outcast.
Hear our prayers
on behalf of all who are abused:

For children,
who suffer at the hands
of parents whom they trust and love;
for spouses,
beaten and destroyed
by the very one
who promised to love
and to cherish them for ever;
for all people
ignored, hated, and cheated,
by the very neighbour
who could be the closest one
to offer your love.

Hear the cry of the oppressed.
Let the fire of your Spirit fill their hearts
with the power of vision, and hope.
Grant to them empowerment to act,
that they may not be passive victims
of violence and hatred.
Fulfil for them the promises you have made,
that their lives may be transformed
and their oppression ended.

Turn the hearts of the oppressor unto you
that their living may be changed
by your forgiving love;
and their abusive actions
and oppressive ways brought to an end.

In the name of Jesus Christ,
who came to liberate the world, we pray.
Through Christ and in us
may your holy name be praised,
this day and for ever.
So be it.

Vienna Cobb Anderson

Jesus, our brother and friend,   *230*
look with kindness and compassion
on those who were sexually abused.
You see the lost child within
still crying alone in the darkness
where the hidden wounds of childhood
still hurt, and make them afraid.
When they feel abandoned, give them hope,
when they feel ashamed, give them comfort,
when they feel unloved, give them faith,
when they feel betrayed, give them peace.
In the power of your resurrection
may love triumph over fear,
light shine in the darkness,
and the long reign of terror be ended.

Tracy Hansen

THE BEREAVED

Most loving God,   *231*
losing a child is devastating.
Bless all women,
and especially — ,
who have had a miscarriage.
Comfort them in their loss.
Give them hope
for children to come.
Bless them with an abundance of love
that as their bodies heal, so too may their hearts.
Give them courage to face each new day
in the confidence of your love;
in the name of Jesus Christ we pray.

Vienna Cobb Anderson

232

God of all consolation,
in your unending love and mercy for us
you turn the darkness of death
into the dawn of new life.
Show compassion to your people in their sorrow.

Be our refuge and our strength
to lift us from the darkness of this grief
to the peace and light of your presence.

Your son, our Lord Jesus Christ,
by dying for us, conquered death
and by rising again, restored life.

May we then go forward eagerly to meet him,
and after our life on earth
be reunited with our brothers and sisters
where every tear will be wiped away.

Source unknown

233   God our Creator,
from whom all life comes,
comfort this family, grieving for the loss of their hoped-for child.
Help them to find assurance
that with you nothing is wasted or incomplete,
and uphold them with your love,
through Jesus Christ our Saviour.

Anglican Church in Aotearoa, New Zealand and Polynesia.
A New Zealand Prayer Book

234

Please listen, God,
while we talk to you about — who has died.
Take care of him/her,
and please take care of us too.
Thank you for the times we had together.
Thank you for Jesus, who shows us your love.
He is close to —, and he is close to us.
Thank you, God.

Anglican Church in Aotearoa, New Zealand and Polynesia.
A New Zealand Prayer Book
(A prayer that may be used by children)

O God, to me who am left to mourn his departure, grant that I may   235
not sorrow as one without hope for my beloved who sleeps in you;
but, as always remembering his courage, and the love that united us
on earth, I may begin again with new courage to serve you more fervently who are the only source of true love and true fortitude; that
when I have passed a few more days in this valley of tears and this
shadow of death, supported by your rod and staff, I may see him face
to face, in those pastures and beside those waters of comfort where I
believe he already walks with you. O Shepherd of the sheep, have pity
on this darkened soul of mine.

*Edward White Benson, 1829–96 (Written on the death of his young son Martin in
1877)*

Father of mercies and God of all comfort, look in thy tender love and   236
pity, we beseech thee, on thy sorrowing servants. Be thou to them
their refuge and strength, a very present help in trouble; make them
to know the love of Christ, which passeth knowledge; who by death
hath conquered death, and by rising again hath opened the gates of
everlasting life, even Jesus Christ our Lord.

Church of South India

Lord, this dreadful thing has happened, and our minds are baffled,   237
our spirits weighed down with grief.

It is beyond our understanding why this little life should be taken,
or why we should be called upon to suffer so terrible a loss.

Yet we know that life is full of mystery and that many others at this
time are facing the same problem and enduring the same anguish as
ourselves.

Help us to bear our sorrow without bitterness, and not to question
your love; for to whom can we look for comfort but to you, O Lord?

Speak your word of peace to our hearts; ease our pain and lift our
darkness; and be to us a very present help in trouble; for Jesus
Christ's sake.

Frank Colquhoun

238 May the cry of widows, orphans and destitute children enter into thine ears, O most loving Saviour. Comfort them with a mother's tenderness, shield them from the perils of this world, and bring them at last to thy heavenly home.

John Cosin, 1595–1672

239 Father of all, stretch out your loving arms to the mother and father who mourn their child, —. Draw them gently to you in their grief; comfort them in the emptiness that is left, and give them strength and courage to face the future.

   Lord, give us understanding and compassion to say the right words and be sensitive to their needs.

Eunice Davies

240 O God, she/he is dead, she is gone,
the best friend I ever had.
My world is empty. Nothing matters.
I find no joy in anything, and wish I could die myself.

Everywhere I turn I see her,
and up come my tears again.
My nights are restless, long,
and all my days are grey.
The ache inside is huge, gaping,
the only thing I feel.

I was not a perfect husband, God. You know that.
How sorry it makes me now.
Why couldn't I see how good and precious she was?
I would have curbed the sharp word,
and let the little things go.
I would have told her and showed her more often how much I loved her.

O God, I don't know what to do.
There seems nothing left for me.
I am a burden to myself, and no good to anyone.

Jesus, Healer of Souls, I need you as never before.
Reach down to me and pull me to my feet.
Call me from the tomb. Breathe on me that I may live.

Kathleen Fischer and Thomas Hart

Grant, O Lord, to all who are bereaved, the spirit of faith and cour-   241
age, that they may have the strength to meet the days to come with
steadfastness and patience; not sorrowing as those without hope, but
in thankful remembrance of thy great goodness in past years, and in
the sure expectation of a joyful reunion in the heavenly places; and
this we ask in the name of Jesus Christ our Lord.

Church of Ireland. Book of Common Prayer

O God, who brought us to birth and in whose arms we die: in our   242
grief and shock contain and comfort us, embrace us with your love,
give us hope in our confusion and grace to let go into new life;
through Jesus Christ our Lord.

Janet Morley

We give them back to thee, dear Lord, who gavest them to us. Yet as   243
thou didst not lose them in giving, so we have not lost them by their
return. What thou gavest thou takest not away, O Lover of souls; for
what is thine is ours also if we are thine. And life is eternal and love is
immortal, and death is only an horizon, and an horizon is nothing
save the limit of our sight. Lift us up, strong Son of God, that we may
see further; cleanse our eyes that we may see more clearly; and draw
us closer to thyself that we may know ourselves to be nearer to our
loved ones who are with thee. And while thou dost prepare for us,
prepare us also for that happy place, that where they are and thou art,
we too may be for evermore.

William Penn, 1624–91

O Lord Jesus Christ, God of all consolation, whose heart was moved   244
to tears at the grave of Lazarus; look with compassion on your children in their loss. Strengthen in them the gift of faith, and give to their
troubled hearts, and to the hearts of all men, the light of hope, that
they may live as one day to be united again, where tears shall be
wiped away, in the kingdom of your love; for you died and were
raised to life with the Father and the Holy Spirit, God, now and for
ever.

Roman Catholic order for a funeral (adapted)

245 Lord I'm so sad.
Since he died I feel so empty inside.
I can't sleep properly.
I don't want to eat.
I don't want to see anybody.
Will you help me Lord?
Will you give me that special peace
which Jesus spoke about?
Help me to feel certain
that with you beside me
everything is going to be all right.
That we are all in your hands,
and that you will never let us go,
even when we die.
Help me to start living again Lord.
I know it won't be the same,
but with your help I think I can cope.
Please let me know that you are with me
every moment of day and night,
and that your strength will see me through.

Frazer Smith

246 O God, you have dealt very mysteriously with us. We have been passing through deep waters; our feet were well-nigh gone, But though you slay us, yet will we trust in you . . . They are gone from us . . . You have reclaimed the lent jewels. Yet, O Lord, shall I not thank you now? I will thank you not only for the children you have left to us, but for those you have reclaimed. I thank you for the blessing of the last ten years, and for all the sweet memories of these lives . . . I thank you for the full assurance that each has gone to the arms of the Good Shepherd, whom each loved according to the capacity of her years. I thank you for the bright hopes of a happy reunion, when we shall meet to part no more. O Lord, for Jesus Christ's sake, comfort our desolate hearts. May we be a united family in heart through the communion of saints; through Jesus Christ our Lord.

Archibald Campbell Tait, 1811–82 (Between 11 March and 8 April 1856 Tait and his wife lost five of their six daughters through scarlet fever)

O Lord our God, from whom neither life nor death can separate *247*
those who trust in thy love, and whose love holds in its remembrance
thy children in this world and the next; so unite us to thyself that in
fellowship with thee we may always be united to our loved ones,
whether here or there; give us courage, constancy and hope; through
him who died and was buried and rose again for us, Jesus Christ our
Lord.

William Temple, 1881–1944

O Lord God, who knowest our frame and rememberest that we are *248*
dust, look in pity upon those who mourn. Make thy loving presence
so real to them that they may feel round about them thine everlasting
arms, upholding and strengthening them.

Grant them such a sense of certainty that their loved one is with
thee, doing thy high service, unhindered by pain, that they may turn
to life's tasks with brave hearts and steady nerves, consoled in the
thought that they will meet their dear one again.

Teach us all to face death unafraid and take us at last in triumph
through the shadows into thine everlasting light where are reunion
and never-ending joy. Through Jesus Christ our Lord.

Leslie D. Weatherhead, 1883–1975

We remember, Lord, the slenderness of the thread which separates *249*
life from death, and the suddenness with which it can be broken.
Help us also to remember that on both sides of that division we are
surrounded by your love.

Persuade our hearts that when our dear ones die neither we nor
they are parted from you.

In you may we find peace, and in you be united with them in the
body of Christ, who has burst the bonds of death and is alive for evermore, our Saviour and theirs for ever and ever.

Dick Williams

250 O Comforting One,
Compassionate One,
be with us all
when we suffer loss
and ache with the pain of grieving.
Give us a glimpse
of the way it will be
when love will never be taken away,
when life itself will not be diminished,
when all that we hold most precious
will live and remain with us for ever.

Miriam Therese Winter

THE DEAD

251 O God righteous and compassionate
Forgive the despair of — for whom we pray.
Heal in him that which is broken,
And in your great love stand with those
Hurt by the violence of his end.
Lord be to him not a judge but a Saviour.
Receive him into that kingdom wherein by your mercy
We sinners also would have place
Through the merits of our wounded Redeemer
Who lives and reigns with you in the Holy Spirit's power
Now and unto the ages of ages.

Elizabeth Bassett

Father of all, we pray to you for those we love but see no longer. *252*
Grant them your peace; let light perpetual shine upon them; and in
your loving wisdom and almighty power, work in them the good purpose of your perfect will, through Jesus Christ our Lord.

Anglican Church of Canada. Alternative Service Book

Welcome, Lord, into your calm and peaceful kingdom those who, *253*
out of this present life, have departed to be with you; grant them rest
and a place with the spirits of the just; and give them the life that
knows not age, the reward that passes not away; through Jesus Christ
our Lord.

Ignatius Loyola, 1491–1556

Remember, O Lord, we beseech thee, the souls of them that have kept *254*
the faith, both those whom we remember and those whom we
remember not; and grant them rest in the land of the living, in the joy
of Paradise, whence all pain and grief have fled away; where the light
of thy countenance shineth for ever; and guide in peace the end of our
lives, O Lord, when thou wilt and as thou wilt, only without shame
and sin; through thine only-begotten Son, our Lord and Saviour Jesus
Christ.

Liturgy of John Chrysostom and Basil the Great

THE DESERTED

255   My God, my God, why have you deserted me?
      Matthew 27.46 (Jerusalem Bible)

256   Mother, God of all,
                           hear our prayer
                           for your children
                           whose mothers
                           have abandoned them.
                           Their pain is unimaginable.
                           Trust has been broken.
                           Fear and suspicion
                           govern their inner being.
                           Grant unto them
                           that peace
                           which you alone can give,
                           the sure and certain knowledge
                           that your trust is unfailing,
                           and your love
                           that makes us all whole;
                           in the name of your Son,
                           Jesus Christ,
                           we pray.

                           Vienna Cobb Anderson

257   Father, we pray for all who have suffered deep loss, through deser-
      tion by parent, partner, friend or child. Come close to them in their
      sense of desolation and keep them from bitterness or despair. Bring
      them a sense of your nearness and your consolation. Through Jesus
      Christ our Lord.

      Mary Batchelor

You were despised and rejected of men, O Lord;   *258*
a man of sorrows and acquainted with grief,
so you can understand when I feel rejected;
you can feel my sorrow and my sadness.
I thank you for your presence
   in all my times of darkness,
     and for giving me light along my way.

Denis Duncan

THOSE IN DESPAIR

God of eternal life,   *259*
bless all who contemplate
taking their own life.
Grant them peace
from the internal fears and doubts,
from the turmoil of failures,
from the pain and suffering in their souls.
Endow them with hope
for the days ahead,
courage to make new beginnings,
and love to strengthen
their resolve to live;
in the name of Christ
we pray.

Vienna Cobb Anderson

260 Comfort, we ask you, most gracious God, all who are cast down and faint of heart amidst the sorrows and difficulties of the world: and grant that, by the quickening power of the Holy Spirit, they may be lifted up to you with hope and courage, and enabled to go upon their way rejoicing in your love; through Jesus Christ our Lord.

Richard Meux Benson, 1824–1915

261   The praise of your salvation, O God,
        has died on lips that are parched.
        The story of your wonders towards us
        has turned hollow, bitter, and sour.
        I doubt any prayer can enter your heart,
        your ear is deaf to my cry.

        Soul-deep I am full of troubles,
        and my life draws near to the grave.
        I totter on the edge of the abyss,
        ghostly, ghastly, shrivelled.
        I am like the wounded in war that stagger;
        like a corpse strewn out on the battlefield.

        I belong no more to my people,
        I am cut off from your presence, O God.
        You have put me in the lowest of dungeons,
        in a pit of scurrying rats.
        To a wall that drips with water I am chained,
        my feet sink into mud.

        I feel nothing but a pounding in my head,
        surges of pain overwhelm me.
        I cannot endure this suffering,
        this furious onslaught, so searing.
        I can remember no time without terror,
        without turmoil and trouble of mind.

        I have been dying since the day of my birth:
        O God, have I ever really existed?
        I have never known who I am,
        and even my friends who once loved me,
        who gave me some sense of belonging,
        have drawn back in horror and left me.
        My sight fails me because of my trouble;

there is no light in the place of deep dark.
I am alone, bewildered, and lost;
yet I cannot abandon you, God.
Day after day I cry out to you,
early in the morning I pray in your absence.

Do you work wonders among the tombs?
Shall the dead rise up and praise you?
Will your loving kindness reach to the grave,
your faithfulness to the place of destruction?
Are the stories of old an illusion?
Will you again do what is right in the land?

Jim Cotter (based on Psalm 88)

In times of despair, O God, rain showers of gentleness upon us, that   262
we may be kindly one to another and also to ourselves. Renew in us
the spirit of hope. Even in the depths of the darkness, may we hear the
approach of the One who harrows hell and greets even Judas with a
kiss.

Jim Cotter

O God, you rule over your creation with tenderness, offering fresh   263
hope in the midst of the most terrible misery. We pray for our brother
whose soul is blackened by despair, infusing him with the pure light
of your love. As he curses the day he was born and yearns for oblivion, reveal to him the miracle of new birth which shall prepare him
for the joys of heaven.

Dimma, 7th century

O merciful Father, who hast taught us in thy holy Word that thou   264
dost not willingly afflict or grieve the children of men: look with pity
upon the sorrows of thy servant for whom our prayers are offered.
Remember him, O Lord, in mercy, nourish his soul with patience,
comfort him with a sense of thy goodness, lift up thy countenance
upon him, and give him peace; through Jesus Christ our Lord.

Episcopal Church of the United States of America. Book of Common Prayer

265

Lord Jesus,
as you bowed your head and died,
a great darkness covered the land.

We lay before you
the despair of all
who find life
without meaning or purpose,
and see no value in themselves,
who suffer the anguish
of inner darkness
that can only lead them
to self-destruction and death.

Lord,
in your passion, you too
felt abandoned, isolated, derelict.

You are one
with all who suffer
pain and torment
of body and mind.

Be to them the light
that has never been mastered.
Pierce the darkness
which surrounds and engulfs them,
so that they may know
within themselves
acceptance, forgiveness, and peace.

We pray for those who,
through the suicide
of one close to them,
suffer the emptiness of loss
and the burden of untold guilt.
May they know
your gift of acceptance,
so that they may be freed
from self-reproach
and mutual recrimination,
and find in the pattern
of your dying and rising,

new understanding, and purpose
for their lives.

Neville Smith

THE DISABLED

Jesus, our Lord and Shepherd,   266
   you had compassion on the weak and disabled
      the two blind beggars
      the crippled at Bethesda,
      the deaf, the dumb,
      the mentally ill,
      and those troubled by evil spirits.

By the anointing of your Spirit
   bring comfort, peace and healing
      to — in his distress.
May he have patience to accept what cannot be changed
   and faith to receive the healing which you offer him
      in body, mind and spirit.

Equip us with discernment and love
   to encourage him to respond to you,
      to the honour and glory of the heavenly Father.

John Gunstone

267 Lord,
There are two frustrations to my disability.
First the physical limitations,
but second the way people's attitudes to those limitations
poison their relationships with me.
Please help me to forgive them.

It feels painful that so many people now see me in terms of what I
    cannot do,
or in terms of what I do differently,
rather than as the person I am.

Being inside this crippled body feels like being on the inside of a
    two-way mirror,
able to look out and see the 'normal' people,
but without their awareness that I am on the other side.

When they look at me and into the mirror from their side they see
    not me,
but a reflection of themselves in my situation.
It is as if they have accidentally walked into a hall of mirrors
at a fun-fair and been suddenly shocked by a grotesquely distorted
    image of themselves,
of their plans, their hopes . . . their futures.

This instinctive reaction is clear in their faces when they meet me,
or look at me from across the street or park.
If they don't look away and are forced to come nearer,
the more obvious this fear of me becomes.
Because it *is* fear they are feeling.
They are afraid of the same thing happening to them.

So, Lord,
please help me to forgive the way they react to me
    because I find it so difficult.
And, Lord,
please forgive me too,
because before I became disabled,
I know that I reacted to disabled people in just the same way.

Peter Lockwood

God our Father, we offer you thanks and praise for life and all its 268
blessings:
  the world of sight and sound, touch and taste and smell;
  the gift of language, the power to communicate with others and
    share our thoughts with them;
  the ties of family life and of friendship, in which giving and
    receiving become one and the same;
  the beacon of high ideals;
  and above all for the sense of eternal things amid all that changes,
    and for hope which dares to stretch out beyond the confines of
    this mortal life.
Father, all these things you give, but not everyone has all of them.
In the name of Jesus who went about doing good and making men
and women whole, we pray now for those who are blind or deaf or
dumb. For the paralysed in body, and the isolated in mind. For those
who have no one to trust, and who feel there is no one to trust and
love them. We pray for all whom force of circumstance condemns to
half-life: and for those also whose worst enemy is themselves.
  All this we see, and yet there is so much we do not see. Our prejudices distort our vision and make our judgments shallow. Keep
restoring our sight, so that we see people in their own right, and not
just for the good or harm they may do us.
Caryl Micklem

O God, the Father of the helpless, we pray for handicapped people 269
and all who suffer from any kind of disability.
  Give them fresh courage to face each day, and the comfort of the
knowledge that you love and care for them.
  Open our eyes and touch our hearts, that we may be sensitive to
their needs and do all that we can to help them; for Jesus Christ's
sake.
Mothers' Union

270　O God, who art the Father of lights, and with whom there is no darkness at all: we thank thee for the good gift of sight which thou hast bestowed upon us, and we pray thee to fill us with thine own compassion for those who have it not.

Direct and prosper the efforts that are made for their welfare. Reveal to them by thy Spirit the things which eye hath not seen, and comfort them with the hope of the light everlasting, to which, of thy great mercy, we beseech thee to bring us all; through Jesus Christ our Saviour.

Arthur W. Robinson, 1856–1928

THE DYING

271　Lord Jesus, receive my spirit!

Acts 7.59

272　　　　　　　O God, give me of thy wisdom,
　　　　　　　O God, give me of thy mercy,
　　　　　　　O God, give me of thy fulness,
　　　　　　　And of thy guidance in face of every strait.

　　　　　　　O God, give me of thy holiness,
　　　　　　　O God, give me of they shielding,
　　　　　　　O God, give me of thy surrounding,
　　　　　　　And of thy peace in the knot of my death.

　　　　　　　O give me of thy surrounding,
　　　　　　　And of thy peace at the hour of my death!

　　　　　　　Source Unknown (Celtic)

God of the dark night,   273
you were with Jesus praying in the garden,
you were with Jesus all the way to the cross
and through the resurrection.
Help us to recognize you now,
as we watch with —,
and wait for what must happen;
help us through any bitterness and despair,
help us accept our distress,
help us to remember that you care for us
and that in your will is our peace.

Anglican Church in Aotearoa, New Zealand and Polynesia.
A New Zealand Prayer Book

Lord Jesus Christ, we thank you that in sharing our life on earth you   274
also entered into the experience of our death and what follows.

As we trust you with our life, so we may surely trust you also with
our death.

When that time comes, give us in your mercy a peaceful end free
from fear, knowing that you are with us and that at the last we shall
be with you in our Father's house for evermore.

Frank Colquhoun

Because I do not hope to turn again   275
Let these words answer
For what is done, not to be done again
May the judgement not be too heavy upon us

Because these wings are no longer wings to fly
But merely vans to beat the air
The air which is now thoroughly small and dry
Smaller and dryer than the will
Teach us to care and not to care
Teach us to sit still.

Pray for us sinners now and at the hour of our death
Pray for us now and at the hour of our death.

T. S. Eliot, 1888–1965

276
    Tie the strings to my life, my Lord,
        Then I am ready to go!
    Just a look at the horses –
        Rapid! That will do!

    Put me in on the firmest side,
        So I shall never fall;
    For we must ride to the Judgment,
        And it's partly down hill.

    But never I mind the bridges
        And never I mind the sea;
    Held fast in everlasting race
        By my own choice and thee.

    Good-by to the life I used to live,
        And the world I used to know;
    And kiss the hills for me, just once;
        Now I am ready to go!

Emily Dickinson, 1830–1886

277
    Father in heaven,
        nothing can separate us from the love of Christ.
    Whether we live or die, we are yours.
    When we walk through the valley of the shadow of death
        we fear no evil, for you are with us.

    We come with — beneath the cross of your beloved Son
        and ask you to wash us in his blood.
    In your mercy, forgive him and us our sins,
        and prepare us to rejoice with your people in Zion,
            where there is no mourning nor crying
            nor any more pain.

    May your Holy Spirit, who raised Jesus from the dead,
        raise — and us to full healing and salvation
    to praise you in eternity.

John Gunstone

Let not mistaken mercy   278
blind my fading sight,
no false euphoria lull me.
I would not unprepared
take this last journey.
Give me a light to guide me
through dark valleys,
a staff to lean upon,
bread to sustain me,
a blessing in my ear
that fear may not assail me.
Then leaving do not hold my hand,
I go to meet a friend –
    that same who traced
    compassion in the sand.

Nancy Hopkins

O Lord, you have freed us from the fear of death. You have made the   279
end of our life here into the beginning of true life for us. You give rest
to our bodies for a time in sleep, and then you awaken them again
with the sound of the last trumpet. Our earthly body, formed by your
hands, you consign in trust to the earth, and then once more you
reclaim it, transfiguring with immortality and grace whatever in us is
mortal or deformed. You have opened for us the way to resurrection,
and given to those that fear you the sign of the holy cross as their
emblem, to destroy the enemy and to save our life.

Eternal God, on you have I depended from my mother's womb,
you have I loved with all the strength of my soul, to you have I dedicated my flesh and my soul from my youth until now. Set by my side
an angel of light, to guide me to the place of repose, where are the
waters of rest, among the holy Fathers. You have broken the fiery
sword and restored to Paradise the thief who was crucified with you
and implored your mercy: remember me also in your kingdom, for I
too have been crucified with you. Let not the dread abyss separate me
from your elect. Let not the envious one bar the way before me. But
forgive me and accept my soul into your hands, spotless and undefiled, as incense in your sight.

Macrina, 4th century

280

Lord Jesus Christ,
Lord of life
and conqueror of death,
look in compassion on all
whose life is drawing to its close.
As they pass
through the valley of the shadow of death
may they know that you are with them.
May they fear no evil.
May they give themselves to you
in trust and faith.
May they find peace and tranquillity
in your nearer presence,
and grant them
a place in your eternal kingdom,
now and for ever.

Heavenly Father,
to your loving care
we commit all those
who watch and wait
with people they know and love.
Enable them to welcome
the moment of death
as friend, not foe,
knowing that all love in this life
flows from your love,
which is stronger than death itself,
as you have shown us
in the living, dying, and rising
of your Son, Jesus Christ our Lord.

Neville Smith

281

At this hour, O Lord, some souls pass
from this life into the unknown world.
May their release be merciful, and may
they find light in thee, who art the God
of all flesh and the victor over the grave.

A Saint Francis Prayer Book

O Christ, be with all who are facing death today in fear or loneliness. 282

United Society for the Propagation of the Gospel

O my most blessed and glorious creator, that hast fed me all my life 283
long, and redeemed me from all evil; seeing it is thy merciful pleasure
to take me out of this frail body, and to wipe away all tears from mine
eyes, and all sorrows from my heart, I do with all humility and willingness consent and submit myself wholly unto thy sacred will. My
most loving redeemer, into thy saving and everlasting arms I commend my spirit; I am ready, my dear Lord, and earnestly expect and
long for thy good pleasure. Come quickly, and receive the soul of thy
servant which trusteth in thee.

Henry Vaughan, 1622–95

THE ELDERLY AND INFIRM

O Lord God, look with mercy on all whose increasing years bring them 284
isolation, distress, or weakness. Provide for them homes of dignity and
peace; give them understanding helpers and the willingness to accept
help; and, as their strength diminishes, increase their faith and their
assurance of your love. We pray in the name of Jesus Christ our Lord.

Anglican Church of Canada. Alternative Service Book

Eternal God, who through the passing years remains ever the same, 285
be near to all who are aged or infirm. Though their bodies fail, let
their spirits be strong in you, that with patience they may bear weari-
ness and distress, and at the last meet death unafraid, through Jesus
Christ our Lord.

New Every Morning

286 Lord Jesus Christ, you are the same yesterday, today and for ever, and have promised to be with us all our days. We pray for all elderly people, especially those who are ill or housebound. In their weakness may they find your strength, and in their loneliness know the joy of your presence. Be to them a sure and certain hope of the life you have prepared for them in heaven.

Mothers' Union

THOSE WITH HIV/AIDS

287 Almighty God, creator of life, sustainer of every good thing I know, my partner with me in the pain of this earth, hear my prayer as I am in the midst of separation and alienation from everything I know to be supportive and healing and true.

AIDS has caused me to feel separated from you. I say, 'Why me? What did I do to deserve this?' . . . Help me to remember that you do not punish your creation by bringing disease, but that you are Emmanuel, God with us. You are as close to me as my next breath.

AIDS has caused a separation between the body I knew and my body now . . . Help me to remember that I am more than my body, and while it pains me greatly to see what has happened to it, I am more than my body . . . I am part of you and you me.

AIDS has separated me from my family . . . O God, help me and them to realize that I haven't changed, I'm still their child, our love for each other is your love for us . . . Help them to overcome their fear, embarrassment and guilt . . . Their love brought me into this world . . . Help them to share as much as possible with me.

AIDS has caused a separation between me and my friends; my friendships have been so important to me. They are especially important now . . . Help me, oh God, to recognize their fear and my increasing need for them to love in any way they can.

AIDS has separated me from society, my whole world and my community . . . It pains me for them to see me differently now . . . Forgive them for allowing their ignorance of this disease and their fear to blind their judgments . . . Help me deal with my anger towards them.

AIDS has caused a separation between me and my church . . . Help the Church restore its ministry to 'the least of these' by reaching out to me and others . . . Help them suspend their judgments and love me as they have before. Help me and them to realize that the Church is the body of Christ . . . that separation and alienation wound the body.

God of my birth and God of my death, help me to know you have been, you are, and you are to come.

Kenneth South

Help us to accept the challenge of AIDS: *288*
    To protect the healthy, calm the fearful;
  to offer courage to those in pain;
  to embrace the dying as they flow
    into love's unendingness;
  to console the bereaved;
  to support all those who attempt to care
    for the sick and the dying.

Enable us to offer our energies,
our imaginations,
and our trusting in the mysteries of love,
to be united with and through one another
    in liberating each other
    from fear of disease.

We offer these thoughts and prayers
    in the mystery of the loving
    that can and does bear all our woundings,
whatever their source,
through the spirit of love's concern
    for each and every person.

Bill Kirkpatrick

289

As those who keep the night watch look for dawn,
so, Lord, we look for your help.
May a cure be found;
May we find love to strengthen us
    and free us from fear;
In the name of him who by dying
    and rising again conquered death
    and is with us now, Jesus Christ.

Ecumenical AIDS Support Team (Edinburgh)

THE HOMELESS AND REFUGEES

290

O God,
you bring hope out of emptiness
energy out of fear
new life out of grief and loss.
As Mary returned to mourn
yet found unspeakable joy,
so comfort all who have lost their homes
through persecution, war, exile,
or deliberate destruction.
Give them security, a place to live,
and neighbours they trust
to be, with them, a new sign of peace to the world.

Janet Morley (Christian Aid)

Our Father, we hold before you in prayer the many homeless people *291*
of our land. We ask the Holy Spirit to open our eyes and our hearts to
their distress and suffering. Though we know that much has been
done to secure more and better housing, we also see the continuing
tragedy of homelessness. Forgive our indifference to the misery
around us, and in your mercy bless and prosper all that is being done
to remedy this evil; for the sake of Jesus Christ our Lord.

Shelter (adapted)

    O God, *292*
    when in Jesus you walked this earth,
    you had no place to call your own,
    no place to lay your head.
    As we stand by the landless and the homeless
    and support those who struggle alongside them,
    may we stand by you,
    seeing your face and image there.

    Barbara Vellacott

THOSE WHO ARE ILL

293   Thank you, O God, for all the people who have looked after me today; for all those who visited today; for all the letters and the get-well cards; for the flowers and gifts friends have sent.

I know that sleep is one of the best medicines for both the body and the mind. Help me to sleep tonight.

Into your strong hands I place all the patients in this ward; the night staff on duty tonight; my loved ones, whose names I now mention; myself, with my fears, my worries and my hopes.

Help me to sleep, thinking of you and your promises.

Source unknown

294   O blessed Jesus, you ministered to all who came to you. Look with compassion upon all who through addiction have lost their health and freedom. Restore to them the assurance of your unfailing mercy; remove the fears that attack them; strengthen them in the work of their recovery; and to those who care for them, give patient understanding and persevering love; for your mercy's sake.

Anglican Church of Canada. Alternative Service Book

295   God of the present moment,
God who in Jesus stills the storm
and soothes the frantic heart;
bring hope and courage to — as he/she/they wait/s in uncertainty.
Bring hope that you will make him/her/them the equal
of whatever lies ahead.
Bring him/her/them courage to endure what cannot be avoided,
for your will is health and wholeness;
you are God, and we need you.

Anglican Church in Aotearoa, New Zealand and Polynesia.
A New Zealand Prayer Book

O heavenly Father, 296
we pray for those suffering from diseases
    for which there is at present no cure.
Give them the victory of trust and hope,
that they may never lose their faith
    in your loving purpose.
Grant your wisdom to all
    who are working to discover the causes of disease,
and the realization that through you
    all things are possible.
We ask this in the name of him
    who went about doing good
    and healing all manner of sickness,
even your Son, Jesus Christ, our Lord.

George Appleton

Healing power of Jesus Christ, 297
fall afresh on me,
Healing power of Jesus Christ,
fall afresh on me.
Touch me, stir me, unfold me, love me.
Healing power of Jesus Christ,
fall afresh on me.

Howard Booth

Almighty, everliving God, maker of all mankind: we beseech thee to 298
have mercy upon this thy servant in his affliction. Give him grace to
take his sickness with patience and courage; and grant that, if it be
thy gracious will, he may recover his bodily health, and serve thee
henceforth in newness of life; through Jesus Christ our Lord.

A Book of Common Prayer, South Africa

299 Lord God, this illness is making me depressed. I am irritated by its aches and pains. I get tired of doing nothing. I worry about the extra work I am causing others. O God, speak to me in the quietness about your majesty, the wonder and beauty of your creation, about your love for me. Speak to me about Jesus Christ my Saviour – the pain of Calvary, about his resurrection life. O God, I will worship you.

Christian Publicity Organisation

300 O Lord Jesus Christ, who went about doing good and healing all manner of sickness: give strength, wisdom and gentleness to all thy ministering servants, our physicians, surgeons and nurses; that always bearing thy presence with them, they may not only heal but bless, and shine as lamps of hope in the darkest hours of distress and fear; who livest and reignest with the Father and the Holy Ghost, ever one God world without end.

Church Missionary Society

301 O God, the Father of lights, from whom cometh down every good and perfect gift: mercifully look upon our frailty and infirmity, and grant us such health of body as thou knowest to be needful for us; that both in body and soul we may evermore serve thee with all our strength; through Jesus Christ our Lord.

John Cosin, 1595–1672

302 O Father of mercies and God of all comfort, our only help in time of need: we humbly beseech thee to behold, visit, and relieve thy sick servant — for whom our prayers are desired. Look upon him with the eyes of thy mercy; comfort him with a sense of thy goodness; preserve him from the temptations of the enemy; and give him patience under his affliction. In thy good time, restore him to health, and enable him to lead the residue of his life in thy fear, and to thy glory; and grant that finally he may dwell with thee in life everlasting; through Jesus Christ our Lord.

Episcopal Church of the United States of America. Book of Common Prayer

O God, the strength of the weak and the comfort of sufferers: mercifully accept our prayers, and grant to your servant — the help of your power, that his sickness may be turned into health, and our sorrow into joy; through Jesus Christ our Lord. 303

Episcopal Church of the United States of America. Book of Common Prayer

O most mighty God and merciful Father, we most humbly beseech thee, if it be thy good pleasure, to continue to us that singular benefit which thou hast given us in the friendship of thy servant, our dear brother, who now lieth on the bed of sickness. Let him abide with us yet awhile for the furtherance of our faith; yet awhile spare him, that he may live to thy honour and our comfort. Thou hast made him a great help and furtherance of the best things among us. O Lord, we beseech thee, restore to us our dear brother, by restoring him to health. 304

Nicholas Ferrar, 1592–1637 (Written for George Herbert, who was gravely ill)

Father of compassion and mercy, who never failest to help and comfort those who cry to thee for succour: give strength and courage to this thy son in his hour of need. Hold thou him up and he shall be safe; enable him to feel that thou art near, and to know that underneath are the everlasting arms; and grant that, resting on thy protection, he may fear no evil, since thou art with him; through Jesus Christ our Lord. 305

Church of Ireland. Book of Common Prayer

Almighty and most merciful Father, whose loving kindness is over all thy works; behold, visit and relieve this thy servant who is grieved with sickness. Grant that the sense of her weakness may add strength to her faith, and seriousness to her repentance. And grant that, by the help of thy Holy Spirit, after the pains and labours of this short life, we may all obtain everlasting happiness, through Jesus Christ our Lord: for whose sake hear our prayers. 306

Samuel Johnson, 1709–86 (Prayed during a farewell visit to a friend)

307 Lord, I'm tired of being ill all the time, sick of minor but exhausting ailments and sick of feeling weak after every effort to accomplish something.

I am tired of hearing people say: 'There is always something wrong with . . .'

True, there *is* always something wrong with me. Nothing serious, nothing which makes others look at me and sadly think: 'It could happen to me . . .'

Not even that. What happens to me is of no great consequence. Minor little illnesses which don't scare anyone: a headache here and a cold there; then something wrong with my stomach, and then something else again. Little nothings.

But there is no end to it. And my patience is running out.

I'm beginning to dream about another life, a life without illness. A strong and healthy life where I get up fresh and rested every morning, ready to meet everything with a smile. A beautiful life: the product of my imagination.

And then I begin to envy people. The healthy ones. I think it's unjust: their relaxed expression, their fresh complexion, their meals without fears and worries. And that smile they put on when they say to me: 'So, what's wrong with you today?' as if they knew what illness was all about.

Forgive me, Lord, for having been unjust. I know that it isn't altogether my fault. But I was nevertheless angry with them. That's stupid.

Teach me, Lord, to understand – that they don't understand.

When I don't feel like doing a thing, give me strength. Strength not to give in, as they say. Strength to try at any rate.

Lord, help me to bear my endless little miseries with some flair.

Paul Geres

Little Boy Sick

308

I am not God's little lamb
I am God's sick tiger.
And I prowl about at night
And what most I love I bite,
And upon the jungle grass I slink,
Snuff the aroma of my mental stink,
Taste the salt tang of tears upon the brink
Of my uncomfortable muzzle.
My tail my beautiful, my lovely tail,
Is warped.
My stripes are matted and my coat once sleek
Hangs rough and undistinguished on my bones,
O God I was so beautiful when I was well.
My heart, my lungs, my sinews and my reins
Consumed a solitary ecstasy,
And light and pride informed each artery.
Then I a temple, now a charnel house.
Then I a high hozannah, now a dirge.
Then I a recompense of God's endeavour,
Now a reproach and earnest of lost toil.
Consider, Lord, a tiger's melancholy
And heed a minished tiger's muted moans,
For thou art sleek and shining bright
And I am weary.
Thy countenance is full of light
And mine is dreary.

Stevie Smith

THE LONELY

309

Lord,
the trouble about life just now
is that I seem to have all the things which don't matter,
and to have lost all the things which do matter.
I have life;
I have enough money to live on;
I have plenty to occupy me:
but I am alone,
and sometimes
I feel that nothing
can make up for that.

Lord,
compel me to see the meaning of my faith.
Make me to realize
that I have a hope
as well as a memory,
and the unseen cloud of witnesses is around me;
that you meant it when you said that
you would be always with me;
and make me realize that
as long as you leave me here
there is something that I am meant to do;
and in doing it,
help me to find the comfort
and the courage
that I need to go on.

Source unknown

O God of love, who art in all places and times, pour the balm of thy *310*
comfort upon every lonely heart. Have pity upon those who are
bereft of human love, and on those to whom it has never come. Be
unto them a strong consolation, and in the end give them fulness of
joy, for the sake of Jesus Christ, thy Son, our Lord.

Source unknown, 19th century

Father, we pray for all the lonely people, especially those who, com- *311*
ing home to an empty house, stand at the door hesitant and afraid to
enter. May all who stand in any doorway with fear in their hearts,
like the two on the Emmaus Road, ask the Living One in. Then, by his
grace, may they find that in loneliness they are never alone, and that
he peoples empty rooms with his presence.

E. M. Farr (Written when sorrowing over the death of his wife, Kathleen)

Accept my prayers, dear Father, for those who have no one to love *312*
them enough to pray for them. Wherever and whoever they are, give
them a share of my blessings, and in thy love let them know that they
are not forgotten.

A Saint Francis Prayer Book

O Lord Jesus *313*
Please abide with me
Dispel my deep loneliness!
No one can be my companion for ever
But you are the Lord who is everywhere
Present at all times
Only you are my dear companion and saviour.

In the long dark night
Along the silent shadowy pathways
I beg you to grasp my hand.
When others have forgotten me
Please remember me in eternity!
In the name of Jesus.

Andrew Song

314 In the depths of our isolation, we cry to you, Lord God; give light in our darkness and bring us out of the prison of our despair; through Jesus Christ our Lord.

David Stancliffe

315 O Lord, we pray for those who, full of confidence and love, once chose a partner for life, and are now alone after final separation. May they receive the gift of time, so that hurt and bitterness may be redeemed by healing and love, personal weakness by your strength, inner despair by the joy of knowing you and serving others; through Jesus Christ our Lord.

Susan Williams

THE MENTALLY
DISTRESSED

316 Heavenly Father, have mercy on all your children who live in mental distress. Restore them to strength of mind and cheerfulness of spirit, and give them health and peace; through Jesus Christ our Lord.

Anglican Church of Canada. Alternative Service Book

Heavenly Father, we bring to you in prayer people who are suffering   *317*
in mind or spirit.
   We remember especially those facing long and incurable illness;
   those cast down by the cares and sorrows of daily life;
   those who have lost their faith and for whom the future is dark.
   In your mercy maintain their courage, lift their burdens and renew
their faith, that they may find in you their strength, their comfort and
their peace; for our Saviour's sake.

Frank Colquhoun

Lord Jesus Christ,   *318*
you healed those who suffered
in mind as well as body.
Look in your compassion
on people among us who are mentally ill.

We pray for all
      who are driven by depression to the depths of despair
      who attempt to end their own lives
      who are victims of obsession
      who are persecuted by the voices they hear
      who live in a world of their own
      who are violent or withdrawn
      who are plagued by religious delusions.

Take from them all unreality.
Help them to know that in the depths
   you search for them
and that in your presence
   you hold them secure.
Grant to them wholeness of mind
so that they may be at peace,
   at one with themselves
   and at one with you.
We ask this for your name's sake.

Neville Smith

319 Lord Jesus Christ, who for love of our souls entered the deep darkness of the cross: we pray that your healing love may surround all
who are in the darkness of great mental distress and who find it
difficult to pray for themselves. May they know that darkness and
light are both alike to you and that you have promised never to fail
them or forsake them.

Llewellyn Cumings

320 Father, we pray for the mentally ill, for all who are of a disturbed and
troubled mind. Be to them light in their darkness, their refuge and
strength in time of fear. Give special skills and tender hearts to all
who care for them, and show them how best to assist in your work of
healing; through Jesus Christ our Lord.

Timothy Dudley-Smith

THE PERSECUTED AND PERSECUTORS

321 Lord, remember not only the men and women of good will, but also
those of ill will. But, do not remember all of the suffering they have
inflicted upon us: instead remember the fruits we have borne because
of this suffering – our fellowship, our loyalty to one another, our
humility, our courage, our generosity, the greatness of heart that has
grown from this trouble. When our persecutors come to be judged by
you, let all of these fruits that we have borne be their forgiveness.

*Source unknown (Found in the clothing of a dead child at Ravensbruck
concentration camp)*

We remember, O Lord,   322
those who suffer from any kind of discrimination;
thy children, and our brothers and sisters,
who are humiliated and oppressed;
we pray for those who are denied fundamental human rights,
for those who are imprisoned,
and especially those who are tortured.
Our thoughts rest a few moments with them . . .
and we pray that thy love and compassion
may sustain them always.

Source unknown (Written for the Week of Prayer for World Peace)

Lord Jesus, you experienced in person torture and death as a prisoner   323
of conscience. You were beaten and flogged and sentenced to an
agonizing death though you had done no wrong. Be now with prisoners of conscience throughout the world. Be with them in their fear
and loneliness, in the agony of physical and mental torture, and in the
face of execution and death. Stretch out your hands in power to break
their chains. Be merciful to the oppressor and the torturer and place a
new heart within them. Forgive all injustice in our lives and transform us to be instruments of your peace, for by your wounds we are
healed.

Amnesty International

God of love and strength, your Son forgave his enemies even while he   324
was suffering shame and death. Strengthen those who suffer for the
sake of conscience. When they are accused, save them from speaking
in hate; when they are rejected, save them from bitterness; when they
are imprisoned, save them from despair. Give us grace to discern the
truth, that our society may be cleansed and strengthened. This we ask
for the sake of our merciful and righteous judge, Jesus Christ our
Lord.

Anglican Church of Canada. Alternative Service Book

325 O God we remember not only our son but also his murderers; not because they killed him in the prime of his youth and made our hearts bleed and our tears flow, not because with this savage act they have brought further disgrace on the name of our country among the civilized nations of the world; but because through their crime we now follow thy footsteps more closely in the way of sacrifice. The terrible fire of this calamity burns up all selfishness and possessiveness in us; its flame reveals the depth of depravity and meanness and suspicion, the dimension of hatred and the measure of sinfulness in human nature; it makes obvious as never before our need to trust in God's love as shown in the cross of Jesus and his resurrection; love which makes us free from hate towards our persecutors; love which brings patience, forbearance, courage, loyalty, humility, generosity, greatness of heart; love which more than ever deepens our trust in God's final victory and his eternal designs for the Church and for the world; love which teaches us how to prepare ourselves to face our own day of death.

O God, our son's blood has multiplied the fruit of the Spirit in the soil of our souls; so when his murderers stand before thee on the day of judgement remember the fruit of the Spirit by which they have enriched our lives. And forgive.

Hassan Dehqani-Tafti (Written when he was the Anglican Bishop in Iran, after the murder of his son)

326 Uphold, O God, all those who are
persecuted or imprisoned for their beliefs.
Be to them a light showing the way ahead;
a rock giving them strength to stand;
a song singing of all things overcome.

Richard Harries

THE POOR AND OPPRESSED

To you, O Lord,   327
on bended knees
our heads we bow in prayer:
that you may hear
our cry for blood-drenched lands
and their exhausted people,
who have seen too much death,
and have been afraid too long
to understand your love,
comprehend your presence,
acknowledge your goodness
and concern for them, a battered people;
yearning for freedom
as they bear your cross.

Lesley G. Anderson

O Heavenly Father, who by thy blessed Son hast taught us to ask of 328
thee our daily bread; have compassion on the millions of our fellow
men who live in poverty and hunger; relieve their distress; make plain
the way of help; and grant thy grace unto us all, that we may bear
each others' burdens according to thy will; through Jesus Christ our
Lord.

George Appleton

Make us worthy, Lord, to serve our fellowmen throughout the world 329
who live and die in poverty and hunger.
Give them, through our hands, this day their daily bread, and by our
understanding love, give peace and joy.

(Mother) Teresa of Calcutta

330   Lord, we remember the millions in our world who must go hungry
      today,
    all those who do not have even the basic necessities of life, and for
      whom life itself has become a burden.
      Out of the depths we cry to you, Lord,
      Hear our cry and listen to our prayer.

    Lord, we remember all those who, because of their caste or class,
      colour or sex, are exploited and marginalized –
      the forces of oppression that trample on people and the unjust
      systems which break the spirit of people, and rob them of their
      rights and dignity.
      Out of the depths we cry to you, Lord,
      Hear our cry and listen to our prayer.

    World Council of Churches

THOSE IN PRISON

331   Lord, thank you for becoming our brother. I ask that you would free
those in prison from the bondage of their shame and disgrace. Let
them see prison as a time to share in the sufferings of their brothers –
and to know that you share those pains as well.

    Charles W. Colson

332   O God, let the sighing of the prisoner come before thee, and mercifully grant unto us that we may be delivered by thine almighty power
from all bonds and chains of sin whether in our bodies or in our souls,
through Jesus Christ our Lord.

    Roman Breviary

Lord, open our eyes   *333*
to the sufferings of our imprisoned brothers and sisters
so that, by our understanding and love,
we may bring them your peace and joy.
You came to set us free.
May your light shine on the captives,
relieve their suffering,
and enable us all to grow toward true freedom
in justice and harmony.

Pax Christi

THOSE IN TROUBLE
AND DISTRESS

God of love, whose compassion never fails; we bring before thee the   *334*
troubles and perils of people and nations, the sighing of prisoners and
captives, the sorrows of the bereaved, the necessities of strangers, the
helplessness of the weak, the despondency of the weary, the failing
powers of the aged. O Lord, draw near to each; for the sake of Jesus
Christ our Lord.

Anselm, 1033–1109

335

O my Lord – Wash me,
     Wash me of this relationship;
Wash me of the pain of it,
Wash me of the hurt of it,
Wash me of the disappointment of it,
Wash me of the resentment of it,
Wash me of the attachment to it,
Wash me of the hurtful memories of it
That come back in quietness, and in prayer time,
That come back in the silent night hours
And rend my body and very heart
With an agony of writhing tears.

I give myself into your hands, Lord,
O Wash me, as I lie still before you.
Do for me what I cannot do for myself.
     Heal me, Lord . . .
Under your healing touch
Hour by hour, and day by day
I shall be set free, until
the intention of my heart is pure love,
And until all my actions give your lovely name
the glory that can flow from a pure heart.

Source unknown

336

O Christ our Lord,
As in times past,
Not all the sick and suffering
Found their own way to your side,
But had to have their hands taken,
   or their bodies carried,
   or their names mentioned;
So we, confident of your goodness,
Bring others to you.

As in times past,
You looked at the faith of friends
And let peace and healing be known,
Look on our faith,
Even our little faith,
And let your kingdom come.

We name before you
Those for whom pain is the greatest problem;
Who are remembered more for their distress
    than for their potential;
Who at night cry, 'I wish to God it were morning.'
And in the morning cry, 'I wish to God it were night.' . . .
Bring healing, bring peace.

We name before you
Those whose problem is not physical;
Those who are haunted by the nightmares of their past
    or the spectres of their future,
Those whose minds are shackled to neuroses,
    depression and fears,
Who do not know what is wrong
And do not know what to pray . . .

Lord Jesus Christ, Lover of all,
Bring healing, bring peace.

We name before you
Those in whose experience light has turned to darkness,
As the end of a life
Or the breaking of a relationship
Leaves them stunned in their souls
    and silent in their conversation,
Not knowing where to turn or who to turn to
or whether life has a purpose any more . . .

Lord Jesus Christ, Lover of all
Bring healing, bring peace.

And others whose troubles we do not know
Or whose names we would not say aloud,
We mention now in the silence which you understand . . .

Lord Jesus Christ, Lover of all
Bring healing, bring peace.

Lord God,
You alone are skilled to know the cure
For every sickness and every soul.
If by our lives your grace may be known
Then in us, through us,

And, if need be, despite us,
Let your kingdom come.

On all who tend the sick,
  counsel the distressed,
  sit with the dying,
  or develop medical research
We ask your blessing,
That in caring for your people
They may meet and serve their Lord.

And for those who, in this land,
Administer the agencies of health and welfare,
We ask your guidance that in all they do
Human worth may be valued,
And the service of human need fully resourced.
This we ask in the name of him
Whose flesh and blood have made all God's children special.

John Bell (Iona Community)

337 We humbly beseech thee, of thy goodness, O Lord, to comfort and
succour all them who in this transitory life are in trouble, sorrow,
need, sickness, or any other adversity: help us to minister to them thy
strength and consolation, and so endow us with the grace of sympathy and compassion that we may bring to them both help and healing; through Jesus Christ our Lord.

Church of England. Book of Common Prayer

338 Lord, hear my prayer when trouble glooms,
  Let sorrow find a way,
  and when the day of trouble comes,
  Turn not thy face away:
  My bones like hearthstones burn away,
  My life like vapoury smoke decays.

  My heart is smitten like the grass,
  That withered lies and dead,
  And I, so lost to what I was,
  Forget to eat my bread.
  My voice is groaning all the day,
  My bones prick through this skin of clay.

The wilderness' pelican,
The desert's lonely owl –
I am their like, a desert man
In ways as lone and foul.
As sparrows on the cottagetop
I wait till I with fainting drop.

I hear my enemies reproach,
All silently I mourn;
They on my private peace encroach,
Against me they are sworn.
Ashes as bread my trouble shares,
And mix my food with weeping cares.

Yet not for them is sorrow's toil,
I fear no mortal's frowns –
But thou hast held me up awhile
And thou has cast me down.
My days like shadows waste from view,
I mourn like withered grass in dew.

But thou, Lord, shalt endure for ever,
All generations through;
Thou shalt to Zion be the giver
Of joy and mercy too.
Her very stones are in thy trust,
Thy servants reverence her dust.

Heathens shall hear and fear thy name,
All kings of earth thy glory know
When thou shalt build up Zion's fame
And live in glory there below.
He'll not despise their prayers, though mute,
But still regard the destitute.

John Clare, 1793–1864 (based on Psalm 102)

We beseech thee, Master, to be our helper and protector. Save the   339
afflicted among us; have mercy on the lowly; raise up the fallen;
appear to the needy; heal the ungodly; restore the wanderers of thy
people; feed the hungry; ransom our prisoners; raise up the sick;
comfort the faint-hearted.

Clement of Rome, 1st century

340 In these days of violent crime we remember before you, our God, the victims of terrorism, hooliganism and muggings.

We pray for the physically injured; for those who have been robbed of their possessions; and the many whose minds are darkened by fear.

Lord, you once suffered at the hands of men.

Look in mercy on those who suffer today, and bring them your healing love and strength, for your name's sake.

Frank Colquhoun

341 God of the heights and the depths,
we bring to you
those driven into the desert,
those suffering with difficult decisions.

May they choose life.

God of the light and the darkness,
we bring to you
those lost in the mist of drugs or drink,
those dazzled by the use of power.

May they choose life.

God of the wild beast and the ministering angel,
we bring to you
those savaged by others' greed,
those exhausted by caring for others.

May they feel your healing touch.

Christ tempted and triumphant,
we bring ourselves to you,
tired of difficult choices,
anxious about the future,
drained by the loss of a loved one.

May we feel your healing touch.

May we feel your healing touch,
know God's presence in all things
and receive the crown of life
through the Holy Spirit of compassion.

Kate McIlhagga

Our Father, for those in need we make our prayer: 342
    the sick in mind and body;
    the blind and the deaf;
    the fatherless and the widow;
    the sorrowing and the anxious.
    In all their troubles and afflictions give them comfort and courage,
and your peace in their hearts; through Jesus Christ our Lord.

Frank Colquhoun

Liberating God, 343
hear our prayers for people who are oppressed today,
as you heard the cries of your people enslaved in Egypt
and raised up Moses to lead them to freedom.

Walk with people who are:

    coming out of long-stay psychiatric hospitals
    unsure of their place and their welcome
    in the communities where they want to live;

    coming out of prison after long sentences
    unsure of their ability to break the pattern
    of former behaviour and association;

    coming out of the darkness after years of anguish,
    rejection and open hostility and learning not to be
    ashamed to be Lesbian or Gay;

    coming through the bleakness of giving up drugs or alcohol
    unsure of their ability to face life without these supports;

    coming through the waters of grief and loss
    unsure of their ability to live alone.

Walk with all who counsel and support them. . . .

Walk with all who were once enslaved on their journey
to freedom.
Say to them through us, 'I will be your God and I will make you
my people.'

Jean Mortimer

344   Father of purity and light, goodness and love, with whom there are no shades of grey or passing shadows: we bring before you many young people who by accident of birth live often in the shadows; some without a father, some with parents who are mentally ill, some bursting with stifled intelligence, some innocently caught up with a bad gang; those in detention or those who are slaves to drink or drugs from an early age. Father of light, allow that great light to shine through us on the people who walk in darkness; through the Light of the World, Jesus Christ our Lord.

Eddie Neale

345   Our heavenly Father, we commend to your mercy those for whom life does not spell freedom: prisoners of conscience, the homeless and the handicapped, the sick in body and mind, the elderly who are confined to their homes, those who are enslaved by their passions, and those who are addicted to drugs. Grant that, whatever their outward circumstances, they may find inward freedom, through him who proclaimed release to captives, Jesus Christ our Saviour.

John R. W. Stott

THOSE WITHOUT WORK

Our Father, in praying for the unemployed we think especially of *346*
those who through no fault of their own have lost their jobs and are
now searching for other work for the sake of their families.

May they not grow despondent or come to regard themselves as
useless.

Help them to employ their skills and gifts in other directions and to
find a measure of fulfilment in the service of the church or community
till employment comes their way again.

Frank Colquhoun

O God who rejoices in both our work and our play,   *347*
   I come before you
      unemployed,
      afraid,
      shaken in my trust.
When I lose courage and hope while searching for work,
   be my rock of safety.
When I find it hard to believe in my talents,
   revive in me an appreciation of the gifts you have given me.
When I begin to doubt my worth,
   help me to remember that I do not need to earn your love.
When my fears take hold and start to overwhelm me,
   let me find comfort in your care for me and those I love, and in their
      love for me.
Thank you for all those who continue to support and encourage me
   during this difficult time.
   May it somehow bring us closer to one another and to you.

Kathleen Fischer and Thomas Hart

348 Father, I pray for those who have no paid employment and who have no colleagues, that they may not despair but may find other ways of working for the well-being of society and may find fellowship in common enterprise. Bless those whose days of retirement have separated them from colleagues and give them a sense of their continuing worth as your children. Enlarge our experience of community life that we may see each other as fellow workers in your wider kingdom, because we all belong to one another in Christ.

More Everyday Prayers

349 Lord Christ, you said to your disciples, 'My Father has worked till now, and I work': we pray for those who through no fault of their own have been deprived of the work that leads towards the fulfilment of their lives.

Inspire and guide those who bear the responsibility of finding the answer to our industrial problems.

Open their minds to the truth, that they may discern in the events of our time the direction of your will; and give them the courage to declare what they believe to be right, and the power to carry it through.

Basil Naylor

—✠—

PRAYERS FOR THE WORLD

—✠—

Let justice roll down like waters, and righteousness like an everflowing stream.

Amos 5.24

REVERENCE FOR CREATION

O God, enlarge within us the sense of fellowship with all living   350
things, our brothers the animals to whom thou gavest the earth as
their home in common with us.

We remember with shame that in the past we have exercised the
high dominion of man with ruthless cruelty so that the voice of the
earth, which should have gone up to thee in song, has been a groan of
travail. May we realize that they live not for us alone but for themselves and for thee, and that they love the sweetness of life.

Basil the Great, c.330–379

> God of creation, the earth is yours   351
> with all its beauty and goodness,
> its rich and overflowing provision.
>
> But we have claimed it for our own,
> plundered its beauty for profit,
> grabbed its resources for ourselves.
>
> God of creation, forgive us.
> May we no longer abuse your trust,
> but care gently and with justice for your earth.
>
> *Jan Berry*

Almighty God, in giving us dominion over things on earth, you made   352
us fellow workers in your creation. Give us wisdom and reverence so
to use the resources of nature that no one may suffer from our abuse
of them, and that generations yet to come may continue to praise you
for your bounty; through Jesus Christ our Lord.

Episcopal Church of the United States of America. Book of Common Prayer
(adapted)

353 Show us, O God, how to love not only animals, birds, and all green and growing things, but the soil, air and water by which we live, so that we may not exploit or pollute them for our own profit or convenience.

Help us to cherish these necessities for our survival; and guide those in authority to ensure that the human spirit may not be starved in pursuit of material comfort and wealth.

Phoebe Hesketh

354 Lord God Almighty, our Creator, teach us to understand more and more profoundly that every human life is sacred, whether it belongs to an unborn infant or to a terminally-ill patient, to a handicapped child or to a disabled adult.

Remind us, heavenly Father, that each individual has been made in your image and likeness and has been redeemed by Christ.

Help us to see each other with your eyes, so that we may reverence, preserve and sustain your gift of life in them, and use our own lives more faithfully in your service.

We ask this through Christ our Lord.

Basil Hume

355   Creator God, who spoke,
              brought forth and it was good,
          who holds this now distorted world
              still in your hands,
          we remember that Christ has come
              to make all things new.

      As we see urban abuse around us,
      we pray for a live conscience.
      May we create clean hearts in our cities, O God.

      As we hear of raped forests and stripped mountains,
      we pray for an understanding
          of the delicacy of nature.
      *Put a new and right spirit in us
      that we may restore and recover.*

      As we experience global oil spills and pollution
      and mourn marine life lost and birds maimed,
      we pray for enlightenment in our policies.

Break down our angry destruction
that our beaches and rivers
   may speak again of your wonders.

As we touch the darkened lives of many people
who long for a bit of sun
   in the battle for survival,
we pray for compassion
   and generous giving of time.
Open up our ears
that we may hear their cries of anguish.

Mother-father God, whose beauty has not changed,
we also give thanks for the things in creation
   that delight us.
To you, God of creation,
   we sing a new song of praise:
a song of trees planted by streams of living water,
a song of mountains clapping their hands for joy,
a song of cities delighting in heavenly harmony,
a song of people that were lost
   and have been found.
For the earth is the Lord's,
   and we shall be glad in it.
Hallelujah.

Dorothy McCrae-McMahon

Lord, purge our eyes to see   *356*
Within the seed a tree,
Within the glowing egg a bird,
Within the shroud a butterfly.
Till, taught by such we see
Beyond all creatures, thee
And hearken to thy tender word
And hear its 'Fear not; it is I'.

Christina Rossetti, 1830–94

357 Forgive us, God,
that we have taken your creation for granted.
You have given us
the run of the land,
the pick of the crop
and we have squandered these resources;
distributed them unfairly,
vandalized their beauty,
violated their purity.

Forgive us, God,
that we have taken your kingdom for granted.
You have given us
the seeds of faith,
the fruits of the spirit,
and we have misused these resources; displayed them rarely,
bestowed them grudgingly,
ignored them blithely.

Thank you, God,
that you are stronger than our destructiveness
and greater than our meanness,
that you give us a fresh start, a second chance.
Overwhelm us with the power of your resurrected love.
Compel us with the challenge you issue for change.
Lead us in the conquest of our own limits and restrictions.
Drive us towards a new life of justice, peace and integrity.

Janet Orchard

358 Eternal Father, source of life and light, whose love extends to all
people, all creatures, all things: grant us that reverence for life which
becomes those who believe in you; lest we despise it, degrade it, or
come callously to destroy it. Rather let us save it, serve it, and sanctify
it, after the example of your Son, Jesus Christ our Lord.

Robert Runcie

Hear our humble prayer, O God, for our friends the animals, espe- *359* cially for animals who are suffering; for any that are hunted or lost or deserted or frightened or hungry; for all that must be put to death. We entreat for them all thy mercy and pity and for those who deal with them we ask a heart of compassion, gentle hands and kindly words. Make us ourselves to be true friends to animals and so to share the blessing of the merciful.

Albert Schweitzer, 1875–1965

Come down, O love divine,   *360*
Fulfil the promised time
When we on earth shall see that Second Coming.
O comforter, draw near,
Within our world appear,
For all creation waits with eager longing.

Alas the hour is late –
The world awaits her fate
As life to dust and ashes we are turning.
Now nature's pattern breaks,
And poison fills her lakes,
The forests of the future we are burning.

Earth groans amid her chains,
Consumed by famine's pains;
The Beast defiles the face of God's creation.
Behold the horsemen four
Ride to the final war.
Now breaks the seal upon God's revelation.

Come, Holy Wisdom, down,
See now her twelve-starred crown –
Here is redeemed God's lovely spoiled creation.
O holy city, come!
Peace rules Jerusalem,
And all God's creatures share in God's salvation.

Angela West

361 Creator of Earth
and of all earth's children,
Creator of soil and sea and sky
and the tapestries of stars,
we turn to you for guidance
as we look on our mutilated planet,
and pray it is not too late for us
to rescue our wounded world.
We have been so careless.
We have failed to nurture the fragile life
You entrusted to our keeping.
We beg you for forgiveness
and we ask you to begin again.
Be with us in our commitment to earth.
Let all the earth say: Amen.

Miriam Therese Winter

SOCIAL JUSTICE

362 Heavenly Father, may your Holy Spirit lead the rich nations to support the poor, and the strong nations to protect the weak; so that every nation may develop in its own way, and work together with other nations in true partnership for the promotion of peace and the good of all mankind; through Jesus Christ our Lord.

Source unknown

O God, whose Son Jesus Christ cared for the welfare of everyone and   363
went about doing good; grant us the imagination and perseverance to
create in this country and throughout the world a just and loving
society for the family of man; and make us agents of your compassion
to the suffering, the persecuted and the oppressed, through the Spirit
of your Son, who shared the suffering of men, our pattern and our
redeemer, Jesus Christ.

Source unknown

> Here is a gaping sore, Lord: 364
>   half the world diets,
>   the other half hungers;
>   half the world is housed,
>   the other half homeless;
>   half the world pursues profit,
>   the other half senses loss.
> Redeem our souls,
> redeem our peoples,
> redeem our times.
>
> *John Bell (Iona Community)*

Strengthen us, O God, to relieve the oppressed, to hear the groans of   365
poor prisoners, to reform the abuses of all professions; that many be
made not poor to make a few rich; for Jesus Christ's sake.

*Oliver Cromwell, 1599–1658 (Adapted from a letter which he wrote after the
Battle of Dunbar, 1650)*

Look with pity, O heavenly Father, upon the people in this land who   366
live with injustice, terror, disease, and death as their constant companions. Have mercy upon us. Help us to eliminate our cruelty to
these our neighbours. Strengthen those who spend their lives estab-
lishing equal protection of the law and equal opportunities for all.
And grant that every one of us may enjoy a fair portion of the riches
of this land; through Jesus Christ our Lord.

Episcopal Church of the United States of America. Book of Common Prayer

367 Oh my heart's heart, in love and anger I will turn to you,
for my soul cries out, 'Where is justice,
when will the balance be redressed
for the fearful dreams of children who sleep with knives,
for the beaten women, and the shamed and helpless men?'
Where is justice?
For the agony of hunger is not to be set
against the insatiable appetites of jaded palates.

In the villages and camps, the children lie bleeding,
and great wounds gape in their throats and sides.
In the city, there is no safety for them;
as the leaves blow through the night streets,
they are swept away, they disappear without trace
as if they had never been.

In the marketplace, weapons are bought and sold;
they change hands as easily as onions from a market woman,
and killing comes lightly everywhere.
The value of people is weighed out on crooked scales
and found wanting,
they are discarded like bruised apples
because they lack the appearance of perfection.

But you, my heart's heart, you are careful;
like a thrifty housewife, who sees no waste in anything,
you gather up that which has been cast aside,
knowing its sweetness,
and take it home with you.

And I will see you in the camps and villages,
working late into the night,
showing patience in the midst of confusion,
reweaving the web of life.
I will see you in the cities,
seated in a circle, making new plans,
drawing attention,
naming the forgotten names.

I will see you in the marketplace,
dressed in black,
with the carved face of an old woman saying 'no' to war,
and you will stand your ground,
and you will seem beautiful to me.
For you are my sanctuary and my light,
my firm ground when the earth cracks
under the weight of warring gods.
As a woman in mortal danger flees to her sisters
and finds refuge,
so you will comfort me, and dress my wounds with tenderness.
And when the flame of courage burns low in me,
your breath, as gentle as a sleeping child,
will stir the ashes of my heart.

Teach me to know your judgement as my friend,
that I may never be ashamed of justice,
or so proud that I flee from mercy.
For your love is never less than justice,
and your strength is tenderness.
You contain my soul's yearning,
and in your encompassing, I am free.

Kathy Galloway (Iona Community)

We cannot pray for those who suffer without being conscious of our   368
own responsibility for some part of that suffering.

Lord, as we listen and watch the events unfolding in our world,
especially in —, we know our own failure as a nation and as a community of nations to prevent the violence and the starvation and the
forced expulsion from their homes of so many of our human family.

Bring us to the point where we demand of our leaders that they put
peace and justice and the care of the weakest first, so that we can help
others to hold up their heads as people who are cared about, just as
Jesus went to the poor and the helpless and the outcast of the world.
We ask it for the sake of Jesus Christ our Lord.

Christopher Avon Lamb

369 Father, source of all power, we confess that we do not always use the powers you have given us as you intend. Sometimes we are afraid of the power we wield, and so do not use it at all; at other times we are careless in our use of it and harm others; at yet other times we deliberately misuse it to achieve our own selfish ends. We confess our misuse of our God-given powers, and ask for your grace to use them properly in the future.

We think of the power of the nations of the world. In international affairs it so often seems that events are out of our control, and rule us. Father, help us to see how national power can be wielded for the fulfilment of your will.

We think of the power of economic systems. Often we feel enmeshed in a system which is not fair and yet cannot be changed without causing immense hardship. Father, help us to become masters of economic forces and to order them for the purposes of justice.

We think of the power of governments. They now touch our personal lives at so many points. Father, may politicians and civil servants use their powers responsibly and respect the rights of individuals.

Give us the courage to challenge them when they are wrong, and willingness to share in the processes of government ourselves. May the power of governments everywhere be used for the good of all.

Father, yours is the ultimate power. We see evidence of it everywhere in the world, but most of all in Jesus Christ. In him we see the power of your love: weakness and death did not destroy him and you raised him from death. May that same power of love be in us.

Caryl Micklem

370   O God of integrity,
of the fair measure and the just weight,
may we show forth your holiness
not only in our worship
but in our business deals:
that the world may be freed
from its slavery to unjust trade,
through Jesus Christ.

Janet Morley (Christian Aid)

Vulnerable God,   371
you challenge the powers that rule this world
through the needy, the compassionate,
and those who are filled with longing.
Make us hunger and thirst to see right prevail,
and single-minded in seeking peace;
that we may see your face
and be satisfied in you,
through Jesus Christ.

Janet Morley

God our deliverer, defender of the poor and needy: when the found- 372
ations of the earth are shaking give strength to your people to uphold
justice and fight all wrong in the name of your Son, Jesus Christ our
Lord.

David Stancliffe

O God, the King of righteousness, lead us, we pray you, in the ways of 373
justice and of peace; inspire us to break down all tyranny and oppression, to gain for every man his due reward and from every man his
due service; that each may live for all, and all may care for each, in the
name of Jesus Christ.

William Temple, 1881–1944

Behold, O Lord God, our strivings after a truer and more abiding 374
order. Give us visions that bring back a lost glory to the earth, and
dreams that foreshadow the better order which you have prepared
for us.

Scatter every excuse of frailty and unworthiness: consecrate us all
with a heavenly mission: open to us a clearer prospect of our work.
Give us strength according to our day gladly to welcome and gratefully to fulfil it; through Jesus Christ our Lord.

Brooke Foss Westcott, 1825–1901

PEACE AND RECONCILIATION

375 Eternal God, in whose perfect kingdom no sword is drawn but the sword of righteousness, and no strength known but the strength of love: we pray thee so mightily to shed and spread abroad thy Spirit, that all peoples and ranks may be gathered under one banner, of the Prince of Peace; as children of one God and Father of all; to whom be dominion and glory now and for ever.

Source unknown

376 Lord, make me an instrument of thy peace.
Where there is hatred, let me sow love.
Where there is injury, pardon.
Where there is discord, vision.
Where there is doubt, faith.
Where there is despair, hope.
Where there is darkness, light.
Where there is sadness, joy.
O divine Master,
grant that I may not so much seek to be consoled as to console;
to be understood as to understand;
to be loved, as to love;
for it is in giving that we receive,
it is in pardoning that we are pardoned,
and it is in dying that we are born to eternal life.

Source unknown (Attributed to Francis of Assisi, 1181–1226)

O God, whose longing is to reconcile the whole universe inside your 377
love, pour out your abundant mercy on your Church, and on your
world so fragmented and torn apart.

For the long history of pain and travail, of oppression and prejudice
inflicted on women, within the Church and in the world,

O God forgive us and pour out your mercy.

For our failure to be open and responsive to the possibility of new
freedom and new hopes,

O God forgive us and pour out your mercy.

For our failure to resist the bitterness which poisons and sours the
gospel of love and reconciliation,

O God forgive us and pour out your mercy.

For our failure to present a wounded world with hope for
reconciliation in a true and loving community of women and men,

O God forgive us and pour out your mercy.

O God, whose longing is to reconcile the whole universe inside your
love, pour out your abundant mercy on your Church and your
world so fragmented and torn apart; this we plead through the love
of Jesus Christ which already surrounds us.

*Source unknown (From the service of rejoicing for the fortieth anniversary of the
ordination of Florence Li Tim Oi, Sheffield Cathedral, January 1984)*

We pray for the United Nations Organization and other inter- 378
national organizations which serve peace and understanding, that
they may be strong in helping settle differences fairly, with respect for
the rights of people, and without recourse to violence; we pray for
political leaders who negotiate peace, that they may learn to trust
each other and that the agreements they achieve may be respected.
We pray for the superpowers that they may be aware of the value and
responsibility of each nation in the family of nations and that they
may turn from the paths that could lead to war.

Source unknown

379   We pray to you, O God,
       the lover of all,
       for those whom we have named our enemies.
       Deliver us from the hardness of heart
       that keeps us locked in confrontation.
       Deliver us from the hatred
       that binds us in old ways.
       Grant unto all people
       the blessing of your love.
       And grant unto us
       such transformation of our lives
       that we may make peace with our enemies,
       and that together we might make this world
       a safer place for all;
       in Christ's name, we pray.

       Vienna Cobb Anderson

380   Grant us to look with your eyes of compassion,
       O merciful God, at the long travail of mankind:
       the wars, the hungry millions,
       the countless refugees,
       the natural disasters,
       the cruel and needless deaths,
       men's inhumanity to one another,
       the heartbreak and hopelessness of so many lives.
       Hasten the coming of the messianic age
       when the nations shall be at peace,
       and men shall live free from fear and free from want
       and there shall be no more pain or tears,
       in the security of your will,
       the assurance of your love,
       the coming of your Kingdom,
       O God of righteousness, O Lord of compassion.

       George Appleton

O God of many names,   381
lover of all people;
we pray for peace
in our hearts and homes,
in our nations and our world;
the peace of your will,
the peace of our need.

Dear Christ, our friend and our guide,
pioneer through the shadow of death,
passing through darkness to make it light,
be our companion that we may fear no evil,
and bring us to life and to glory.

For the hungry and the overfed
May we have enough.

For the mourners and the mockers
May we laugh together.

For the victims and the oppressors
May we share power wisely.

For the peacemakers and the warmongers
May clear truth and stern love lead us to harmony.

For the silenced and the propagandists
May we speak our own words in truth.

For the unemployed and the overworked
May our impress on the earth be kindly and creative.

For the troubled and the sleek
May we live together as wounded healers.

For the homeless and the cosseted
May our homes be simple, warm and welcoming.

For the vibrant and the dying
May we all die to live.

May God kindle in us
the fire of love
to bring us alive
and give warmth to the world.

Lead me from death to life,
from falsehood to truth;
lead me from despair to hope,
from fear to trust;
lead me from hate to love,
from war to peace.
Let peace fill our heart,
our world, our universe.

Anglican Church of Aotearoa, New Zealand and Polynesia

382   God, we believe that you have called us together
      to broaden our experience of you and of each other.
      We believe that we have been called
      to help in healing the many wounds of society
      and in reconciling man to man and man to God.
      Help us, as individuals or together,
      to work, in love, for peace, and never to lose heart.
      We commit ourselves to each other –
      in joy and sorrow.
      We commit ourselves to all who share our belief in reconciliation –
      to support and stand by them.
      We commit ourselves to the way of peace –
      in thought and deed.
      We commit ourselves to you –
      as our guide and friend.

      Corrymeela Community (Northern Ireland)

383   O God, who hast made of one blood all nations of men for to dwell
      on the face of the earth, and didst send thy blessed Son, Jesus Christ,
      to preach peace to them that are afar off, and to them that are nigh;
      grant that all the peoples of the world may feel after thee and find
      thee; hasten, O God, the fulfilment of thy promise to pour out thy
      Spirit upon all flesh, through Jesus Christ our Lord.

      George Cotton, 1813–66

The story, Lord, is as old as history, 384
   as remorseless as man:
Man the raider, the plunderer, the terrorist,
   the conqueror,
Defiling the light of dawn with
The conspiracies of night,
Perverting to evil the fine instruments of nature,
Dealing fear among the tents and the homesteads
Of the unsuspecting or the weak,
Confiscating, purloining, devastating.

The passions are more subtle in our time –
The fire-power of bombs for the dust-clouds of cavalry,
Napalm and incendiary and machines in the skies,
Devices for war decrying the stars,
New skills with the same curse of destruction,
The sanctity of mankind in the jeopardy of techniques,
Gracelessness against the majesty on high.

By the truth of the eternal exposure,
By the reckoning of the eternal justice,
By compassion upon kin and kind,
By the awe of thy sovereignty,
Turn our deeds, O good Lord,
Repair our ravages,
Forgive our perversities.
O God, give peace, grateful peace.

Kenneth Cragg

O God, you make men to be of one mind in an house and have called 385
us into the fellowship of your dear Son; draw into closer unity the
peoples of all races in this and every land, that, in fellowship with
you, they may understand and help one another, and that, serving
you, they may find their perfect freedom; through the same your Son
Jesus Christ our Lord.

Joost de Blank

386 God of mercy and love, fill my heart anew with your divine love.
Fill my thinking with your touchstone of grace and understanding.
Guide my judgment of others made in your image.
Help me to be your instrument of reconciliation.
Help me to overcome human reaction to people and events with
    something of your love for others.
Forgive me when I doubt your power to heal relationships and make
    all things new.

Robert H. A. Eames

387   We light this candle for peace, Lord.
        May its light scatter the darkness;
        may its flame be a symbol of hope;
        may its burning be a sign of faith
        joining with many other lights for peace.
    We light this candle for peace.
        May our lives be an expression of peacemaking;
        may we seek to be lights in a dark world,
            pointing to you, Jesus, the Prince of Peace,
                and following you in the way of peace.
    Let the candle burn, as a sign for peace,
        offered to you.

John Johansen-Berg

388 Lord, forgive us the hatreds and prejudices and malice which pull the
rug from under all our so-called love for others and for you. Black
and White, Catholic and Protestant, Jew and Arab, Croat, Muslim
and Serb – so many peoples feed on hatred for one another, endlessly
suppressing the truth of our common humanity.

    Lord, give courage and compassion, a liberation of the spirit, an
opening of heart and mind, so that those thought of only as aliens and
enemies may become simply people.

    We make our prayer through the Friend of sinners, Jesus Christ our
Lord.

Christopher Avon Lamb

To you, Creator of nature and humanity, of truth and beauty, I pray: *389*

Hear my voice, for it is the voice of the victims of all wars and violence among individuals and nations.

Hear my voice, for it is the voice of all children who suffer and will suffer when people put their faith in weapons and war.

Hear my voice when I beg you to instil into the hearts of all human beings the wisdom of peace, the strength of justice and the joy of fellowship.

Hear my voice, for I speak for the multitudes in every country and in every period of history who do not want war and are ready to walk the road of peace.

Hear my voice and grant insight and strength so that we may always respond to hatred with love, to injustice with total dedication to justice, to need with the sharing of self, to war with peace.

O God, hear my voice, and grant unto the world your everlasting peace.

(Pope) John Paul II

God, what kind of world is this that the adult people are going to   *390* leave for us children? There is fighting everywhere and they tell us we live in a time of peace. You are the only one who can help us. Lord, give us a new world in which we can be happy, in which we can have friends and work together for a good future. A world in which there will not be any cruel people who seek to destroy us and our world in so many ways.

A Liberian child

Christ died that we might be reconciled to you, Father, and to one   *391* another. People cannot believe in reconciliation with you unless there are human reconciliations which reflect it. And so we pray for the healing of the broken bonds of human life.

We pray for reconciliation between nations. We do not believe that the true interests of nations ever conflict sharply enough for war to be necessary. And yet we know that peace has often been exploited by those who love to oppress, making war a grim necessity. Give us true peace, founded on justice and respect for human rights.

We pray for reconciliation between races, especially in countries where different races live side by side. May the principle of equal citizenship and equal opportunity be accepted everywhere. May the laws strengthen the hands of people of goodwill. May different races learn to speak the truth in love to each other. May wisdom and patience mean that the day of bloody revolution need never come.

We pray for reconciliation between generations. It is hard for parents to realize that their authority is not absolute and that their values may be questioned. It is hard for young people to realize that they lack experience and may have no more staying power than their elders. It is especially hard when one generation is given opportunities and choices the other did not have. Grant, Lord, that both may learn from each other, and that the common problems of our world may be faced together.

We pray for reconciliation between the sexes. We thank you for the new opportunities women have to follow their careers and take part in public life. Help men and women to understand the ways in which their roles have changed and must change, and to work together on equal terms and with mutual respect. Help husbands and wives to achieve harmony in marriage, despite the stresses of modern life.

We pray for reconciliation between churches. Break down the inertia which keeps us apart when the original causes of division no longer matter. Help us to judge whether present differences are sufficient to be allowed to obscure the unity we have in Christ. And may unions of churches take place in such a way that they do not become the occasion for new divisions.

We pray for reconciliation between religions. May those who profess one faith no longer suspect and misrepresent those who profess another. May good be recognized wherever it exists. May all people hold to truth as they see it, and bear witness to it, but with goodwill and respect.

May the Christ who once reconciled Jew and Gentile, slave and freeman into one body continue to break down the walls which divide us.

Caryl Micklem

O God, Giver of Life, Bearer of Pain, Maker of Love,   392
    you are able to accept in us what we cannot even acknowledge:
    you are able to name in us what we cannot bear to speak of;
    you are able to hold in your memory what we have tried to forget;
    you are able to hold out to us the glory that we cannot conceive of.
Reconcile us through your cross to all that we have rejected in our selves, that we may find no part of your creation to be alien or strange to us, and that we ourselves may be made whole. Through Jesus Christ, our lover and our friend.

Janet Morley

Lord, we pray this day mindful of the sorry confusion of our world. 393 Look with mercy upon this generation of your children so steeped in misery of their own contriving, so far strayed from your ways and so blinded by passions. We pray for the victims of tyranny, that they may resist oppression with courage. We pray for wicked and cruel men, whose arrogance reveals to us what the sin of our own hearts is like when it has conceived and brought forth its final fruit.

We pray for ourselves who live in peace and quietness, that we may not regard our good fortune as proof of our virtue, or rest content to have our ease at the price of other men's sorrow and tribulation.

We pray for all who have some vision of your will, despite the confusions and betrayals of human sin, that they may humbly and resolutely plan for and fashion the foundations of a just peace between men, even while they seek to preserve what is fair and just among us against the threat of malignant powers.

Reinhold Niebuhr, 1892–1971

O Lord, our Lord, who hast decided that all men, whatever their col- 394 our or race, are equal before thee: break down the hatred between men, especially hatred due to national differences. We ask thee to help those in whose hands are the various governments of the world. Reconcile them to one another, so that each may respect the rights of the other. We ask all this in the name of our Saviour, Jesus Christ.

Student Christian Movement (Zambia)

395   God, our Heavenly Father, we draw near to thee with thankful hearts because of all thy great love for us. We thank thee most of all for the gift of thy dear Son, in whom alone we may be one. We are different one from another in race and language, in material things, in gifts, in opportunities, but each of us has a human heart, knowing joy and sorrow, pleasure and pain. We are one in our need of thy forgiveness, thy strength, thy love; make us one in our common response to thee, that bound by a common love and freed from selfish aims we may work for the good of all and the advancement of thy kingdom. Through Jesus Christ, our Lord.

(Queen) Salote (Tonga)

396   O God, who art the unsearchable abyss of peace,
    the ineffable sea of love, the fountain of blessings
    and the bestower of affection,
    who sendest peace to those that receive it;
Open to us this day the sea of thy love
    and water us with plenteous streams
    from the riches of thy grace
    and from the most sweet springs of thy kindness.
Make us children of quietness and heirs of peace,
    enkindle in us the fire of thy love;
    sow in us thy fear;
    strengthen our weakness by thy power;
    bind us closely to thee and to each other
    in our firm and indissoluble bond of unity.

Syrian Clementine Liturgy

397   O God, our Leader and our Master and our Friend, forgive our imperfections and our little motives, take us and make us one with thy great purpose, use us and do not reject us, make us all servants of thy kingdom, weave our lives into thy struggle to conquer and to bring peace and union to the world.

We are small and feeble creatures, we are feeble in speech, feebler still in action, nevertheless let but thy light shine upon us, and there is not one of us who cannot be lit by thy fire and who cannot lose himself in thy salvation. Take us into thy purposes, O God, let thy kingdom come into our hearts and into this world.

H. G. Wells, 1866–1946

Eternal God, whose image lies in the hearts of all people,   398
We live among peoples whose ways are different from ours,
    whose faiths are foreign to us,
    whose tongues are unintelligible to us.
Help us to remember that you love all people with your great love,
    that all religion is an attempt to respond to you,
      that the yearnings of other hearts are much like our own and are
        known to you.
Help us to recognize you in the words of truth, the things of beauty,
    the actions of love about us.
We pray through Christ, who is a stranger to no one land more than
    another, and to every land no less than to another.

World Council of Churches (based on a prayer by Robert H. Adams, Jr.)

NATIONAL WELL-BEING

Father in heaven, we give thanks for life, and the experience life   399
brings us. We thank you for our joys, sorrows, trials, failures and
triumphs. Above all we thank you for the hope we have in Christ that
we shall find fulfilment in him.

    We praise you for our country, its beauty, the riches it has for us
and the gifts it showers on us. We thank you for your peoples, the gift
of languages we speak, the variety of races we have, the cultural heritage we cherish and the latent possibilities there are for our country to
be great. Grant that we accept these gifts with thankfulness, and use
them for the good of the human race and to bring glory to you.
Through Jesus Christ our Lord. Amen.

Source unknown (India)

400   O God, the Father of all mankind,
we beseech thee so to inspire the people of this land
with the spirit of justice, truth, and love,
that in all our dealings one with another
we may show forth our brotherhood in thee,
for the sake of Jesus Christ our Lord.

A Book of Common Prayer, South Africa

401   Almighty God, our heavenly Father, to forget whom is to stumble and fall, to remember whom is to rise again: we pray thee to draw the people of this country to thyself. Prosper all efforts to make known to them thy truth, that many may learn their need of thee and thy love for them; so that thy Church and kingdom may be established among us to the glory of thy Name; through Jesus Christ our Lord.

Randall T. Davidson, 1848–1930

402   Almighty God, who hast ordained that men should serve thee in serving one another by their labours: have regard, we pray thee, to this nation, oppressed at this time by many burdens. Grant to its citizens grace to work together with honest and faithful hearts, each caring for the good of all; that seeking first thy kingdom and its righteousness, they may have added to them all things needful for their daily sustenance and the common good; through Jesus Christ our Lord.

Geoffrey F. Fisher, 1887–1972

403   Almighty God, you have proclaimed your eternal truth by the voice of prophets and evangelists: direct and bless, we ask you, those who in this our generation speak where many listen and write what many read: that they may do their part in making the heart of the people wise, its mind sound and its will righteous, to the honour of Jesus Christ, our Lord.

Norman Goodacre

Vouchsafe, O Lord, to prosper with your blessing the work of all uni- 404
versities, colleges and schools, that they who serve you therein, as
teachers or learners, may set your holy will ever before them, and be
led to the knowledge of your truth; that so both church and world
may benefit from their studies, and they themselves become worthy
partakers of eternal life; through Jesus Christ, our Lord.

Norman Goodacre

God bless —, 405
Guard her peoples,
Guide her leaders,
And give peace,
For Jesus Christ's sake.

Trevor Huddleston

O God the Father of all, watch over the men and women of other 406
countries who live and work among us. Guide them in strange surroundings. Protect them in temptation. Preserve in them all that is
good in their own traditions, and help them to understand and share
what is good in the way of life of the country they have come to. Give
to us all humility, love and patience, and help us to build together a
community in which every contribution is welcomed and every one's
dignity is respected.

John Kingsnorth (USPG)

Let your mercy and blessing, O Lord of lords, rest upon our land and 407
nation; upon all the powers which you have ordained over us: our
Queen and those in authority under her, the ministers of state, and
the great councils of the nation; that we may lead a quiet and peaceable life in all godliness and honesty. Rule the hearts of our people in
your faith and fear; rebuke the power of unbelief and superstition;
and preserve to us your pure Word in its liberty and glory even to the
end of days; through Jesus Christ our Lord.

Handley C. G. Moule, 1841–1920

RULERS AND LEADERS

408 O God, Almighty Father, King of kings and Lord of all our rulers, grant that the hearts and minds of all who go out as leaders before us, the statesmen, the judges, the men of learning, and the men of wealth, may be so filled with the love of thy laws, and of that which is righteous and life-giving, that they may serve as a wholesome salt unto the earth, and be worthy stewards of thy good and perfect gifts; through Jesus Christ our Lord.

Source unknown, 1348 (Prayer of the Order of the Garter)

409 O righteous Lord, that lovest righteousness, may thy Holy Spirit be with our rulers, with our sovereign and all in authority under her, that they may govern in thy faith and fear, striving to put down all that is evil and to encourage all that is good. Give thy spirit of wisdom to those who make our laws, grant that they may understand how great a work thou hast given them to do; that they may not do it lightly, but gravely and soberly, to the putting away of all wrong and oppression and to the advancement of the true welfare of thy people.

Thomas Arnold, 1795–1842

410 Lord God, in our prayers for our country we remember especially the men and women who powerfully influence the life of society:
>   those who fashion our politics,
>   those who frame and administer our laws,
>   those who mould public opinion through the press, radio and television,
>   those who write what many read.

May all such recognize their responsibility to you and to the nation, that people may be influenced for what is good, not evil; for what is true, not false; for the glory of your name.

Frank Colquhoun

O God, give wisdom to those who govern us,   *411*
a sense of justice to those who wield power,
that they may frame laws that are life-giving,
that the poor and the weak may breathe freely.
May they defend the cause of the needy,
save the abandoned and orphans,
disarm the rebellious and violent.

May such wisdom endure like the sun and moon,
giving light from one age to the next.
May justice rain down like showers
that water the new-sown fields.
In our days may justice flourish
and abundance of peace till the moon be no more.

May wisdom reign from sea to sea,
following the great rivers to the end of the earth.
May folly bow down to truth,
the enemies of justice lick the dust.
May all the rulers of the peoples seek wisdom,
the nations serve the ways of justice and truth.

Those who are wise deliver the needy when they call,
the weak and those who have no one to speak for them.
They will rescue them from oppression and violence,
and their lives are precious in their sight.

So may there be abundance of grain in the land,
to the tops of the hills may it wave.
Let the mountains be laden with peace,
with prosperity that follows from justice.
May the corn swell with the gentle rains,
the sheaves thicken like the grass of the meadows.

May prayer be made for those in high office,
that they may bear their burdens with wisdom.
May blessings be invoked on them day by day,
may they be heartened by the prayers of the people.

Blessed be the God of all the earth,
who alone is all wisdom and justice,
who alone does great wonders.
Blessed be the glorious name of God:
may the universe be filled with God's glory.
Let the Amen echo with praise.

Jim Cotter (based on Psalm 72)

412 King of kings, and Lord of lords,
We pray today for statesmen, leaders and rulers,
May they be quiet in spirit, clear in judgment,
Able to understand the issues that face them.
May they think often of the common people on whose behalf they
    must speak and act.
May they remember that in keeping thy laws is
    man's only good and happiness.
Grant them patience, grant them courage,
Grant them foresight and great faith,
In their anxieties be thou their security,
In their opportunities be thou their inspiration,
By their plans and their actions may thy kingdom come,
thy will be done.

Lilian Cox

413 Lord of grace and gentleness, we pray for a world in which even ordinary humanity fails so often. We pray for those who are called government ministers – servants – in every nation. We pray that those
who lead and take on themselves great responsibilities may not
simply wish to seem great in the eyes of others, but may genuinely
serve their peoples, searching continually for policies and strategies
which will be for the good of all, especially for the weakest and most
vulnerable. We ask this for the sake of him who is both servant and
Lord, Jesus Christ.

Christopher Avon Lamb

Heavenly Father, 414

You give us responsibility which we must exercise, and call upon us to make decisions at the risk of making mistakes. We remember all who are brought to such a test, and find themselves on their own.

We remember scientists of all kinds, who know that the results of their work could become a blessing or a curse. We pray that they may be careful not to be compromised in evil experiments; that they may put their trust in revealing the truth; and that they may keep their integrity in whatever dilemma they may find themselves.

We remember those national leaders who alone have access to confidential information, and must make up their minds what course of action to take. We pray that they may have a just motive, clear judgement and consistent thought.

We remember educators, preachers, leaders and speakers of all kinds, who have power to influence opinion. We pray that they may always remain servants of the truth, and not try to manipulate people's loyalty.

We remember industrialists and employers, whose decisions affect the lives of millions. We pray that they may insist upon quality in production, and provide good conditions of work; that they may be honest in their dealings, and never become cynical about power or treat it as a game.

So we pray for many who bear the burden of responsibility, that they may accept your guidance and be very wise.

Through Jesus Christ our Lord.

Caryl Micklem

Sovereign Lord of men and nations, we pray for rulers and statesmen 415 who are called to leadership among their fellow countrymen; give them vision to see far into the issues of their time, courage to uphold what they believe to be right, and integrity in their words and motives; and may their service to their people promote the welfare and peace of mankind; through Jesus Christ our Lord.

Basil Naylor

416   Almighty God, from whom all thoughts of truth and peace proceed: kindle, we pray thee, in the hearts of all men the true love of peace, and guide with thy pure and peaceable wisdom those who take counsel for the nations of the earth; that in tranquillity thy kingdom may go forward, till the earth is filled with the knowledge of thy love; through Jesus Christ our Lord.

Francis Paget, 1851–1911

417   Almighty God, whose is the eternal only power,
and other men's power but borrowed of thee:
we beseech thee for all those who hold office that,
holding it first from thee, they may use it for
the general good and to thine honour: through
Jesus Christ our Lord.

William Tyndale, c.1494–1536 (adapted)

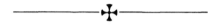

PRAYERS FOR GOD'S

HELP AND STRENGTH

**In everything by prayer and supplication
with thanksgiving let your requests be
made known to God.**

Philippians 4.6-7

Father, I fall on my knees before you. I ask you from the wealth of 418
your glory to give me power through your Spirit to be strong in my
inner self. I pray that Christ will make his home in my heart, that I
may have the power to understand how broad and long, how high
and deep, is Christ's love. For by means of your power working in me
you are able to do so much more than I can ever ask for, or even think
of. To you, Father, be the glory in the Church and in Christ Jesus for
all time, for ever and ever!

Ephesians 3.14–21 (Good News Bible, adapted)

You have called us, O God, to be your people. You have loved us and 419
chosen us for your own. Clothe us with your compassion, your kindness, your humility, your gentleness and your patience. Help us forgive one another as you have forgiven us. And bind us all together in
the perfect unity of your love.

Colossians 3.12–14 (Good News Bible, adapted)

Give us, Lord, a bit o'sun 420
A bit o' work and a bit o' fun
Give us all in th' struggle and splutter
Our daily bread and a bit o' butter.
Give us health, our keep to make,
An' a bit to spare for poor folks' sake,
Give us sense, for we are some of us duffers,
An' a heart to feel for all that suffers.

Source unknown

God guide me with thy wisdom, 421
God chastise me with thy justice,
God help me with thy mercy,
God protect me with thy strength,
God shield me with thy shade,
God fill me with thy grace,
For the sake of thine anointed Son.

Source unknown (Early Scottish)

422 Grant, O God, your protection; and in your protection, strength; and in strength, understanding; and in understanding, knowledge; and in knowledge, the knowledge of justice; and in the knowledge of justice, the love of it; and in that love, the love of existence; and in the love of all existence, the love of God, God and all goodness.

Source unknown (Early Welsh)

423 Grant us, Lord, to know in weakness the strength of thy incarnation: in pain the triumph of thy passion: in poverty the riches of thy Godhead: in reproach the satisfaction of thy sympathy: in loneliness the comfort of thy continual presence: in difficulty the efficacy of thy intercession: in perplexity the guidance of thy wisdom; and by thy glorious death and resurrection bring us at last to the joy of seeing thee face to face.

Source unknown

424 Guard for me my eyes, Jesus Son of Mary, lest seeing another's
    wealth make me covetous.
Guard for me my ears, lest they hearken to slander, lest they listen to
    folly in the sinful world.
Guard for me my heart, O Christ, in thy love,
    lest I ponder wretchedly the desire of any iniquity.
Guard for me my hands, that they be not stretched out for quarrelling
    or practise shameful supplication.
Guard for me my feet upon the gentle earth . . .
    lest they be bent on profitless errands.

Source unknown (Early Irish)

425   I am only a spark. Make me a fire.
        I am only a string. Make me a lyre.
        I am only a drop. Make me a fountain.
        I am only an ant-hill. Make me a mountain.
        I am only a feather. Make me a wing.
        I am only a rag. Make me a king!

        Source unknown (Mexico)

Lord of my heart, give me vision to inspire me, that, working or rest-   426
ing, I may always think of you.

Lord of my heart, give me light to guide me, that, at home or
abroad, I may always walk in your way.

Lord of my heart, give me wisdom to direct me, that, thinking or
acting, I may always discern right from wrong.

Lord of my heart, give me courage to strengthen me, that, amongst
friends or enemies, I may always proclaim your justice.

Lord of my heart, give me trust to console me, that, hungry or well-
fed, I may always rely on your mercy.

Lord of my heart, save me from empty praise, that I may always
boast of you.

Lord of my heart, save me from worldly wealth, that I may always
look to the riches of heaven.

Lord of my heart, save me from military prowess, that I may
always seek your protection.

Lord of my heart, save me from vain knowledge, that I may always
study your word.

Lord of my heart, save me from unnatural pleasures, that I may
always find joy in your wonderful creation.

Heart of my own heart, whatever befall me, rule over my thoughts
and feelings, my words and action.

Source unknown

Lord, thou knowest better than I know myself that I am getting older   427
and will some day be old. Keep me from the fatal habit of thinking I
must say something on every subject and on every occasion. Release
me from craving to straighten out everybody's affairs. Make me
thoughtful but not moody: helpful but not bossy. With my vast store
of wisdom it seems a pity not to use it all, but thou knowest, Lord,
that I want a few friends at the end.

Keep my mind free from the recital of endless details; give me
wings to get to the point. Seal my lips on my aches and pains. They are
increasing and love of rehearsing them is becoming sweeter as the
years go by. I dare not ask for grace enough to enjoy the tales of
others' pains, but help me to endure them with patience.

I dare not ask for improved memory, but for a growing humility
and lessening cocksureness when my memory seems to clash with the
memories of others. Teach me the glorious lesson that occasionally I
may be mistaken.

Keep me reasonably sweet; I do not want to be a saint – some of them are so hard to live with – but a sour old person is one of the crowning works of the devil. Give me the ability to see good things in unexpected places, and talents in unexpected people. And, give me, O Lord, the grace to tell them so.

Source unknown, 17th century

428   O eternal Father,
who hast sent thy blessed Spirit to abide in me,
to form me after the likeness of thy dear Son
   in all purity and goodness;
help me, I beseech thee, to bring forth in my life
   those fruits of the Spirit which belong to thy true children:
   the fruit of love,
      that I may love thee above all things,
      and all others in thee and for thy sake;
   the fruit of joy,
      that I may find thy service my delight;
   the fruit of peace,
      that, pardoned and accepted through thy mercy,
      I may repose on thy love;
   the fruit of long-suffering,
      that I may bear with patient submission to thy will
      all crosses and afflictions;
   the fruit of gentleness,
      that I may subdue all risings of temper,
      and take calmly and sweetly all trials
      and provocations;
   the fruit of meekness,
      that I may forgive freely all who may hurt me
      either by word or deed,
      and endure with patience
      all that may be laid upon me;
   the fruit of temperance and chastity,
      that I may restrain all my desires
      and keep under my body,
      bringing it into subjection in all things
      to thy holy will.
And grant, O gracious Father, that
   thus striving to please thee here on earth,

I may be found meet to behold
the glorious vision of thee hereafter;
through the merits of thy dearly beloved Son
Jesus Christ our Lord.

Source unknown

O Lord Jesus Christ, only-begotten Son of thine eternal Father, thou   429
hast said that without thee we can do nothing. O Lord, I embrace
with faith and with my whole heart and soul what thou hast said.
Help me, a sinner, to finish the work which I now undertake for thee;
in the name of the Father, and of the Son, and of the Holy Spirit.

Source unknown (Eastern Orthodox)

O Lord, give us yourself above all things.   430
It is in your coming alone that we are enriched.
It is in your coming that your true gifts come.
Come, Lord, that we may share the gifts of your presence.
Come, Lord, with healing of the past,
Come and calm our memories,
Come with joy for the present,
Come and give life to our existence,
Come with hope for the future,
Come and give a sense of eternity.
Come with strength for our wills,
Come with power for our thoughts,
Come with love for our heart,
Come and give affection to our being.
Come, Lord, give yourself above all things
And help us to give ourselves to you.

David Adam

431 O thou God of peace, unite our hearts by thy bond of peace, that we may live with one another continually in gentleness and humility, in peace and unity. O thou God of patience, give us patience in the time of trial, and steadfastness to endure to the end. O thou spirit of prayer, awaken our hearts, that we may lift up holy hands to God, and cry unto him in all our distresses. O thou gentle wind, cool and refresh our hearts in all heat and anguish. Be our defence and shade in the time of need, our help in trial, our consolation when all things are against us. Come, O thou eternal light, salvation, comfort, be our light in darkness, our salvation in life, our comfort in death; and lead us in the straight way to everlasting life, that we may praise thee, forever.

Bernhard Albrecht, 1569–1636

432   Give me, O Lord, I pray thee,
         firm faith, unwavering hope,
         perfect charity.
         Pour into my heart
         the spirit of wisdom and understanding,
         the spirit of counsel and spiritual strength,
         the spirit of knowledge and true godliness,
         and the spirit of thy holy fear.
         Light eternal, shine in my heart:
         Power eternal, deliver me from evil:
         Wisdom eternal, scatter the darkness of my ignorance:
         Might eternal, pity me.
         Grant that I may ever seek thy face,
         with all my heart and soul and strength;
         and, in thine infinite mercy,
         bring me at last to thy holy presence,
         where I shall behold thy glory
         and possess thy promised joys.

         Alcuin, 735–804

Be, Lord, within me to strengthen me, without me to preserve, over 433
me to shelter, beneath to support, before me to direct, behind me to
bring back, round about me to fortify.

Lancelot Andrewes, 1555–1626

O merciful God, fill our hearts, we pray, with the graces of thy Holy 434
Spirit; with love, joy, peace, patience, gentleness, goodness, faithfulness, humility and self-control. Teach us to love those who hate us; to
pray for those who despitefully use us; that we may be the children of
thy love, our Father, who makes the sun to rise on the evil and the
good, and sends rain on the just and on the unjust. In adversity grant
us grace to be patient; in prosperity keep us humble; may we guard
the door of our lips; may we lightly esteem the pleasures of this
world, and thirst after heavenly things; through Jesus Christ our
Lord.

Anselm, 1033–1109

O God, from whom to be turned is to fall, 435
to whom to be turned is to rise,
and in whom to stand is to abide for ever:
grant us in all our duties thy help,
in all our perplexities thy guidance,
in all our dangers thy protection,
and in all our sorrows thy peace;
through Jesus Christ our Lord.

Augustine, 354–430

Almighty God, give us wisdom to perceive you, intellect to under- 436
stand you, diligence to seek you, patience to wait for you, eyes to
behold you, a heart to meditate upon you and life to proclaim you,
through the power of the Spirit of our Lord Jesus Christ.

Benedict, 480–543

437 Help me, O God, to put off all pretences and to find my true self.
Help me, O God, to discard all false pictures of you, whatever the
cost to my comfort.
Help me, O God, to let go all my problems, and fix my mind on you.
Help me, O God, to see my own sins, never to judge my neighbour,
and may the glory be all yours.
Into your hands I commend my spirit.
Your will, not mine, be done.

Anthony Bloom

438 Lord, who hast given all for us: help us to give all for thee.

George W. Briggs, 1875–1959

439 I am tired, Lord. Too tired to think, too tired to pray, too tired to do
anything. Too tired, drained of resources, 'labouring at the oars
against a head wind', pressed down by a force as strong as the sea.
Lord of all power and might, 'your way was through the sea, your
path through the great waters'; calm my soul, take control, Lord of
all power and might.

Rex Chapman

440 Let thy mighty hand, O Lord God, and outstretched arm be our
defence; thy mercy and loving-kindness in Jesus Christ, thy dear Son,
our salvation; thy all-true Word, our instruction; the grace of the life-
giving Spirit, our comfort and our consolation, unto the end and in
the end.

Church of Scotland. Book of Common Order

441 Lord, since you exist, we exist. Since you are beautiful, we are beautiful. Since you are good, we are good. By our existence we honour
you. By our beauty we glorify you. By our goodness we love you.
   Lord, through your power all things were made. Through your
wisdom all things are governed. Through your grace all things are
sustained. Give us power to serve you, wisdom to discern your laws,
and grace to obey those at all times.

Edmund of Abingdon, c.1180–1240

Lord, by this sweet and saving sign,   442
Defend us from our foes and thine.

Jesus, by thy wounded feet,
    Direct our path aright:
Jesus, by thy nailed hands,
    Move ours to deeds of love:
Jesus, by thy pierced side,
    Cleanse our desires:
Jesus, by thy crown of thorns,
    Annihilate our pride:
Jesus, by thy silence,
    Shame our complaints:
Jesus, by thy parched lips,
    Curb our cruel speech:
Jesus, by thy closing eyes,
    Look on our sin no more:
Jesus, by thy broken heart,
    Knit ours to thee.

And by this sweet and saving sign,
Lord, draw us to our peace and thine.

Richard Crashaw, 1613–49, and others
(Obsecration before the crucifix)

Almighty and merciful God, who art the strength of the weak, the   443
refreshment of the weary, the comfort of the sad, the help of the
tempted, the life of the dying, the God of patience and of all consolation; thou knowest full well the inner weakness of our nature, how
we tremble and quiver before pain, and cannot bear the cross without
thy divine help and support. Help me, then, O eternal and pitying
God, help me to possess my soul in patience, to maintain unshaken
hope in thee, to keep that childlike trust which feels a Father's heart
hidden beneath the cross; so shall I be strengthened with power
according to thy glorious might, in all patience and long-suffering; I
shall be enabled to endure pain and temptation, and, in the very
depth of my suffering, to praise thee with a joyful heart.

Johann Habermann, 1516–90

444 O Lord, we beseech thee mercifully to receive the prayers of thy people who call upon thee; and grant that they may both perceive and know what things they ought to do; and also may have grace and power faithfully to fulfil the same; through Jesus Christ our Lord.

Gregorian Sacramentary, 6th century

445
O eternal God,
Now let it please you
To burn in that love
So that we become those limbs
Which you made in that same love
When you gave birth to your Son
In the first dawn
Before all creatures,
And look on this need
Which falls upon us.
Take it from us
For the sake of your Son
And lead us into the bliss of salvation.

Hildegard of Bingen, 1098–1179

446 You, who said, 'Come unto me all ye who are weary and heavy-laden and I will give you rest,' I come to you now.

For I am weary indeed. Mentally and physically I am bone-tired. I am all wound up, locked up tight with tension. I am too tired to eat. Too tired to think. Too tired even to sleep. I feel close to the point of exhaustion.

Lord, let your healing love flow through me.

I can feel it easing my tensions. Thank you. I can feel my body relaxing. Thank you. I can feel my mind begin to go calm and quiet and composed.

Thank you for unwinding me, Lord, for unlocking me. I am no longer tight and frozen with tiredness, but flowing freely, softly, gently into your healing rest.

Marjorie Holmes

O Holy Ghost,   447
Come down from heaven's height,
Give us thy light.

O Father of the poor,
All gifts to men are thine
Within us shine.

Comforter beyond man's comforting,
O stranger sweet
Our hearts await thy feet.

In passion thou art peace,
Rest for our labouring,
Our cooling spring.

O solace of our tears,
Upon the secrets of our sins and fears,
Pour thy great light.

Apart from thee,
Man has no truth unfeigned,
No good unstained.

Our hearts are dry.
O River, flow thou through the parched ground,
Quicken those near to die.

Our hearts are hard,
O bend them to thy will, Eternal Lord,
To go thy way.

Thy sevenfold power
Give to thy faithful folk
Who bear thy yoke.

Give strength to endure,
And then to die in peace
And live for ever in thy blessedness.

Stephen Langton, 1151–1228

448

Jesus, Creator,
   Recreate and renew me.

Jesu, Saviour,
   Save me from sin,
   Save me from self.

Jesu, High Priest,
   Pity me,
   Plead for me,
   Pardon and purify me.

Jesu, Prophet,
   Waken and warn me.

Jesu, King,
   Rule me.

Jesu, the Way,
Jesu, my friend,
   Go with me always.

Jesu, the Truth,
   Teach me and counsel me,
   Make me all true.

Jesu, true Light,
   Scatter my darkness.

Jesu, true Bread,
   Strengthen my weakness.

Jesu, good Shepherd,
   Lead me and feed me.

Jesu, the Life,
   Live in me always,
      that I may adore thee,
      my Lord and my God,
      evermore.

Eric Milner-White, 1884–1963

O Lord Christ, Lamb of God, Lord of Lords,   449
  call us, who are called to be saints,
    along the way of thy cross:
  draw us, who would draw nearer our King,
    to the foot of thy cross:
  cleanse us, who are not worthy to approach,
    with the pardon of thy cross:
  instruct us, the ignorant and blind,
    in the school of thy cross:
  arm us, for the battles of holiness,
    by the might of thy cross:
  bring us, in the fellowship of thy sufferings
    to the victory of thy cross:
  and seal us in the kingdom of thy glory
    among the servants of thy cross,
      O crucified Lord;
  who with the Father and the Holy Ghost
    livest and reignest one God almighty,
    eternal, world without end.

Eric Milner-White, 1884–1963

Father, give to us, and to all your people, in times of anxiety, serenity;   450
in times of hardship, courage; in times of uncertainty, patience; and,
at all time, a quiet trust in your wisdom and love; through Jesus
Christ our Lord.

New Every Morning

Give me, Lord, a stout heart to bear my own burdens, a tender heart   451
to bear the burdens of others, and a believing heart to lay all my burdens on you, for you care for us.

Lesslie Newbigin

O Lord my God, rescue me from myself, and give me to thee; take   452
away from me everything which draws me from thee; give me all
those things which lead me to thee; for Jesus Christ's sake.

Precationes Piae, 1564

453 Let me never forget, O my God, that seasons of consolation are refreshments here, and nothing more; not our abiding state. They will not remain with us, except in heaven. Here they are only intended to prepare us for doing and suffering. I pray Thee, O my God, to give them to me from time to time. Shed over me the sweetness of thy presence, lest I faint by the way; lest I find religious service wearisome, through my exceeding infirmity, and give over prayer and meditation; lest I go about my daily work in a dry spirit, or am tempted to take pleasure in it for its own sake, and not for thee. Give me thy divine consolations from time to time; but let me not rest in them. Let me use them for the purpose for which thou givest them. Let me not think it grievous, let me not be downcast, if they go. Let them carry me forward to the thought and the desire of heaven.

John Henry Newman, 1801–90

454
Holy God, who madest me
And all things else to worship thee;
Keep me fit in mind and heart,
Body and soul to take my part.
Fit to stand, and fit to run,
Fit for sorrow, fit for fun,
Fit for work, and fit for play,
Fit to face life day by day.
Holy God, who madest me,
Make me fit to worship thee.

Orders of Service for Children's Worship

455 O God, today I need to be as strong as I can bear.
Help me put aside both cowardice and selfish pride;
Give me O God instead the courage to hear what must be said.
My weakness I confess; give me the strength of openness,
Help me to trust in honesty, and not to flinch from fear.

John Simon

456
May my eyes not see that face again
which I know as a fist knows its glove
without the strength to see, O Lord,
my shame, and the eyes of your love.

John Simon

Almighty and ever-living God, 457
by your Holy Spirit in the burning bush, in chariots of fire,
and in tongues of flame,
you have made your people partakers
    in the radiance of your transfigured One;
strengthen the hearts of your servants:
give us courage in temptation and comfort in desolation;
show us your paths in the desert
    that we may find streams of living water;
make us a holocaust for your people,
pure channels of your love,
and receive us into the fire of your life.

Maggie Ross

Gracious God, 458
    Send us anywhere in this world you would have us go,
only go thou with us.
    Place upon us any burden you desire,
only stand by us to sustain us.
    Break any tie that binds us
except the tie that binds us to thee.
And the blessing of God,
    Creating Presence,
    Redeeming Christ,
    and Life-Giving Spirit
be with you now
and for evermore.

John Shelby Spong

O God, I am hellishly angry; I think so-and-so is a swine; I am tor- 459
tured by worry about this or that; I am pretty certain that I have
missed my chances in life; this or that has left me feeling terribly
depressed. But nonetheless here I am like this, feeling both bloody
and bloody-minded, and I am going to stay here for ten minutes. You
are most unlikely to give me anything. I know that. But I am going to
stay for the ten minutes nonetheless.

Harry Williams

460   *E Tenebris*

Come down, O Christ, and help me! reach thy hand,
    For I am drowning in a stormier sea
    Than Simon on thy lake of Galilee:
The wine of life is spilt upon the sand,
My heart is in some famine-murdered land
    Whence all good things have perished utterly,
    And well I know my soul in hell must lie
If I this night before God's throne should stand.
'He sleeps perchance, or rideth to the chase,
    Like Baal, when his prophets howled that name
    From morn to noon on Carmel's smitten height.'
Nay, peace, I shall behold, before the night,
    The feet of brass, the robe more white than flame,
The wounded hands, the weary human face.

Oscar Wilde, 1854–1900

461   O Lord, in confidence of thy great mercy and goodness to all that truly repent and resolve to do better, I most humbly implore the grace and assistance of the Holy Spirit to enable me to become every day better. Grant me the wisdom and understanding to know my duty, and the heart and will to do it. Endue me, O Lord, with the true fear and love of thee, and with a prudent zeal for thy glory. Increase in me the graces of charity and meekness, of truth and justice, of humility and patience, and a firmness of spirit to bear every condition with constancy and equality of mind.

(King) William III, 1650–1702

462   Helper of all who are helpless,
we call on you in times of stress
and in times of devastation.
Pick up the broken pieces
of our hearts, our homes, our history
and restore them to the way they were,
or give us the means of starting over
when everything seems lost.
O God, our help in ages past,
we place all our hope in you.

Miriam Therese Winter

COMPASSION
AND KINDNESS

O thou whose divine tenderness ever outsoars the narrow loves and   463
charities of earth, grant us a kind and gentle heart towards all that
live. Let us not ruthlessly hurt any creature of thine. Let us take
thought also for the welfare of little children, and of those who are
sick, and the poor; remembering that what we do unto the least of
these his brethren we do unto Jesus Christ our Lord.

John Baillie, 1886–1960

> Open my eyes that they may see   464
> the deepest needs of people;
> move my hands that they may feed the hungry;
> touch my heart that it may bring warmth to the despairing;
> teach me the generosity that welcomes strangers;
> let me share my possessions to clothe the naked;
> give me the care that strengthens the sick;
> make me share in the quest to set the prisoner free.
> In sharing our anxieties and our love,
> our poverty and our prosperity,
> we partake of your divine presence.
>
> *Canaan Banana*

O Lord, baptize our hearts into a sense of the conditions and needs of   465
all men.

George Fox, 1624–91

466 Lord of the Universe
look in love upon your people.
Pour the healing oil of your compassion
on a world that is wounded and dying.
Send us out in search of the lost,
to comfort the afflicted,
to bind up the broken,
and to free those trapped
under the rubble of their fallen dreams.

Sheila Cassidy

467 Tender God, touch us.
Be touched by us;
make us lovers of humanity
compassionate friends of all creation.
Gracious God, hear us into speech;
speak us into acting;
and through us, recreate the world.

Carter Heyward

468 O Lord, open my eyes
that I may see the need of others,
open my ears that I may hear their cries,
open my heart so that they need not be without succour.
Let me not be afraid to defend the weak
because of the anger of the strong,
nor afraid to defend the poor
because of the anger of the rich.
Show me where love and hope and faith are needed,
and use me to bring them to these places.
Open my eyes and ears that I may, this coming day,
be able to do some work of peace for thee.

Alan Paton

469 Teach me to feel another's woe;
   To hide the fault I see;
That mercy I to others show,
   That mercy show to me.

Alexander Pope, 1688–1744

Gracious Lord, in whom are laid up all the treasures of knowledge 470
and wisdom, direct me in the ways of life; remove from me the ways
of death. Give me a soft and meek spirit, that I may help the succour-
less, and comfort the comfortless. O my dear Lord, pardon me for the
neglect of this duty, and make me to redeem the time with a cheerful
constancy.

The Penitent Pilgrim, 1641

We give you thanks, 471
Gentle One who has touched our soul.
You have loved us from the moment of our first waking
and have held us in joy and in grief.
Stay with us, we pray.
Grace us with your presence
and with it, the fullness of our own humanity.
Help us claim our strength and need,
our awesomeness and fragile beauty,
that encouraged by the truth
we might work to restore
compassion to the human family
and renew the face of the earth.

Janet Schaffran and Pat Kozak

O God, the father of the forsaken, the help of the weak, the supplier 472
of the needy; you teach us that love towards the race of man is the
bond of perfectness and the imitation of your blessed self.

Open and touch our hearts that we may see and do, both for this
world and that which is to come, the things that belong to our peace.
Strengthen us in the work which we have undertaken; give us wisdom, perseverance, faith and zeal, and in your own time and according to your pleasure prosper the issue; for the love of your Son, Christ
Jesus.

(Lord) Shaftesbury, 1801–85

473 Grant us grace, O Father, not to pass by suffering or joy without eyes to see. Give us understanding and sympathy, and guard us from self-ishness, that we may enter into the joys and sufferings of others. Use us to gladden and strengthen those who are weak and suffering; that by our lives we may help others to believe and serve thee, and shed forth thy light which is the light of life.

H. R. L. (Dick) Sheppherd, 1880–1937

474 Dearest Lord, may I see you today and every day in the person of your sick, and whilst nursing minister to you.

Though you hide yourself behind the unattractive disguise of the irritable, the exacting, the unreasonable, may I still recognize you and say: 'Jesus, my patient, how sweet it is to serve you.'

Lord, give me this seeing faith, then my work will never be monotonous. I will ever find joy in humouring the fancies and gratify-ing the wishes of all poor sufferers.

O beloved sick, how doubly dear you are to me, when you per-sonify Christ; and what a privilege is mine to be allowed to tend you.

Sweetest Lord, make me appreciative of the dignity of my high voc-ation, and its many responsibilities. Never permit me to disgrace it by giving way to coldness, unkindness, or impatience.

And, O God, while you are Jesus, my patient, deign also to be to me a patient Jesus, bearing with my faults, looking only to my intention, which is to love and serve you in the person of each of your sick.

Lord, increase my faith, bless my efforts and work, now and for evermore.

(Mother) Teresa of Calcutta (Her daily prayer)

475 Christ, I see thy crown of thorns in every eye, thy bleeding, wounded naked body in every soul; thy death liveth in every memory; thy wounded body is embalmed in every affection; thy pierced feet are bathed in everyone's tears; and it is my privilege to enter with thee into every soul.

Thomas Traherne, 1636–74

CONTENTMENT

Almighty God, who knowest our necessities before we ask, and our   476
ignorance in asking: set free thy servants from all anxious thoughts
for the morrow; give us contentment with thy good gifts; and confirm
our faith that according as we seek thy kingdom, thou wilt not suffer
us to lack any good thing; through Jesus Christ our Lord.

Augustine, 354–430

O God, make us more thankful for what we have received, more con-   477
tent with what we have, and more mindful of other people in need:
we ask it for his sake who lived for us in poverty, Jesus Christ our
Lord.

Simon H. Baynes

He that is down needs fear no fall,   478
He that is low, no pride:
He that is humble ever shall
Have God to be his guide.

I am content with what I have,
Little be it or much:
And, Lord, contentment still I crave;
Because thou savest such.

John Bunyan, 1628–88

479   When I was a child, Lord, I didn't know. I didn't know that you can be tired, tired of yourself, and that you can feel that you have missed out on life.

I've known many temptations, but these are the worst: to wish for better health, higher intelligence, a stronger body, a better education, another job and some of the appreciation shown to others.

To see others have countless opportunities which I should have liked and advantages I never had. To know that it is high time to live and too late to dream. To know that the impossible will never happen.

To know this, Lord, is to have a guiding light. The dreams are over. What is left now is my life – the real life which I must love! My life such as it is, my poor health, my poor job, and all the rest I never wanted.

I should like to accept all this, Lord. And accept myself, as poor as I am. Help me no longer to torment myself with thoughts of what 'might have been', but to find happiness in doing what I can.

Paul Geres

480   Grant me, O most sweet and loving Jesus, to rest in thee above every creature, above all health and beauty, above all glory and honour, above all power and dignity, above all knowledge and subtlety, above all riches and arts, above all joy and exultation, above all fame and praise, above all sweetness and consolation, above all hope and promise, above all desert and desire, above all gifts and presents which thou art able to bestow or infuse, above all joy and gladness which the mind is capable of receiving and feeling; finally, above angels and archangels, and above all the heavenly host, above all things visible and invisible, and above all that thou art not, O my God!

Thomas a Kempis, c.1380–1471

COURAGE AND CONFIDENCE

Lord, help me to understand that you ain't gwine to let nuthin' come 481
my way that you and me together can't handle.

Source unknown

O Holy Spirit, give me faith that will protect me from despair, from 482
passions, and from vice; give me such love for God and men as will
blot out all hatred and bitterness; give me the hope that will deliver
me from fear and faint-heartedness.

Dietrich Bonhoeffer (Prayed as he awaited trial for his part in a plot against Hitler)

> Grant, O God, 483
> that I may speak so boldly
> and so lovingly
> that the greatness of Christ
> may shine out clearly in my person,
> through the indwelling of your Holy Spirit.
>
> *Donald Coggan*

> Teach us to look, in all our ends, 484
> On thee for judge, and not our friends;
> That we, with thee, may walk uncowed
> By fear or favour of the crowd.
>
> *Rudyard Kipling, 1865–1936*

485

You, Springtime Jesus,
just as I'd settled down for winter,
you broke into my heart
and danced your love right across it
in a mad excess of giving.
Just as I'd got comfortable
with bare branches and unfeeling,
just as my world was neatly black and white,
there you were,
kicking up flowers
all over the place.
Springtime Jesus,
I tried to find a way to tell you
that there were places
where you could or could not dance.
I wanted to guide you on my paths
and have you sign the visitors' book;
but you laughed right through my words
and sang to me your melting song,
causing sap to fire the branches,
causing the flames of buds
to flicker into green bonfires,
causing a windquake of blossom,
causing growth-pain,
causing life.

Springtime Jesus,
the fullness of life can be frightening
and I'm lacking in courage.
It isn't easy to live with a heart
that's wide open to invasion.
Teach me, Jesus, how to move with you,
step for step, in your love dance.
Touch my fears with your melting song.
Gift me with your laughter,
and, in the mystery of your Springtime,
show me the truth of the blossoming Cross.

Joy Cowley

May he give us 486
   all the courage that we need
      to go the way he shepherds us.

That when he calls
   we may go unfrightened.

If he bids us come to him
   across the waters,
      that unfrightened we may go.

And if he bids us climb a hill,
   may we not notice that it is a hill,
      mindful only of
         the happiness of his company.

He made us for himself,
   that we should travel with him
      and see him at the last
         in his unveiled beauty
      in the abiding city where
      he is light
         and happiness
            and endless home.

Bede Jarrett, 1881–1934

Empower me 487
to be a bold participant,
rather than a timid saint in waiting,
in the difficult ordinariness of now;
to exercise the authority of honesty,
rather than to defer to power,
or deceive to get it;
to influence someone for justice,
rather than impress anyone for gain;
and, by grace, to find treasures
of joy, of friendship, of peace
hidden in the fields of the daily
you give me to plough.

Ted Loder

488   Make us, O blessed Master, strong in heart, full of courage, fearless of danger, holding pain and danger cheap when they lie in the path of duty. May we be strengthened with all might by thy Spirit in our hearts.

F. B. Meyer, 1847–1929

489   O Lord, who, when thine hour was near, didst go without fear among those who sought thy life; give us such boldness to confess thee before men, and such readiness to bear thy cross, that hereafter thou mayest confess us before thy Father which is in heaven.

Joseph Houldsworth Oldham, 1874–1969

490   What shall befall us hereafter we know not; but to God, who cares for all men, who will one day reveal the secrets of all hearts, we commit ourselves wholly, with all who are near and dear to us. And we beseech the same most merciful and almighty God, that for the time to come we may so bear the reproach of Christ with unbroken courage, as ever to remember that here we have no continuing city, but may seek one to come, by the grace and mercy of our Lord Jesus Christ; to whom with the Father, and the Holy Ghost, be all honour and dominion, world without end.

Matthew Parker, 1504–75

491   Give us courage, O Lord, to stand up and be counted, to stand up for others who cannot stand up for themselves. To stand up for ourselves when it is needful to do so.

Let us fear nothing more than we fear thee.

Let us love nothing more than we love thee, for then we shall fear nothing also.

Let us have no other God before thee, whether nation or party or state or church. Let us seek no other peace but the peace which is thine, and make us its instruments, opening our eyes and our ears and our hearts, so that we should know always what work of peace we should do for thee.

Alan Paton

Lord, help me to say 'yes'.   492
Michel Quoist

Dear God,   493
Somehow many of us have grown to adulthood believing we are not intelligent, experienced, or wise enough to give our opinion and share our insight. We passively wait for leaders to solve every problem. Keep us aware that each of us has something to offer – a personal wisdom different from anyone else's. And we can never know what influence we might have unless we speak up in the spirit of Christian love. Give us courage to share what you have revealed to us.
Mary Zimmer

FAITH AND TRUST

I believe; help my unbelief!   494
Mark 9.24

Almighty God, who in thy wisdom hast so ordered our earthly life   495
that we needs must walk by faith and not by sight; grant us such faith in thee that, amidst all things that pass our understanding, we may believe in thy fatherly care, and ever be strengthened by the assurance that underneath are the everlasting arms; through Jesus Christ our Lord.
Source unknown

496 Eternal God and Father, help us to entrust the past to your mercy, the present to your love, and the future to your wisdom, in the name of Jesus Christ our Lord, who is the same yesterday, and today, and for ever.

Source unknown

497
Holy and eternal God,
    give us such trust in your sure purpose,
that we measure our lives
not by what we have done or failed to do,
but by our faithfulness to you.

Anglican Church in Aotearoa, New Zealand and Polynesia.
A New Zealand Prayer Book

498
While faith is with me, I am blest;
It turns my darkest night to day;
But, while I clasp it to my breast,
I often feel it slide away.

What shall I do if all my love,
My hopes, my toil, are cast away?
And if there be no God above
To hear and bless me when I pray?

Oh, help me, God! For thou alone
Canst my distracted soul relieve.
Forsake it not: it is thine own,
Though weak, yet longing to believe.

Anne Brontë, 1820–49

499
Dear God, it is so hard for us not to be anxious.
We worry about work and money,
    about food and health,
    about weather and crops,
    about war and politics,
    about loving and being loved.
Show us how perfect love casts out fear.

Monica Furlong

O God our Father, help us to a deeper trust in the life everlasting. *500*
May we feel that this love which is now, ever shall be; this robe of the
flesh is thy gift to thy child, and, when it is worn out, thou wilt clothe
him again; this work of life is the work thou hast given us to do, and,
when it is done, thou wilt give us more; this love, that makes all our
life so glad, flows from thee, for thou art love, and we shall love
forever. Help us to feel how, day by day, we see some dim shadow of
the eternal day that will break upon us at the last. May the gospel of
thy Son, the whisper of thy Spirit, unite to make our faith in the life to
come, strong and clear; then shall we be glad when thou shalt call us,
and enter into thy glory in Jesus Christ.

Robert Collyer, 1823–1912

Lord, *501*
I'm bored.
I've lost my vision.
I've lost my sense of vocation.

Nothing seems to have any meaning any more.

I keep on putting one foot in front of the other;
but where am I going, and why?
What's the use?

Everything used to be full of life;
now it's all silent and empty.

Lord, if only I were somewhere else,
    if only things had turned out differently,
    if only I could see where it's all leading,
    if only. . . .
    if only I didn't feel so depressed!

But these are the circumstances you've given me:
it's here
    and not somewhere else
    that I have to learn to trust you
    in patience and humility.

Lord, help me to remember
    that they that wait upon the Lord
shall renew their strength.

Margaret Dewey (USPG)

502 O most merciful Father, we beseech thee, for thy mercy's sake, continue thy grace and favour towards us. Let not the sun of thy gospel ever go down out of our hearts; let thy truth abide and be established among us for ever. Help our unbelief, increase our faith, and give us hearts to consider the time of our visitation. Through faith clothe us with Christ, that he may live in us, and thy name may be glorified through us in all the world.

John Jewel, 1522–71

503 Teach us, O God not to torture ourselves, not to make martyrs of ourselves through stifling reflection; but rather teach us to breathe deeply in faith, through Jesus, our Lord.

Søren Kierkegaard, 1813–55

504 Lord, our heavenly Father, who orderest all things for our eternal good, mercifully enlighten our minds, and give us a firm and abiding trust in thy love and care. Silence our murmurings, quiet our fears, and dispel our doubts, that rising above our afflictions and our anxieties, we may rest on thee, the rock of everlasting strength.

New Church Book of Worship, 1876

505 May the Lord Jesus put his hands on our eyes also, for then we too shall begin to look not at what is seen but at what is not seen. May he open the eyes that are concerned not with the present but with what is yet to come, may he unseal the heart's vision, that we may gaze on God in the Spirit, through the same Lord, Jesus Christ, whose glory and power will endure throughout the unending succession of ages.

Origen, c.185–c.254

506 Hold us fast, O Lord of Hosts, that we fall not from thee. Grant us thankful and obedient hearts, that we may increase daily in the love, knowledge and fear of thee. Increase our faith, and help our unbelief; that being provided for and relieved of all our needs by thy fatherly care and providence, we may live a godly life, to the praise and good example of thy people, and after this life may reign with thee for ever; through Jesus Christ our Saviour.

James Pilkington, 1520–76

What is before us, we know not, whether we shall live or die; but this 507 we know, that all things are ordered and sure. Everything is ordered with unerring wisdom and unbounded love, by thee, our God, who art love. Grant us in all things to see thy hand; through Jesus Christ our Lord.

Charles Simeon, 1759–1836

Lord, I believe in thee; help thou mine unbelief. I love thee, yet not 508 with a perfect heart as I would; I long for thee, yet not with my full strength; I trust in thee, yet not with my whole mind. Accept my faith, my love, my longing to know and serve thee, my trust in thy power to keep me. What is cold do thou kindle, what is lacking do thou make up. I wait thy blessing; through Jesus Christ our Lord.

Malcolm Spencer

O Lord Jesus Christ, who didst invite the heavy laden to come to thee, 509 and didst promise to give them rest and never to cast them out, help us so to come to thee that we find rest in thee, and so to believe thy promise that we may know that thou hast received us, for the glory of thy name, who with the Father and the Holy Spirit art ever worthy to be trusted and adored.

John R. W. Stott

Help us, 510
O Keeper of Faith,
to keep the faith entrusted to us,
faith in a world worth saving,
faith in a dream worth sharing,
faith in a heritage worth keeping
even as we reinvigorate it
to have meaning for us now.
Help us keep faith in you,
and help us not lose faith in ourselves,
for faith is the substance of our hope,
and hope, the assurance of love.
Praise to you, O Faithful One,
now and forever.

Miriam Therese Winter

GOODNESS AND HOLINESS

511 O Lord God, destroy and root out whatever the adversary plants in me, that with my sins destroyed you may sow understanding and good work in my mouth and heart; so that in act and in truth I may serve only you and know how to fulfil the commandments of Christ and to seek yourself. Give me love, give me chastity, give me faith, give me all things which you know belong to the profit of my soul. O Lord, work good in me, and provide me with what you know that I need.

Columbanus, c.550–615

512 May I be no man's enemy, and may I be the friend of that which is eternal and abides.

May I never quarrel with those nearest me: and if I do, may I be reconciled quickly.

May I love, seek, and attain only that which is good.

May I wish for all men's happiness and envy none.

May I never rejoice in the ill-fortune of one who has wronged me.

When I have done or said what is wrong, may I never wait for the rebuke of others, but always rebuke myself until I make amends.

May I win no victory that harms either me or my opponent.

May I reconcile friends who are angry with one another.

May I, to the extent of my power, give all needful help to my friends and all who are in want.

May I never fail a friend who is in danger.

When visiting those in grief may I be able by gentle and healing words to soften their pain.

May I respect myself.

May I always keep tame that which rages within me.

May I accustom myself to be gentle, and never be angry with people because of circumstances.

May I never discuss who is wicked and what wicked things he has done, but know good men and follow in their footsteps.

Eusebius, 3rd century

Lord, make us to walk in your way: 513
'Where there is love and wisdom, there is neither fear nor ignorance;
where there is patience and humility, there is neither anger nor
    annoyance;
where there is poverty and joy, there is neither greed nor avarice;
where there is peace and contemplation, there is neither care nor
    restlessness;
where there is the fear of God to guard the dwelling, there no enemy
    can enter;
where there is mercy and prudence, there is neither excess nor
    harshness';
this we know through your Son, Jesus Christ our Lord.

Francis of Assisi, 1182–1226

If only I possessed the grace, good Jesus, to be utterly at one with you! 514
Amidst all the variety of worldly things around me, Lord, the only
thing I crave is unity with you. You are all my soul needs. Unite, dear
friend of my heart, this unique little soul of mine to your perfect
goodness. You are all mine; when shall I be yours? Lord Jesus, my
beloved, be the magnet of my heart; clasp, press, unite me for ever to
your sacred heart. You have made me for yourself; make me one with
you. Absorb this tiny drop of life into the ocean of goodness whence
it came.

Francis de Sales, 1567–1622

May God himself, the God of peace, make us holy in every part; and 515
keep us sound in spirit, soul, and body, without fault when our Lord
Jesus Christ comes. He who calls us is to be trusted: he will do it.

    For ecstasy of body, for exchange of mind, and for unity of the
spirit in love, praise God.

Daphne Fraser

O Lord Jesus, who camest down from heaven to redeem us from all 516
iniquity, we beseech thee to write thy word in our hearts that we may
know thee, and the power of thy resurrection, and express it in turning from our iniquities. Rule in our hearts by faith, that being dead
unto sin and living unto righteousness, we may have our fruit unto
holiness and grow in grace and in the practical knowledge of thee.

Henry Hammond, 1605–60

517   O God, grant that looking upon the face of the Lord, as into a glass, we may be changed into his likeness, from glory to glory. Take out of us all pride and vanity, boasting and forwardness; and give us the true courage which shows itself by gentleness; the true wisdom which shows itself by simplicity; and the true power which shows itself by modesty.

Charles Kingsley, 1819–75

518   O God, who madest me for thyself,
to show forth thy goodness in me:
manifest, I humbly beseech thee,
the life-giving power of thy holy nature within me;
help me to such a true and living faith in thee,
such strength of hunger and thirst after
   the birth, life and spirit of thy holy Jesus
   in my soul,
that all that is within me
may be turned from every inward thought
   or outward work
that is not thee, thy holy Jesus,
and heavenly workings in my soul.

William Law, 1686–1761

519   Give me, good Lord, an humble, lowly, quiet, peaceable, patient, charitable, kind and filial and tender mind, every shade, in fact, of charity, with all my words and all my works, and all my thoughts, to have a taste of thy holy blessed Spirit.

(Sir) Thomas More, 1478–1535

520   God, stay with me; let no word cross my lips that is not your word, no thoughts enter my mind that are not your thoughts, no deed ever be done or entertained by me that is not your deed.

Malcolm Muggeridge

521   Cleanse me, O God, by the bright fountain of thy mercy, and water me with the dew of thine abundant grace, that, being purified from my sins, I may grow up in good works, truly serving thee in holiness and righteousness all the days of my life.

Private Devotions, 1560

O Lord, prepare my heart, I beseech thee, to reverence thee, to adore 522
thee, to love thee; to hate, for love of thee, all my sins, imperfections,
shortcomings, whatever in me displeaseth thee; and to love all which
thou lovest, and whom thou lovest. Give me, Lord, fervour of love,
shame for my unthankfulness, sorrow for my sins, longing for thy
grace, and to be wholly united with thee. Let my very coldness call for
the glow of thy love; let my emptiness and dryness, like a barren and
thirsty land, thirst for thee, call on thee to come into my soul, who
refreshest those who are weary. Let my heart ache to thee and for
thee, who stillest the aching of the heart. Let my mute longings praise
thee, crave to thee, who satisfiest the empty soul, that waits on thee.

Edward Bouverie Pusey, 1800–82

Hear our prayers, O Lord, and consider our desires. Give unto us true 523
humility, a meek and quiet spirit, a loving and friendly, a holy and a
useful manner of life; bearing the burdens of our neighbours, denying
ourselves, and studying to benefit others, and to please thee in all
things. Grant us to be righteous in performing promises, loving to our
relatives, careful of our charges; to be gentle and easy to be entreated,
slow to anger, and readily prepared for every good work.

Jeremy Taylor, 1613–67

O God the Holy Ghost, most loving Comforter of the fainthearted, I 524
beseech thee ever to turn that which is evil in me into good and that
which is good into that which is better; turn my mourning into joy,
my wandering feet into the right path, my ignorance into knowledge
of thy truth, my lukewarmness into zeal, my fear into love, all my
material good into a spiritual gift, all my earthly desires into
heavenly, all that is transient into that which lasts for ever, everything
human into that which is divine, everything created and finite into
that sovereign and immeasurable good, which thou thyself art, O my
God and Saviour.

Thomas a Kempis, c.1380–1471

525   Grant us, O Lord, to know that which is worth knowing, to love that which is worth loving, to praise that which can bear with praise, to hate what in thy sight is unworthy, to prize what to thee is precious, and, above all, to search out and to do what is well-pleasing unto thee; through Jesus Christ our Lord.

Thomas a Kempis, c.1380–1471

526   You have accomplished a deed so sublime that my mind cannot grasp it. You have come down to earth and saved me. It is the wonder of all wonders, the miracle of all miracles. I believe in you, I confess your name, I preach to others your gospel of salvation, I marvel that you have shown such love towards me, and I want others to receive such love for themselves. O Lover of men, my Lover, I implore you to grant me a place in heaven. Yet I am still a sinner, I am still distorted by evil thoughts and feelings. Do not delay. Redeem your promise now. Make me fit for heaven, even while I live on earth. Make me holy, as you are holy, that I may glorify you in every thought, every feeling, and every action.

Tychon of Zadonsk, 1724–83

GRATITUDE

527   Lord of all mercy and goodness, suffer us not by any ingratitude or hardness of heart to forget the wonderful benefits that thou hast bestowed upon us this and every day; but grant that we may be mindful all the days of our life of the incomparable gifts which thou ever givest us through Jesus Christ our Lord.

Source unknown (Early Scottish)

Thou that hast given so much to me,   *528*
Give one thing more, a grateful heart.
See how thy beggar works on thee
    By art.

Wherefore I cry, and cry again;
And in no quiet canst thou be,
Till I a thankful heart obtain
    Of thee:

Not thankful, when it pleaseth me:
As if thy blessings had spare days:
But such a heart, whose pulse may be
    Thy praise.

George Herbert, 1593–1633

O glorious God, the whole of creation proclaims your marvellous   *529*
work: increase in us a capacity to wonder and delight in it, that
heaven's praise may echo in our hearts and our lives be spent as good
stewards of the earth; through Jesus Christ our Lord.

Christopher Irvine

O Lord, that lends me life,   *530*
Lend me a heart replete with thankfulness.

William Shakespeare, 1564–1616

Give us, O Lord God, a deep sense of thy holiness; how thou art of   *531*
purer eyes than to behold iniquity, and canst not overlook or pass by
that which is evil. Give us no less, O Lord, a deep sense of thy wonderful love towards us; how thou wouldest not let us alone in our ruin,
but didst come after us, in the Person of thy Son Jesus Christ to bring
us back to our true home with thee. Quicken in us, O Lord, the spirit
of gratitude, of loyalty and of sacrifice, that we may seek in all things
to please him who humbled himself for us, even to the death of the
cross, by dying unto sin and living unto righteousness; through the
same Jesus Christ our Lord.

Charles John Vaughan, 1816–97

HOPE

532   O God, who never forsakest those that hope in thee: grant that we may ever keep that hope which thou hast given us by thy Word as an anchor of our souls, to preserve us sure and steadfast, unshaken and secure in all the storms of life; through Jesus Christ our Lord.

Source unknown

533   O God, the author and fountain of hope, enable us to rely with confident expectation on thy promises, knowing that the trials and hindrances of the present time are not worthy to be compared with the glory that shall be revealed, and having our faces steadfastly set towards the light that shineth more and more to the perfect day; through Jesus Christ our Lord.

A Devotional Diary

534   O Lord, in whom is our hope, remove far from us, we pray thee, empty hopes and presumptuous confidence. Make our hearts so right with thy most holy and loving heart, that hoping in thee we may do good; until that day when faith and hope shall be abolished by sight and possession, and love shall be all in all.

Christina Rossetti, 1830–94

535   O Lord, who art the hope of all the ends of the earth, let me never be destitute of a well-grounded hope, nor yet possessed with a vain presumption: suffer me not to think thou wilt either be reconciled to my sins, or reject my repentance; but give me, I beseech thee, such a hope as may be answerable to the only ground of hope, thy promises, and such as may both encourage and enable me to purify myself from all filthiness, both of flesh and spirit; that so, it may indeed become to me an anchor of the soul both sure and steadfast.

The Whole Duty of Man, 1658

Grant, O God, that amidst all the discouragements, difficulties and   *536*
dangers, distress and darkness of this mortal life, I may depend upon
thy mercy, and on this build my hopes, as on a sure foundation. Let
thine infinite mercy in Christ Jesus deliver me from despair, both now
and at the hour of death.

Thomas Wilson, 1663–1755

HUMILITY

Dear Lord, I thank you for calling me to share with others your pre-   *537*
cious gift of laughter. May I never forget that it is your gift and my
privilege. As your children are rebuked in their self-importance and
cheered in their sadness, help me to remember that your foolishness is
wiser than men's wisdom.

Source unknown ('The Clown's Prayer')

O Father, give us the humility which   *538*
    Realizes its ignorance,
    Admits its mistakes,
    Recognizes its need,
    Welcomes advice,
    Accepts rebuke.
Help us always
    To praise rather than to criticize,
    To sympathize rather than to condemn.
    To encourage rather than to discourage,
    To build rather than to destroy,
    And to think of people at their best rather than at their worst.
This we ask for thy name's sake.

William Barclay

539 Dear God,
I would like to become a little child and rest my soul in you.
I'm tired of the loneliness, tired of the struggle,
I want to surrender but I don't know how.
You see, I have this problem of being adult.
I belong to the generation which makes decisions, plans, works,
accepts responsibility, takes pride in being independent.
Adults are supposed to manage their lives.
They are concerned with owning things and
making things happen, and they don't like to look small or foolish.
Dear God, for a long time I've been living at the centre of a world
which has prevented me from entering the Kingdom of Heaven.

Father God, Mother God,
show me how to become your child.
I am aware of the advice that Jesus gives.
He does not say that we should remain in infancy.
He says that we should become as little children.
This tells me that I need to know the futility of independence before
I can let go of it.
It is the letting go which is difficult.
I know you are there, waiting to give yourself to me, but I'm afraid to
commit myself.
Please help me to loosen this grip on my pride
so that I can hold out my arms to you and be enfolded in your love.

Joy Cowley

540 O Thou who in almighty power wast weak, and in perfect excellency
wast lowly, grant unto us the same mind. All that we have which is
our own is naught; if we have any good in us it is wholly thy gift. O
Saviour, since thou, the Lord of heaven and earth, didst humble thyself, grant unto us true humility, and make us like thyself; and then,
of thine infinite goodness, raise us to thine everlasting glory; who
livest and reignest with the Father and the Holy Ghost for ever and
ever.

Thomas Cranmer, 1489–1556

Give us a sense of humour, Lord and also things to laugh about; give *541*
us the grace to take a joke against ourselves, and to see the funny side
of the things we do; save us from annoyance, bad temper, resentful-
ness against our friends. Help us to laugh even in the face of trouble,
fill our minds with the love of Jesus; for his name's sake.

Michael Hollings and Etta Gullick

O Lord Jesus Christ, who didst humble thyself to become man, and to *542*
be born into the world for our salvation: teach us the grace of humility, root out of our hearts all pride and haughtiness, and so fashion us
after thy holy likeness in this world, that in the world to come we may
be made like unto thee in thy eternal kingdom.

William Walsham How, 1823–97

O Saviour, meek and lowly of heart, let not our pride refuse thy bid- *543*
ding, to become as little children, in joy and simplicity, in trustfulness
one toward another, in lowliness of heart; and by this thine own
glory, bring us unto ours; for thy majesty and thy mercy's sake.

Eric Milner-White, 1884–1963

Lord, help me not to despise or oppose what I do not understand. *544*

William Penn, 1644–1718

Lord! going out from this silence, teach me to be more alert, humble, *545*
expectant, than I have been in the past: ever ready to encounter you in
quiet, homely ways: in every appeal to my compassion, every act of
unselfish love which shows up and humbles my imperfect love, may I
recognize you: still walking through the world. Give me that grace of
simplicity which alone can receive your mystery.

> Come and abide with me!
> Meet me, walk with me!
> Enlighten my mind!

And then, Come in! Enter my humble life with its poverty and its limitations as you entered the stable of Bethlehem, the workshop of
Nazareth, the cottage of Emmaus.

> Bless and consecrate the material of that small and ordinary life.
> Feed and possess my soul.

Evelyn Underhill, 1875–1941

546 Lord, give us a heart to turn all knowledge to thy glory and not to our own. Keep us from being deluded with the lights of vain philosophies. Keep us from the pride of human reason. Let us not think our own thoughts; but in all things acting under the guidance of the Holy Spirit, may we find thee everywhere, and live in all simplicity, humility and singleness of heart unto the Lord.

Henry Kirke White, 1785–1806

547   The pinnacle of the Temple is a very lonely place.
You will not be waiting for me there.
Your method,
    your prayer,
    your disclosure of God,
    take the lowliest path.
Your tabernacle among us is in the cave and the cottage.
I must come down like Zacchaeus
if I would have you dwell with me,
    on the country roads of Galilee,
    in the villages and on the shore,
    down among the cares,
        the sins,
        labours
        and sufferings of ordinary men –
there we shall find you.

'O teach me your ways
and hold up my going in your paths
that my footsteps slip not.'

Your paths are well-trodden.
Along them you and your saints have carried
healing and love
to ordinary men and women where they are.
Teach me to serve them as you serve –
    with patience,
    simplicity,
    reverence
    and love.

Your saints never presumed to grasp at
their spiritual privileges,
or use them for their own advantage:

nor sought extraordinary grace.
They loved to follow you along ordinary ways.
Help me to love those ways too.

Your spirit is not given that we may escape
life's friction and demands,
but so that we may live the common life
as you would have it lived –
in earth as in heaven.

Evelyn Underhill, 1875–1941

JOY

Help me, my God, to be joyful always, to pray at all times, and be   548
thankful in all circumstances.

1 Thessalonians 5.16–18 (Good News Bible, adapted)

Lord, renew our spirits and draw our hearts unto thyself, that our   549
work may not be to us a burden, but a delight. Oh, let us not serve
thee with the spirit of bondage as slaves, but with the cheerfulness
and gladness of children, delighting ourselves in thee, and rejoicing in
thy work.

Benjamin Jenks, 1646–1724

550 Almighty and Holy Spirit, the comforter, pure, living, true, – illuminate, govern, sanctify me, and confirm my heart and mind in the faith, and in all genuine consolation; preserve and rule over me that, dwelling in the house of the Lord all the days of my life, to behold the beauty of the Lord, I may be and remain forever in the temple of the Lord, and praise him with a joyful spirit, and in union with all the heavenly Church.

Philip Melanchthon, 1497–1560

551 Grant to us, O Lord, the royalty of inward happiness, and the serenity which comes from living close to thee. Daily renew in us the sense of joy, and let the eternal Spirit of the Father dwell in our souls and bodies, filling every corner of our hearts with light and grace; so that, bearing about with us the infection of good courage, we may be diffusers of life, and may meet all ills and cross accidents with gallant and high-hearted happiness, giving thee thanks always for all things.

Robert Louis Stevenson, 1850–94

552 O Lord Christ, help us to maintain ourselves in simplicity, and in joy, the joy of the merciful, the joy of brotherly love. Grant that, renouncing henceforth all thought of looking back, and joyful with infinite gratitude, we may never fear to precede the dawn, to praise and bless and sing to the Christ our Lord.

Taizé Community

553 Tender God, gentle protector in time of trouble: pierce the gloom of despair and give us, with all your people, the song of freedom and the shout of praise, in Jesus Christ our Lord.

Michael Vasey

PATIENCE AND
GENTLENESS

Bestow on me, O Lord, a genial spirit and unwearied forbearance; a   *554*
mild, loving, patient heart; kindly looks, pleasant, cordial speech and
manners in the exchanges of daily life; that I may give offence to
none, but as much as in me lies live in charity with all men.

Johann Arndt, 1555–1621

O God, give us patience when those who are wicked hurt us. O how   *555*
impatient and angry we are when we think ourselves unjustly slan-
dered, reviled and hurt! Christ suffers blows upon his cheek, the
innocent for the guilty; yet we may not abide one rough word for his
sake. O Lord, grant us virtue and patience, power and strength, that
we may take all adversity with goodwill, and with a gentle mind overcome it. And if necessity and thy honour require us to speak, grant
that we may do so with meekness and patience, that the truth and thy
glory may be defended, and our patience and steadfast continuance
perceived.

Miles Coverdale, 1488–1568

O thou Prince of Peace, who, when thou wast reviled reviledst not   *556*
again, and on the cross didst pray for thy murderers, implant in our
hearts the virtues of gentleness and patience, that we may overcome
evil with good, for thy sake love our enemies, and as children of our
heavenly Father seek thy peace, and evermore rejoice in thy love;
through Jesus Christ our Saviour.

Treasury of Devotion, 1869

557   Jesus, you cared for all the sick
        who came to you.
         I want to care with loving compassion,
           to attend to details with gentleness.
         But I become weary and impatient,
           angry and abrupt.
         It is hard to watch the suffering of someone I love,
           hard to find energy for all I must do.
         I grow discouraged and resentful.
         Let me learn from your life of compassion.
      Spirit of healing and comfort,
         Be with me in these difficult times.
         Teach me to take time for myself,
           to be gentle with my own limits,
           to ask for help from others.
         May your grace allow me
           to forgive myself when I fail,
           to let go of my expectations,
           to grieve all my losses.
         Send your healing power to me and the one for
           whom I care. We trust in your love.

Kathleen Fischer

PEACE AND SERENITY

May the Light of lights come
To my dark heart from thy place;
May the Spirit's wisdom come
To my heart's tablet from my Saviour.
Be the peace of the Spirit mine this night,
Be the peace of the Son mine this night,
Be the peace of the Father mine this night,
The peace of all peace be mine this night,
Each morning and evening of my life.

Source unknown (Celtic)

558

O Father of lights, with whom there is no variation nor shadow of turning, who abidest steadfast as the stars of heaven: give us grace to rest upon thy eternal changelessness, and in thy faithfulness find peace; through Jesus Christ our Lord.

George W. Briggs, 1875–1959

559

O God, make us children of quietness and heirs of peace.

Clement of Rome, 1st century

560

O thou lover of mankind, send down into our hearts that peace which the world cannot give, and give us peace in this world. O King of Peace, keep us in love and charity; be our God, for we have none other beside thee; grant unto our souls the life of righteousness, that the death of sin may not prevail against us, or against any of thy people.

Walter Farquhar Hook, 1798–1875

561

562   O Lord Jesus Christ, who didst say that in thee we may have peace, and hast bidden us to be of good cheer, since thou hast overcome the world: give us ears to hear and faith to receive thy Word; that in all the tensions and confusion of this present time, with mind serene and steadfast purpose, we may continue to abide in thee, who livest and wast dead and art alive for evermore.

Frederick B. Macnutt, 1873–1949

563   In the name of Jesus Christ, who was never in a hurry, we pray, O God, that thou wilt slow us down, for we know that we live too fast. With all of eternity before us, make us take time to live – time to get acquainted with thee, time to enjoy thy blessings, and time to know each other.

Peter Marshall

564   The Lord is my pace-setter, I shall not rush,
He makes me stop and rest for quiet intervals,
He provides me with images of stillness, which restore my serenity.
He leads me in the ways of efficiency; through calmness of mind,
And his guidance is peace.
Even though I have a great many things to accomplish each day,
I will not fret for his presence is here.
His timelessness, his all-importance will keep me in balance.
He prepares refreshment and renewal in the midst of my activity
By anointing my mind with his oils of tranquillity,
My cup of joyous energy overflows.
Surely harmony and effectiveness shall be the fruits of my hours,
For I shall walk in the pace of my Lord, and dwell in his house
    for ever.

Toki Miyashina (based on Psalm 23)

565   Grant calmness and control of thought to those who are facing uncertainty and anxiety: let their heart stand fast, believing in the Lord. Be thou all things to all men, knowing each one and his petition, each house and its need, for the sake of Jesus Christ.

Russian Liturgy, 6th century

O Lord God, heavenly Father, who didst give up thine only-begotten 566
Son into grief and sorrow, that we might have peace through him:
grant us so surely to found our faith upon him alone that we may
have peace in our souls. Quicken us with thy Word; grant already
here on earth the peace which is a foretaste of the rest that remaineth
for thy people. And while the cares and tumults of this life beset us
round about, guide us in all our undertakings by thy Holy Spirit, that
we may abide in thy peace; through Jesus Christ our Lord.

Swedish Liturgy

Slow me down Lord! Ease the pounding of my heart by the quieting 567
of my mind. Steady my hurried pace with a vision of the eternal reach
of time. Give me amidst the confusion of my day the calmness of the
everlasting hills. Allow me to know the magical restoring power of
sleep. Teach me the art of taking one-minute vacations . . . of slowing
down to look at a flower, to pat a dog, to read a few lines from a good
book. Let me look up into the branches of the towering oak and
know that it grew great and strong because it grew slowly and well.

Slow me down Lord, and inspire me to send my roots deep into the
soil of life's enduring values that I may grow toward the stars of my
greater destiny.

Toc H

Drop thy still dews of quietness, 568
Till all our strivings cease;
Take from our souls the strain and stress,
And let our ordered lives confess
The beauty of thy peace.

Breathe through the heats of our desire
Thy coolness and thy balm;
Let sense be dumb, let flesh retire;
Speak through the earthquake, wind, and fire,
O still small voice of calm!

John Greenleaf Whittier, 1807–92

PERSEVERANCE

569   O Lord God, when thou givest to thy servants to endeavour any great matter; grant us also to know that it is not the beginning but the continuing of the same until it is thoroughly finished which yieldeth the true glory. Through him who, for the finishing of thy work, laid down his life for us, our redeemer, Jesus Christ.

Source unknown (based on a saying of Sir Francis Drake, c.1540–96)

570   O God our Father, let us find grace in thy sight so as to have grace to serve thee acceptably with reverence and godly fear, and further grace not to receive thy grace in vain, not to neglect it and fall from it, and to persevere in it unto the end of our lives; through Jesus Christ our Lord.

Lancelot Andrewes, 1555–1626

571   I pray you, O most gentle Jesus, having redeemed me by baptism from original sin, so now by your precious blood, which is offered and received throughout the world, deliver me from all evils, past, present and to come. By your most cruel death give me lively faith, a firm hope and perfect charity, so that I may love you will all my heart and all my soul and all my strength. Make me firm and steadfast in good works and grant me perseverance in your service so that I may be able to please you always.

Clare of Assisi, 1194–1253

572   Give us, O God, the power to go on, to carry our share of thy burden through to the end, to live all the years of our life faithful to the highest we have seen, with no pandering to the second best, no leniency to our own lower selves; no looking backward, no cowardice. Give us the power to give ourselves, to break the bread of our lives unto starving humanity; in humble self-subjection to serve others, as thou, O God, dost serve the world.

J. S. Hoyland

O God, who hast promised that they who endure to the end shall be 573
saved, give us grace to persevere in thy holy service all our days, that
we may reach the end of our faith, even the salvation of our souls:
through Jesus Christ our Lord.

The Narrow Way

Lord, give us grace to hold to you 574
    when all is weariness and fear
    and sin abounds within, without
    when love itself is tested by the doubt . . .
    that love is false, or dead within the soul,
    when every act brings new confusion, new distress,
    new opportunities, new misunderstandings,
    and every thought new accusation.

Lord, give us grace that we may know
    that in the darkness pressing round
    it is the mist of sin that hides your face,
    that you are there
    and you do know we love you still
    and our dependence and endurance in your will
    is still our gift of love.

Gilbert Shaw, 1886–1967

PURITY OF HEART

575   Almighty God, in whom we live and move and have our being, thou hast made us for thyself, so that our hearts are restless until they find rest in thee; grant us purity of heart and strength of purpose, that no selfish passion may hinder us from knowing thy will, no weakness from doing it; but that in thy light we may see light, and in thy service find perfect freedom; through Jesus Christ our Lord.

Augustine, 354–430

576   Lord Jesus, our Saviour, let us now come to thee:
Our hearts are cold; Lord, warm them with thy selfless love.
Our hearts are sinful; cleanse them with thy precious blood.
Our hearts are weak; strengthen them with thy joyous Spirit.
Our hearts are empty; fill them with thy divine presence.
Lord Jesus, our hearts are thine; possess them always
   and only for thyself.

Augustine, 354–430

577   Almighty God, unto whom all hearts are open, all desires known, and from whom no secrets are hid; cleanse the thoughts of our hearts by the inspiration of thy Holy Spirit, that we may perfectly love thee, and worthily magnify thy holy Name, through Jesus Christ our Lord.

Gregorian Sacramentary, 6th century

578   Write deeply upon our minds, O Lord God, the lesson of thy holy word, that only the pure in heart can see thee. Leave us not in the bondage of any sinful inclination. May we neither deceive ourselves with the thought that we have no sin, nor acquiesce idly in aught of which our conscience accuses us. Strengthen us by thy Holy Spirit to fight the good fight of faith, and grant that no day may pass without its victory; through Jesus Christ our Lord.

Charles John Vaughan, 1816–97

O eternal God, who hast taught us by thy holy word that our bodies *579* are temples of thy Spirit; keep us, we most humbly beseech thee, temperate and holy in thought, word and deed, that at the last we, with all the pure in heart, may see thee and be made like unto thee in thy heavenly kingdom; through Jesus Christ our Lord.

Brooke Foss Westcott, 1825–1901

Make and keep me pure within. *580*

Charles Wesley, 1707–88

SELF-CONTROL

Father, make me quick to listen, but slow to speak, and slow to *581* become angry.

James 1.19 (Good News Bible, adapted)

God, Let me put right before interest, *582*
Let me put others before self,
Let me put the things of the spirit
before the things of the body.
Let me put the attainment of noble ends
above the enjoyment of present pleasures
Let me put principle above reputation.
Let me put thee before all else.

John Baillie, 1886–1960

583 O my Lord, I discern in my anger a sense of self-righteousness which is much too close to pleasure. And I think of you, Lord. You were never angry in your own defence, and you took no pleasure in anger: else why the Cross? But you were angry for God: you were angry with those who sold him as a commodity; you were angry with those who used him for their own status; or who treated him as belonging only to them.

O Lord, implant in me a holy fear of the wrong kind of anger, which ministers to my own sense of self-importance, or is simply an indulgence of my own frustration. Forgive me, Lord, for all such occasions.

Ruth Etchells

584 O God, we hold in your presence the anger that this day will bring forth. Teach us to really care, so that our anger is not occasioned by trifles to do with our comfort and status, but by what outrages your heart of love.

Richard Harries

585 O Lord help us to be masters of ourselves that we may be the servants of others.

(Sir) Alexander Henry Paterson, 1884–1947

586 Grant Lord, that I may not, for one moment, admit willingly into my soul any thought contrary to thy love.

Edward Bouverie Pusey, 1800–82

TRUTH

Lord, let me not love in just words and talk; but let my love be true, showing itself in action.

1 John 3.18 (Good News Bible, adapted)

587

> From the cowardice that shrinks from new truths,
> from the laziness that is content with half-truth,
> from the arrogance that thinks it knows all truth,
> O God of truth, deliver us.
>
> *Source unknown*

O Lord almighty, Father of Jesus Christ our Lord, grant us, we pray thee, to be grounded and settled in thy truth by the coming down of thy Holy Spirit in our hearts. That which we know not do thou reveal; that which is wanting in us, do thou fill up; that which we know do thou confirm, and keep us blameless in thy service, through the same Jesus Christ our Lord.

Clement of Rome, 1st century

589

Dear Lord, give me the truths which are veiled by the doctrines and articles of faith, which are masked by the pious words of sermons and books. Let my eyes penetrate the veil, and tear off the mask, that I can see your truth face to face.

John of the Cross, 1542–91

590

Lord, give us weak eyes for things which are of no account and clear eyes for all your truth.

Søren Kierkegaard, 1813–55

591

592   *Come, Holy Spirit, and show us what is true.*
                             Come, Holy Spirit, and show us what is true.
                             In a world of great wealth
                             where many go hungry
                             and fortunes are won and lost
                             by trading in money,
                             come, Holy Spirit, and show us what is true.

In a world of great knowledge
where many die of ignorance
and every piece of information
has a price in the marketplace,
come, Holy Spirit, and show us what is true.

In a world of easy communication
where words leap between continents
and we expect to see a picture
to illustrate each item of the news,
come, Holy Spirit, and show us what is true.

In a Church touched by the flame of the Pentecost
moved to generous sacrifice and costly love
interpreting the will of God with new insight,
come, Holy Spirit, and show us what is true.

Stephen Orchard

593   God, make me single and sincere; take away all that is not true, all that hinders thy work in me; for only so shall I serve thee.

A Saint Francis Prayer Book

594   Almighty God who hast sent the Spirit of truth unto us to guide us into all truth: so rule our lives by thy power that we may be truthful in thought and word and deed. May no fear or hope ever make us false in act or speech; cast out from us whatsoever loveth or maketh a lie, and bring us all into the perfect freedom of thy truth; through Jesus Christ our Lord.

Brooke Foss Westcott, 1825–1901

UNSELFISHNESS

O Lord, give us more charity, more self-denial, more likeness to thee. *595*
Teach us to sacrifice our comforts to others, and our likings for the
sake of doing good. Make us kindly in thought, gentle in word, generous in deed. Teach us that it is better to give than to receive; better to
forget ourselves than to put ourselves forward; better to minister
than to be ministered unto. And unto thee, the God of love, be glory
and praise for ever.

Henry Alford, 1810–71

O Saviour, pour upon me thy spirit of meekness and love, annihilate *596*
the selfhood in me, be thou all my life. Guide thou my hand which
trembles exceedingly upon the rock of ages.

William Blake, 1757–1827

Pour into our hearts the spirit of unselfishness, so that, when our cup *597*
overflows, we may seek to share our happiness with our brethren. O
thou God of love, who makest thy sun to rise on the evil and on the
good, and sendest rain on the just and the unjust, grant that we may
become more and more thy true children, by receiving into our souls
more of thine own spirit of ungrudging and unwearying kindness;
which we ask in the name of Jesus Christ.

John Hunter, 1849–1917

O God, in whom nothing can live but as it lives in love, grant us the *598*
spirit of love which does not want to be rewarded, honoured or
esteemed, but only to become the blessing and happiness of everything that wants it; love which is the very joy of life, and thine own
goodness and truth within the soul; who thyself art Love, and by love
our Redeemer, from eternity to eternity.

William Law, 1686–1761

599 We let the world overcome us; we live too much in continual fear of the chances and changes of mortal life. We let things go too much their own way. We try too much to get what we can by our own selfish wits, without considering our neighbour. We follow too much the ways and fashions of the day, doing and saying and thinking anything that comes uppermost, just because there is so much around us. Free us from our selfish interests, and guide us, good Lord, to see thy way and to do thy will.

Charles Kingsley, 1819–75

600   This is the day that the Lord has made.
Let us rejoice and be glad in it.
We will not offer to God
Offerings that cost us nothing.

Spirit of God,
brooding over the waters
of our chaos,
inspire us to
generous living.

Wind of God,
dancing over the desert
of our reluctance,
lead us to the oasis
of celebration.

Breath of God,
inspiring communication
among strangers,
make us channels
of your peace,

that we may give
in deep thankfulness,
placing the overflowing basket
of our gifts
on the table
of rejoicing.

Kate McIlhagga

Lord, teach us to understand that your Son died to save us, not from *601*
suffering, but from ourselves; not from injustice, far less from justice,
but from being unjust. He died that we might live – but live as he lives,
by dying as he died who died to himself.

George Macdonald, 1824–1905

I'm glad to be alive – to breathe and walk; to laugh and cry; to see *602*
life's beauty and its grandeur. I know, too, its beastliness, squalor; its
poverty, disease and hate. As I give thanks for all my blessings, give
me, Lord, the will to share with others what I have so undeservedly
been given. Make me loving, courteous, considerate; give me a listening ear, a compassionate heart and a generous mind. Let me live my
life in your sight for others so that they, too, may find you and give
thanks.

(Brother) John Charles Vockler

WISDOM AND UNDERSTANDING

O Lord, thou greatest and most true Light, whence the light of the *603*
day doth spring! O Light, which dost lighten every man that cometh
into the world! O thou Wisdom of the eternal Father, lighten my
mind, that I may see only those things that please thee, and may be
blinded to all other things. Grant that I may walk in thy ways, and
that nothing else may be light and pleasant.

John Bradford, 1510–55

604   O God, by whom the meek are guided in judgement, and light rises up in darkness for the godly; give us, in all our doubts and uncertainties the grace to ask what thou wouldst have us to do; that the spirit of wisdom may save us from all false choices, and that in thy light we may see light and in thy straight path may not stumble; through Jesus Christ our Lord.

William Bright, 1824–1901

605   O Lord, heavenly Father, in whom is the fulness of light and wisdom, enlighten our minds by thy Holy Spirit, and give us grace to receive thy word with reverence and humility, without which no man can understand thy truth, for Christ's sake.

John Calvin, 1509–64

606   Holy Spirit, think through me till your ideas are my ideas.

Amy Carmichael, 1868–1951

607   You are Wisdom, uncreated and eternal,
     the supreme first cause, above all being,
     sovereign Godhead, sovereign goodness,
     watching unseen the God-inspired wisdom of Christian people.
Raise us, we pray, that we may totally respond
     to the supreme, unknown, ultimate, and splendid height
     of your words, mysterious and inspired.
There all God's secret matters lie covered and hidden
     under darkness both profound and brilliant, silent and wise.
You make what is ultimate and beyond brightness
     secretly to shine in all that is most dark.
In your way, ever unseen and intangible,
     you fill to the full with most beautiful splendour
     those souls who close their eyes that they may see.
And I, please, with love that goes on beyond mind
     to all that is beyond mind,
     seek to gain such for myself through this prayer.

The Cloud of Unknowing, 14th century ('St Denis's prayer')

O Lord Jesu Christ, who as a child didst learn and grow in wisdom: *608*
grant me so to learn thy holy Word, that I may walk in thy ways and
daily grow more like unto thee; who are my Saviour and my Lord.
Church of Ireland. Book of Common Prayer

O God, the Father of lights, who by the entrance of thy Word giveth   *609*
light unto the soul: grant to us the spirit of wisdom and understanding; that, being taught of thee in holy scripture, we may receive with
faith the words of eternal life, and be made wise unto salvation;
through Jesus Christ our Lord.
Church of Scotland. Book of Common Order

Almighty God, the giver of wisdom, without whose help resolutions   *610*
are vain, without whose blessing study is ineffectual; enable me, if it
be thy will, to attain such knowledge as may qualify me to direct the
doubtful, and instruct the ignorant; to prevent wrongs and terminate
contentions; and grant that I may use that knowledge which I shall
attain, to thy glory and my own salvation, for Jesus Christ's sake.
Samuel Johnson, 1709–86

Teach me, O my Lord Jesus, instruct me, that I may learn from thee   *611*
what I ought to teach concerning thee.
William Laud, 1573–1645

Let us have clean hearts ready inside us for the Lord Jesus, so that he   *612*
will be glad to come in, gratefully accepting the hospitality of those
worlds, our hearts: he whose glory and power will endure throughout the ages.
Origen, c.185–c.254

O heavenly Father, the author and fountain of all truth, the bottom-   *613*
less sea of all understanding, send, we beseech thee, thy Holy Spirit
into our hearts, and lighten our understandings with the beams of thy
heavenly grace. We ask this, O merciful Father, for thy dear Son, our
Saviour, Jesus Christ's sake.
Nicholas Ridley, c.1500–55

614 In times of doubt and questions, when our belief is perplexed by new teaching, new thought, when our faith is strained by creeds, by doctrines, by mysteries beyond our understanding, give us the faithfulness of learners, and the courage of believers in thee; give us boldness to examine and faith to trust all truth, stability to hold fast our tradition with enlightened interpretation, to grasp new knowledge and combine it loyally and honestly with old; alike from stubborn rejection of new revelation and from hasty assurance that we are wiser than our Fathers, save us and help us, O Lord.

(Bishop) Ridding

615 Lord Jesus, merciful and patient, grant us grace, I beseech thee, ever to teach in a teachable spirit; learning along with those we teach, and learning from them whenever thou so pleasest. Word of God, speak to us, what thou wilt. Wisdom of God, instruct us, instruct by us, if and whom thou wilt. Eternal truth, reveal thyself to us, reveal thyself by us, in whatsoever measure thou wilt; that we and they may all be taught by God.

Christina Rossetti, 1830–94

616 O Lord Jesus Christ, Wisdom and Word of God, dwell in our hearts, we beseech thee, by thy most Holy Spirit, that out of the abundance of our hearts our mouths may speak thy praise.

Christina Rossetti, 1830–94

617   As one who travels in the heat
  longs for cool waters,
  so do I yearn for wisdom;
  and as one who is weary with walking,
  so shall I sit at her well and drink.

  For her words are like streams in the desert;
  she is like rain on parched ground,
  like a fountain whose waters fail not.
  Whoever hears her voice
  will be content with nothing less;
  and whoever drinks of her will long for more.

But who can find wisdom's dwelling place,
and who has searched her out?
for many have said to me, lo, here is wisdom,
and there you shall find understanding;
here is true worship of God,
and thus shall your soul be satisfied.

But there was no delight in my soul;
all my senses were held in check.
My body became alien to me,
and my heart was shrivelled within me.

For I sought understanding without justice;
discernment without the fear of God.
I would have filled my belly with the husks of knowledge,
and quenched my thirst with what was already stagnant.

But you have blessed me with emptiness, O God;
you have spared me to remain unsatisfied.

And now I yearn for justice;
like an infant that cries for the breast,
and cannot be pacified,
I hunger and thirst for oppression to be removed,
and to see the right prevail.

So while I live I will seek your wisdom, O God;
while I have strength to search, I will follow her ways.
For her words are like rivers in the desert;
she is like rain on parched ground,
like a fountain whose waters fail not.

Then shall my soul spring up like grass,
and my heart recover her greenness;
and from the deepest places of my soul
shall flow streams of living water.

St Hilda Community

618   Arise, O sun of righteousness, upon us, with healing in thy wings; make us children of the light and of the day. Show us the way in which we should walk, for unto thee, O Lord, do we lift up our souls. Dispel all mists of ignorance which cloud our understandings. Let no false suggestion either withdraw our hearts from the love of thy truth, or from the practice of it in all the actions of our lives; for the sake of Jesus Christ our Lord.

Thomas Sherlock, 1678–1761

619   Blessed Lord, by whose providence all holy scriptures were written and preserved for our instruction, give us grace to study them this and every day with patience and love. Strengthen our souls with the fullness of their divine teaching. Keep from us all pride and irreverence. Guide us in the deep things of thy heavenly wisdom, and of thy great mercy lead us by thy Word unto everlasting life; through Jesus Christ our Lord and Saviour.

Brooke Foss Westcott, 1825–1901

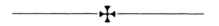

CONFESSION

AND FORGIVENESS

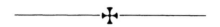

If we confess our sins, he who is faithful
and just will forgive us our sins and cleanse
us from all unrighteousness.

1 John 1.9

God, have mercy on me, a sinner! 620

Luke 18.13

Have mercy on me, O God, according to your loving-kindness; 621
 in your great compassion blot out my offences.
Wash me through and through from my wickedness and cleanse me
 from my sin.

Holy God,
holy and mighty,
holy immortal one,
have mercy upon us.

Source unknown (Eastern Orthodox)

Lord, for thy tender mercies' sake, lay not our sins to our charge, but 622
forgive that is past and give us grace to amend our lives; to decline
from sin and incline to virtue, that we may walk with a perfect heart
before thee, now and evermore.

Source unknown, 16th century

Lord Jesus Christ, I admit that I am a sinner. I confess my sins to you, 623
especially those upon my conscience. I firmly believe that you died for
me to bear away my sins. And now, according to your promise, I
open my heart to you. Come in, Lord Jesus, and be my Saviour and
Friend for ever.

Source unknown

Lord Jesus Christ, Son of God, have mercy on me, a sinner. 624

Source unknown (Eastern Orthodox 'Jesus prayer')

O Lord, forgive what I have been, sanctify what I am, and order what 625
I shall be.

Source unknown

626 Almighty and merciful God, the fountain of all goodness, who knowest the thoughts of our hearts, we confess unto thee that we have sinned against thee, and done evil in thy sight. Wash us, we beseech thee, from the stains of our past sins, and give us grace and power to put away all hurtful things; so that, being delivered from the bondage of sin, we may bring forth worthy fruits of repentance, through Jesus Christ our Lord.

Alcuin, 735–804

627 O Lord, who hast mercy upon all, take away from me my sins, and mercifully kindle in me the fire of thy Holy Spirit. Take away from me the heart of stone, and give me a heart of flesh, a heart to love and adore thee, a heart to delight in thee, to follow and to enjoy thee, for Christ's sake.

Ambrose of Milan, c.339–97

628   Forgive me my sins, O Lord;
              forgive me the sins of my youth and the sins of my age,
              the sins of my soul and the sins of my body,
              my secret and my whispering sins,
              my presumptuous and my crying sins,
              the sins that I have done to please myself,
              and the sins I have done to please others.
              Forgive me the sins which I know,
              and those sins which I know not;
              forgive them, O Lord,
              forgive them all of thy great goodness.

Lancelot Andrewes, 1555–1626

629   The sins of the world,
              such dreadful sins,
              not just the personal sins
              but the solidarity of sin
              greater than the total
                  of individual sins,
              nuclear evil in endless fission,
                  O Lamb of God.

The sin of racial pride
that sees not the faith
that all men are divinely made . . .
that each is the sibling
for whom Christ died.

The burgeoning greed
that never heeds the needs of others
involved in a merciless system,
looking only at profit and dividend,
the lust of possessions
that cannot accompany us
at our last migration.
Take away these sins,
O Lamb of God.

The massive sin of war . . .
billions of pounds wasted
on weapons, bombs . . .
the hungry still unfed,
grief stalking unnumbered homes:
Weep over us,
O Lamb of God.

The sin of the world,
alienation from thee
not just weakness
but evil intention . . .
O Lamb of God
take away this sin.

Begin with me,
O Lamb of God,
forgive my sins,
cleanse my heart,
disarm my will
and let me fight
armed with thy truth, righteousness and love
with thy cross of love
incised upon my heart,
O Lamb of God.

George Appleton (adapted)

630   O Spirit of God,
  who dost speak to spirits
    created in thine own likeness,
Penetrate into the depth of our spirits
  into the storehouse of memories
    remembered and forgotten,
  into the depths of being,
    the very springs of personality,
And cleanse and forgive, making us whole and holy,
That we may be thine,
  and live in the new being
  of Christ our Lord.

George Appleton

631   O thou gracious and gentle and condescending God, thou God of peace, Father of mercy, God of all comfort; see, I lament before thee the evil of my heart; I acknowledge that I am too much disposed to anger, jealousy, and revenge, to ambition and pride, which often give rise to discord and bitter feelings between me and others. Too often have I thus offended and grieved both thee, O long-suffering Father, and my fellow-men. Oh forgive me this sin, and suffer me to partake of the blessing which thou hast promised to the peacemakers, who shall be called the children of God.

Johann Arndt, 1558–1621

632   O Lord, the house of my soul is narrow; enlarge it, that you may enter in. It is ruinous, O repair it! It displeases your sight; I confess it, I know. But who shall cleanse it, to whom shall I cry but to you? Cleanse me from my secret faults, O Lord, and spare your servant from strange sins.

Augustine, 354–430

I was slow to love you, Lord,

633

your age-old beauty is still as new to me:
I was so slow to love you!
You were within me,
yet I stayed outside
seeking you there;
in my ugliness I grabbed at
the beautiful things of your creation.
Already you were with me,
but I was still far from you.
The things of this world kept me away:
I did not know then
that if they had not existed through you
they would not have existed at all.
Then you called me
and your cry overcame my deafness;
you shone out
and your light overcame my blindness;
you surrounded me with your fragrance
and I breathed it in,
so that now I yearn for more of you;
I tasted you
and now I am hungry and thirsty for you;
you touched me,
and now I burn with longing for your peace.

Augustine, 354–430

For my deceitful heart and crooked thoughts:

634

For barbed words spoken deliberately:
For thoughtless words spoken hastily:
For envious and prying eyes:
For ears that rejoice in iniquity and rejoice not in the truth:
For greedy hands:
For wandering and loitering feet:
For haughty looks:
Have mercy upon me, O God.

John Baillie, 1886–1960

635 Forgive us, O Lord, for everything that has spoiled our home life: for the moodiness and irritability which made us difficult to live with; for the insensitiveness which made us careless of the feelings of others; for selfishness which made life harder for others.

Forgive us, O Lord, for everything that has spoiled our witness for thee; that so often men would never have known that we had been with Jesus and pledged ourselves to him: that we have so often denied with our lives that which we said with our lips; for the difference between our creed and our conduct, our profession and our practice; for any example which made it easier for men to criticize thy Church or for another to sin.

When we think of ourselves and of the meanness and ugliness and weakness of our lives, we thank thee for Jesus Christ our Saviour. Grant unto us a true penitence for our sins. Grant that at the foot of the Cross, we may find our burdens rolled away. And so strengthen us by thy Spirit that in the days to come, we may live more nearly as we ought. Through Jesus Christ our Lord.

William Barclay

636 O Lord our God, you know who we are; men with good consciences and with bad, persons who are content and those who are discontented, the certain and the uncertain, Christians by conviction and Christians by convention, those who believe and those who half-believe, those who disbelieve.

And you know where we have come from: from the circle of relatives, acquaintances and friends, or from the greatest loneliness; from a life of quiet prosperity, or from manifold confusion and distress; from family relationships that are well ordered or from those disordered, or under stress; from the inner circle of the Christian community or from its outer edge.

But now we all stand before you, in all our differences, yet alike in that we are all in the wrong with you and with one another, that we must all one day die, that we would be lost without your grace, but also in that your grace is promised and made available to us all in your dear Son, Jesus Christ.

Karl Barth, 1886–1968

God: 637

Take fire and burn our guilt and our lying hypocrisies.

Take water and wash away our brothers' blood which we have caused to be shed.

Take hot sunlight and dry the tears of those we have hurt, and heal the wounded souls, minds, and bodies.

Take love and root it in our hearts, so that brotherhood may grow, transforming the dry desert of our prejudices and hatreds.

Take our imperfect prayers and purify them, so that we mean what we pray and are prepared to give ourselves to you along with our words, through Jesus Christ, who did not disdain to take our humanness upon him and live among us, sharing our life, our joys, and our pains.

Malcolm Boyd

    Oppressed with sin and woe,   638
      A burdened heart I bear;
    Opposed by many a mighty foe,
      Yet I will not despair.

    With this polluted heart,
      I dare to come to thee –
    Holy and mighty as thou art –
      For thou wilt pardon me.

    I feel that I am weak,
      And prone to every sin;
    But thou, who giv'st to those who seek,
      Wilt give me strength within.

    I need not fear my foes;
      I need not yield to care;
    I need not sink beneath my woes,
      For thou wilt answer prayer.

    In my Redeemer's name,
      I give myself to thee;
    And, all unworthy as I am,
      My God will cherish me.

Anne Brontë, 1820–49

639 Ah, Lord, my prayers are dead, my affections dead, and my heart is dead: but thou art a living God and I bear myself upon thee.

William Bridge, 1600–70

640 O Lord Jesus, we confess how quickly we see other people's faults, and how slow we are to recognize our own. Forgive us, and make us more forgiving; through Jesus Christ our Lord.

Beryl Bye

641 Almighty and most merciful Father, look down upon us thy unworthy servants through the mediation and merits of Jesus Christ, in whom only thou art well pleased. Purify our hearts by thy Holy Spirit, and as thou dost add days to our lives, so good Lord, we beseech thee to add repentance to our days; that when we have passed this mortal life we may be partakers of thine everlasting kingdom; through the merits of Jesus Christ our Lord.

(King) Charles I, 1600–49

642   O Lamb of God,
That takest away the sins of the world,
Grant us thy peace.

Church of England. Book of Common Prayer

643 O most merciful Father, who dost put away the sins of those who truly repent, we come before thy throne in the name of Jesus Christ, that for his sake alone thou wilt have compassion upon us, and let not our sins be a cloud between thee and us.

John Colet, 1467–1519

644 Lord our God, great, eternal, wonderful in glory, who keepest covenant and promises for those that love thee with their whole heart, who art the Life of all, the Help of those that flee unto thee, the Hope of those who cry unto thee, cleanse us from our sins, secret and open; and from every thought displeasing to thy goodness, cleanse our bodies and souls, our hearts and consciences, that with a pure heart, and a clean soul, with perfect love and calm hope, we may venture confidently and fearlessly to pray unto thee, through Jesus Christ our Lord.

Coptic Liturgy of St Basil

Forgive me, Lord, my sins – the sins of my youth, the sins of the pres-   645
ent; the sins I laid upon myself in an ill pleasure, the sins I cast upon
others in an ill example; the sins which are manifest to all the world,
the sins which I have laboured to hide from mine acquaintance, from
mine own conscience, and even from my memory; my crying sins and
my whispering sins, my ignorant sins and my wilful; sins against my
superiors, equals, servants, against my lovers and benefactors, sins
against myself, mine own body, mine own soul, sins against thee, O
almighty Father, O merciful Son, O blessed Spirit of God.

Forgive me, O Lord, through the merits of thine anointed, my
Saviour, Jesus Christ.

John Donne, 1573–1631

> Wilt thou forgive that sin where I begun,   646
>   Which was my sin, though it were done before?
> Wilt thou forgive that sin, through which I run,
>   And do run still: though still I do deplore?
>   When thou hast done, thou hast not done,
>   For I have more.
>
> Wilt thou forgive that sin by which I have won
>   Others to sin, and made my sin their door?
> Wilt thou forgive that sin which I did shun
>   A year, or two; but wallowed in, a score?
>   When thou hast done, thou hast not done,
>   For I have more.
>
> I have a sin of fear, that when I've spun
>   My last thread, I shall perish on the shore;
> Swear by thyself that at my death thy Son
>   Shall shine – as he shines now, and heretofore;
> And, having done that, thou hast done,
>   I fear no more.

John Donne, 1573–1631

647 O God, save me from myself, save me from myself; this frivolous self which plays with your creation, this vain self which is clever about your creation, this masterful self which manipulates your creation, this greedy self which exploits your creation, this lazy self which soothes itself with your creation; this self which throws the thick shadow of its own purposes and desires in every direction in which I try to look, so that I cannot see what it is that you, my Lord and God, are showing to me. Teach me to stand out of my own light, and let your daylight shine.

Austin Farrer

648   Lord Christ,
help us to have the courage and humility to name our burdens
and lay them down
so that we are light to walk across the water
to where you beckon us

Our pride,
armouring us,
hardening us,
making us defend our dignity by belittling others
We name it
and we lay it down.

The memory of hurts and insults,
driving us to lash out,
to strike back
We name it
and we lay it down.

Our antagonism against those
whose actions, differences, presence,
threaten our comfort or security,
We name it
and we lay it down.

Our fear,
of unsolved questions,
of the unkown,
of fear itself,
We name it
and we lay it down.

We do not need these burdens,
but we have grown used to carrying them,
have forgotten what it is like to be light.

Beckon us to lightness of being,
for you show us it is not unbearable.
Only so can we close the distance
Only so can we walk upon the water.

It is so.

Blessed are you, Lord Christ, who makes heavy burdens light.
Kathy Galloway (Iona Community)

Lord, nothing is going right tonight. I didn't think I was capable of 649
this. I thought I had got rid of it. But, no!

This time I really feel like letting go of everything. If this is what it
all comes to, I would rather give up at once. For you know, Lord, that
I have tried.

What hurts me deep down is that I must give up the habit of thinking so highly of myself.

Lord, I admit that the thing that bothers me most is wounded
pride.

Lord, I know it isn't good. But I would rather admit it to you
directly, without beating about the bush. My regret isn't pure. I do
regret my sin.

But what I regret most is myself. The self I thought had changed.
The self that I was beginning to feel proud of – like Seneca, I believe it
was, who visited his soul every evening and took pleasure in finding it
in order.

Forgive me, Lord, for having loved myself more than you. For having put myself before you.

Teach me to bear my sin and not just drag it behind me. Help me to
accept with courage that in your eye I am a sinner, and help me not to
sulk about it like a little child.

Give me your forgiveness. For my sin. But also . . . for my wounded
pride.

Lord, I thank you for having made me realize that I am like all
other men.

Paul Geres

650 Lord, we thank thee for all the love that has been given to us, for the love of family and friends, and above all for your love poured out upon us every moment of our lives in steadfast glory. Forgive our unworthiness. Forgive the many times we have disappointed those who love us, have failed them, wearied them, saddened them. Failing them we have failed you, and hurting them we have wounded our Saviour who for love's sake died for us. Lord, have mercy on us, and forgive. You do not fail those who love you. You do not change nor vary. Teach us your own constancy in love, your humility, selflessness and generosity. Look in pity on our small and tarnished loving, protect, foster and strengthen it, that it may be less unworthy to be offered to you and to your children. O Light of the world, teach us how to love.

Elizabeth Goudge

651
    Love bade me welcome; yet my soul drew back
        Guilty of dust and sin.
    But quick-eyed Love observing me grow slack
        From my first entrance in,
    Drew nearer to me, sweetly questioning
        If I lacked anything.

    'A guest,' I answered, 'worthy to be here':
        Love said, 'You shall be he'.
    'I, the unkind, ungrateful? Ah, my dear,
        I cannot look on thee.'
    Love took my hand and smiling did reply,
        'Who made the eyes but I?'

    'Truth, Lord; but I have marr'd them: let my shame
        Go where it doth deserve.'
    'And know you not', says Love, 'Who bore the blame?'
        'My dear, then I will serve.'
    'You must sit down,' says Love, 'and taste my meat.'
        So I did sit and eat.

George Herbert, 1593–1633

Lord, hear; Lord, forgive; Lord, do. 652

Hear what I speak not; forgive what I speak amiss; do what I leave undone;

that, not according to my word or my deed, but according to thy mercy and truth, all may issue to thy glory and the good of thy kingdom.

Maria Hare, 1798–1870

If I have played the truant, or have here 653
Failed in my part; Oh! thou that art my dear,
My mild, my loving tutor, Lord and God,
Correct my errors gently with thy rod.
I know that faults will many here be found,
But where sin dwells, there let thy grace abound.

Robert Herrick, 1591–1674

My spirit is dry within me because it forgets to feed on thee. 654

John of the Cross, 1542–91

Hear me, O God! 655
  A broken heart
  Is my best part:
Use still thy rod
  That I may prove
  Therein thy love.

If thou hadst not
  Been stern to me,
  But left me free,
I had forgot
  Myself and thee.

For sin's so sweet,
  As minds ill-bent
  Rarely repent,
Until they meet
  Their punishment.

Who more can crave
  Than gav'st a son
To free a slave,
  First made of nought,
  With all since bought?

Sin, Death, and Hell
  His glorious Name
  Quite overcame,
Yet I rebel,
  And slight the same.

But I'll come in,
  Before my loss
  Me farther toss,
As sure to win
  Under his cross.

Ben Jonson, 1572–1637

656   *Non Nobis Domine*

Non nobis Domine! –
  Not unto us, O Lord!
The praise or glory be
  Of any deed or word;
For in thy judgement lies
  To crown or bring to nought
All knowledge or device
  That man has reached or wrought.

And we confess our blame –
  How all too high we hold
That noise which men call fame,
  That dross which men call gold.
For these we undergo
  Our hot and godless days,
But in our hearts we know
  Not unto us the praise.

O Power by whom we live –
   Creator, Judge, and Friend,
Upholdingly forgive
   Nor fail us at the end:
But grant us well to see
   In all our piteous ways –
Non nobis Domine! –
   Not unto us the praise!

Rudyard Kipling, 1865–1936

Lord of compassion, you loved me; you called to me as a mother calls   657
to her child. But the more you called to me, the more I turned away.
Yet you were the one who taught me to walk; you took me up in your
arms. But I did not acknowledge that you took care of me. You drew
me to you; you picked me up, and held me to your cheek. You bent
down to me and fed me. Lord of compassion, do not give me up; do
not abandon me. Do not punish me in your anger!

Philip Law (based on Hosea 11.1–9)

From all my lame defeats and oh! much more   658
From all the victories that I seemed to score;
From cleverness shot forth on thy behalf,
At which, while angels weep, the audience laugh;
From all my proofs of thy divinity,
Thou, who wouldst give no sign, deliver me.
Thoughts are but coins. Let me not trust, instead
Of thee, their thin-worn image of thy head.
From all my thoughts, even from my thoughts of thee,
O thou fair silence, fall, and set me free.
Lord of the narrow gate and the needle's eye,
Take from me all my trumpery lest I die.

C. S. Lewis, 1898–1963

659

God, lovegiver,
>the love that dares to speak out,
>the love that listens,
>the love found most powerfully in weakness,
>the love that heals,
this is the love we need and long for,
not counterfeit pretty love, tied with bows,
but lasting love;
love that's there when the sweetness has gone;
love that endures beyond the barrier of pain.

Forgive us
>for worshipping the idols of perfection,
>for failing to see your glory in the vulnerable,
>for attaching more worth to the seen
>than the unseen.
>>*Lord, have mercy.*
>>*Christ, have mercy.*

Forgive us
>for being so full of our own importance
>that we cannot do the one thing needful.
>>*Lord, have mercy.*
>>*Christ, have mercy.*

Forgive us
>our lack of perseverance
>in face of failure, doubt, rejection;
>our failure to make connections
>between politics and health,
>economics and healing.
>>*Lord, have mercy.*
>>*Christ, have mercy.*

>Vulnerable Lovegiver,
>Christ, wounded healer,
>Holy Spirit, compassionate friend,
>grant us love in all its fullness.

Kate McIlhagga

Almighty and merciful God, the fountain of all goodness, who 660
knowest the thoughts of our hearts, we confess unto thee that we
have sinned against thee, and done evil in thy sight. Wash us, we
beseech thee, from the stains of our past sins, and give us grace and
power to put away all hurtful things; so that, being delivered from the
bondage of sin, we may bring forth worthy fruits of repentance.

O eternal light, shine into our hearts. O eternal goodness, deliver
us from evil. O eternal power, be thou our support. Eternal wisdom,
scatter the darkness of our ignorance. Eternal pity, have mercy upon
us. Grant unto us that with all our hearts, and minds, and strength,
we may evermore seek thy face; and finally bring us, in thine infinite
mercy, to thy holy presence. So strengthen our weakness that, following in the footsteps of thy blessed Son, we may obtain thy mercy, and
enter into thy promised joy.

Meuin, 8th century

If my soul has turned perversely to the dark; 661
If I have left some brother wounded by the way;
If I have preferred my aims to thine;
If I have been impatient and would not wait;
If I have marred the pattern drawn out of my life;
If I have cost tears to those I loved;
If my heart has murmured against thy will,
  O Lord, forgive.

F. B. Meyer

O God our Father, help us to nail to the cross of thy dear Son the 662
whole body of our death, the wrong desires of the heart, the sinful
devisings of the mind, the corrupt apprehensions of the eyes, the cruel
words of the tongue, the ill-employment of hands and feet; that the
old man being crucified and done away, the new may live and grow
into the glorious likeness of the same thy Son Jesus Christ, who liveth
and reigneth with thee and the Holy Ghost, one God, world without
end.

Eric Milner-White, 1884–1963

663 Lord, please forgive our sins, and set us free from them.
We confess to the sin of pride:
   we have been sure of our own goodness and importance and have
      looked down on others.
Help us to appreciate the true worth of other people.

We confess to the sin of envy:
   we have been displeased when others have been more successful or
      sought after than we have been.
Help us to be glad when others prosper.

We confess to our sin of anger:
   we have lost our temper and nursed grievances.
Help us to be patient and understanding with everyone.

We confess to our sin of self-indulgence:
   we have had enough and to spare, yet we have neglected the needs
      of others.
Help us to deny ourselves so that others may not be in want.

We confess to our sin of unchastity:
   in one way or another we have used sex wrongly.
Help us to create and uphold right relations between men and
      women, inside marriage and outside it.

We confess to our sin of anxiety:
   we have worried about many things.
Help us to trust you to see us through.

We confess to our sin of laziness:
   we have been lukewarm Christians.
Make us eager to do your will.

Caryl Micklem

664
                    O God, we confess that we often look back.
                 We look back on mistakes we have made,
                       work left undone,
                       people we have hurt,
                       excuses we have made,
                 We see these as things for which we feel guilty.
                 We overwhelm ourselves with regret.

Free us, O God, from self-condemnation that immobilizes us.
Allow us to remember that you call us to look back.
To remember those times of joy.
To remember those people who were kind and compassionate.
To remember that we did the best we were able.
To remember that you journey with us each day of our life.
May we continue to grow in grace and truth,
in the name of Christ.

Rosemary C. Mitchell

O God,   665
We hear and hear, and do not understand.
We see and see, but do not perceive.
Sharpen our memory,
unlock our grief,
teach us to name what is evil
and refuse it:
even when it seems normal
even when it seems necessary
even when it is commanded by religion;
then, now, always.

Janet Morley (Christian Aid)

O thou that beholdest all things, we have sinned against thee in   666
thought, word, and deed; blot out our transgressions, be merciful to
us sinners, and grant that our names may be found written in the
Book of Life, for the sake of Christ Jesus our Saviour.

Nerses of Clajes, 4th century

O Lord, open our minds to see ourselves as you see us,   667
and from all unwillingness to know our weakness and our sin,
Good Lord, deliver us.

From selfishness;
from wishing to be the centre of attraction;
from seeking admiration;
from the desire to have our own way in all things;
from unwillingness to listen to others;
from resentment of criticism,
Good Lord, deliver us.

261

From love of power; from jealousy;
from taking pleasure in the weakness of others,
   Good Lord, deliver us.

From the weakness of indecision; from fear of adventure;
from constant fear of what others are thinking of us; from fear of
   speaking what we know is truth,
and doing what we know is right,
   Good Lord, deliver us.

From possessiveness about material things and people;
from carelessness about the needs of others;
from selfish use of time and money;
from all lack of generosity,
   Good Lord, deliver us.

From laziness of conscience;
from lack of self-discipline; from failure to persevere;
from depression in failure and disappointment,
   Good Lord, deliver us.

From failure to be truthful;
from pretence and acting a part; from hypocrisy;
from all dishonesty with ourselves and with others,
   Good Lord, deliver us.

From impurity in word, in thought, and in action;
from failure to respect the bodies and minds
of ourselves and others;
from any kind of addiction,
   Good Lord, deliver us.

From hatred and anger; from sarcasm;
from lack of sensitivity and division in our community;
from all failure to love and to forgive,
   Good Lord, deliver us.

From failure to see our sin as an affront to God;
from failure to accept the forgiveness he offers,
   Good Lord, deliver us.

Peter Nott

O Lord, our hearts are heavy with the sufferings 668
of the ages, with the crusades and the holocausts
  of a thousand thousand years.
The blood of the victims is still warm,
The cries of anguish still fill the night.

  To you we lift our outspread hands.

  We thirst for you in a thirsty land.

O Lord, who loves us as a father, who cares for us
  as a mother, who came to share our life as a brother,
we confess before you our failure to live
  as your children,
brothers and sisters bound together in love.

  To you we lift our outspread hands.

  We thirst for you in a thirsty land.

We have squandered the gift of life.
The good life of some is built on the pain of many;
the pleasure of a few on the agony of millions.

  To you we lift our outspread hands.

  We thirst for you in a thirsty land.

We worship death in our quest to possess
  ever more things; we worship death
  in our hankering after our own security,
our own survival, our own peace,
as if life were divisible, as if love were divisible,
as if Christ had not died for all of us.

  To you we lift our outspread hands.

  We thirst for you in a thirsty land.

O Lord, forgive our life-denying pursuit of life,
and teach us anew what it means to be your children.

  To you we lift our outspread hands.

  We thirst for you in a thirsty land.
World Council of Churches

263

669   O merciful Lord Jesus, forget not me, as I have forgotten thee.

Christina Rossetti, 1830–94

670   O Lord Jesu Christ, take us to thyself, draw us with cords to the foot of thy cross; for we have no strength to come, and we know not the way. Thou art mighty to save, and none can separate us from thy love. Bring us home to thyself, for we are gone astray. We have wandered: do thou seek us. Under the shadow of thy cross let us live all the rest of our lives, and there we shall be safe.

Frederick Temple, 1821–1902

671   We confess before thee our blindness of heart, our poverty of life, our littleness, our meanness, and our sin. We have not followed after Christ. We have not given love to the loveless and the lost. Change thou our lives, O God. Give us light that we may be light to those whose lives are darkened. Give us life that we may be life-giving to the dying.

Help and uphold us when the temptations of the world press upon us. Show us thy service. Open thy will to us, that we may serve thee aright. Strengthen us when our hearts grow weak, and hope and faith flicker and fail within us. Raise us when we fall; give us the power to stand, and lend us the guiding light of thy cross, O Christ, to lead us home where shadows are no more.

Lauchlan Maclean Watt, 1867–1957

672   Forgive them all, O Lord: our sins of omission and our sins of commission; the sins of our youth and the sins of our riper years; the sins of our souls and the sins of our bodies; our secret and our more open sins; our sins of ignorance and surprise, and our more deliberate and presumptuous sins; the sins we have done to please others; the sins we know and remember, and the sins we have forgotten; the sins we have striven to hide from others and the sins by which we have made others offend; forgive them, O Lord, forgive them all for his sake, who died for our sins and rose for our justification, and now stands at thy right hand to make intercession for us, Jesus Christ our Lord.

John Wesley, 1703–91

Lord Jesus, my Saviour, my heart is cold, warm it with your selfless 673
love; my heart is sinful, cleanse it by your precious blood; my heart is
weak, strengthen it by your joyful Spirit; my heart is empty, fill it with
your divine presence. Lord Jesus, my heart is yours, possess it always
and only for yourself.

Maurice Wood

Almighty God, we confess that we have often misused and ill-treated 674
your creation: hear us, and in your mercy save us and help us.

For every act of carelessness that has treated the world merely as a
playground:
 Father, forgive us –
 save us and help us.

For every act of wastefulness that forgets the crying of the needy:
 Father, forgive us –
 save us and help us.

For every act of selfishness that defies your just rule over our lives:
 Father, forgive us –
 save us and help us.

Cleanse us from our sins through the love of Christ, and set us free for
his service through the power of the Spirit; for the glory of your
name.

Worship Now

IN TIMES OF TEMPTATION

675   I pray, O Lord, that I will not fall into temptation; for the spirit is willing, but the flesh is weak.

Matthew 26.41 (Good News Bible, adapted)

676   Your grace, O Lord, is all I need; for your power is strongest when I am weak.

2 Corinthians 12.9 (Good News Bible, adapted)

677   O God, you are the true God. Keep us safe from false gods.

1 John 5.20–21 (Good News Bible, adapted)

678   God help my thoughts! they stray from me, setting off on the wildest journeys; when I am at prayer, they run off like naughty children, making trouble. When I read the Bible, they fly to a distant place, filled with seductions. My thoughts can cross an ocean with a single leap; they can fly from earth to heaven, and back again, in a single second. They come to me for a fleeting moment, and then away they flee. No chains, no locks can hold them back; no threats of punishment can restrain them, no hiss of a lash can frighten them. They slip from my grasp like tails of eels; they swoop hither and thither like swallows in flight.

Dear, chaste Christ, who can see into every heart, and read every mind, take hold of my thoughts. Bring my thoughts back to me, and clasp me to yourself.

Source unknown (Celtic)

Our Father in heaven, I thank thee that thou has led me into the Light. 679
I thank thee for sending the Saviour to call me from death to life. I
confess that I was dead in sin before I heard his call, but when I heard
him, like Lazarus, I arose. But, O my Father, the grave clothes bind
me still. Old habits that I cannot throw off, old customs that are so
much a part of my life that I am helpless to live the new life that Christ
calls me to live. Give me strength, O Father, to break the bonds; give
me courage to live a new life in thee; give me faith, to believe that with
thy help I cannot fail. And this I ask in the Saviour's name who has
taught me to come to thee.

Source unknown (Taiwan)

O Lord, succour, we beseech thee, us who are tempted. May nothing 680
induce us to distrust thy care over us, nor to use thy gifts to the denial
of thee, their giver. May we never presume upon thy protection when
we are forsaking thy paths, and tempting thee. May we never, for the
sake of any supposed gain or advancement, quench the testimony of
thy Spirit or prove disloyal to thy service. Do thou so support us in all
temptations that, when we have been tried, we may receive the crown
of life, which thou hast prepared for them that love thee.

Henry Alford, 1810–71

O God, by thy mercy strengthen us who lie exposed to the rough 681
storms of troubles and temptations. Help us against our own negli-
gence and cowardice, and defend us from the treachery of our
unfaithful hearts. Succour us, we beseech thee, and bring us to thy
safe haven of peace and felicity.

Augustine, 354–430

O God our Father, hear me, who am trembling in this darkness, and 682
stretch forth thy hand unto me; hold forth thy light before me; recall
me from my wanderings; and, thou being my guide, may I be restored
to myself and to thee.

Augustine, 354–430

683 Preserve me, Lord, from the sin which I fear so much: contempt for thy love. May I never sin against the Holy Spirit who is love and union, harmony and peace. May I never be separated from thy Spirit, from the unity of thy peace, by committing the sin which can never be forgiven, neither here nor in the world to come. Keep me, O Lord, among my brothers and kinsfolk that I may proclaim thy peace. Keep me among those who preserve the unity of the Spirit in the bond of peace.

(Archbishop) Baldwin, 12th century

684 O thou who knowest our hearts, and who seest our temptations and struggles, have pity upon us, and deliver us from the sins which make war upon our souls. Thou art all-powerful, and we are weak and erring. Our trust is in thee, O thou faithful and good God. Deliver us from the bondage of evil, and grant that we may hereafter be thy devoted servants, serving thee in the freedom of holy love, for Christ's sake.

Eugene Bersier, 1831–89

685 O Lord, never suffer us to think that we can stand by ourselves, and not need thee.

John Donne, 1573–1631

686 My strength fails; I feel only weakness, irritation and depression. I am tempted to complain and to despair. What has become of the courage I was so proud of, and that gave me so much self-confidence? In addition to my pain, I have to bear the shame of my fretful feebleness. Lord, destroy my pride; leave it no resource. How happy I shall be if you can teach me by these terrible trials, that I am nothing, that I can do nothing, and that you are all!

François Fénelon, 1651–1715

687 Save us, O Lord, from the snares of a double mind. Deliver us from all cowardly neutralities. Make us to go in the paths of thy commandments, and to trust for our defence in thy mighty arm alone; through Jesus Christ our Lord.

Richard Hurrell Froude, 1803–36

Preserve us this day from the temptations of the world, the flesh, and 688
the devil. Suffer us not to fall into idle habits, and if diligent in business, suffer not our hearts to be so engrossed but that we may serve
thee, the Lord; and grant that thy presence may be with us, giving us
peace in our souls all the day long; through Jesus Christ our Lord.

Thomas Furlong, 19th century

There was a time when I did not exist, 689
And thou hast created me;
I did not beseech thee for a wish,
And thou hast fulfilled it;
I had not come into the light,
And thou hast seen me;
I had not yet appeared,
And thou hast taken pity on me;
I had not invoked thee,
And thou hast taken care of me;
I did not raise my hand,
And thou hast looked at me;
I had not entreated thee,
And thou hast heard me;
I had not groaned,
And thou hast lent an ear;
With prescient eyes thou sawest
The crimes of my guilty self,
And yet thou hast fashioned me.
And now, I who have been created by thee,
And saved by thee,
And have been tended with such care,
Let me not wholly perish by the blow of sin
That is but the slanderer's invention;
Let not the fog of my stubbornness
Triumph over the light of thy forgiveness;
Nor the hardness of my heart
Over thy forbearing goodness;
Nor my material weakness
Over thine unconquerable grandeur.

Gregory of Narek, 951–1001

690 Grant, O God, that we may keep a constant guard upon our thoughts and passions, that they may never lead us into sin; that we may live in perfect charity with all mankind, in affection to those that love us, and in forgiveness of those, if any there are, that hate us. Give us good and virtuous friends. In the name of our blessed Lord and Saviour Jesus Christ.

Warren Hastings, 1732–1818

691 O good shepherd, seek me out, and bring me home to thy fold again. Deal favourably with me according to thy good pleasure, till I may dwell in thy house all the days of my life, and praise thee for ever and ever with them that are there.

Jerome, c.342–420

692 Enlighten our understandings with knowledge of right, and govern our wills by thy laws, that no deceit may mislead us, no temptation corrupt us; that we may always endeavour to do good and hinder evil. Amidst all the hopes and fears of this world, take not thy Holy Spirit from us; for the sake of Jesus Christ our Lord.

Samuel Johnson, 1709–84

693   Oh blessed Lord! How much I need
      Thy light to guide me on my way!
      So many hands, that, without heed,
      Still touch thy wounds and make them bleed,
      So many feet that day by day
      Still wander from thy fold astray!
      Feeble at best is my endeavour!
      I see but cannot reach the height
      That lies for ever in the Light;
      And yet for ever and for ever,
      When seeming just within my grasp,
      I feel my feeble hands unclasp,
      And sink discouraged into night;
      For thine own purpose thou has sent
      The strife and the discouragement.

      Henry Wadsworth Longfellow, 1807–82

Suffer me never to think that I have knowledge enough to need no   694
teaching, wisdom enough to need no correction, talents enough to
need no grace, goodness enough to need no progress, humility
enough to need no repentance, devotion enough to need no quickening, strength sufficient without thy Spirit; lest, standing still, I fall
back for evermore.

Eric Milner-White, 1884–1963

Behold the prodigal! To thee I come,   695
To hail my Father and to seek my home.
Nor refuge could I find, nor friend abroad,
Straying in vice and destitute of God.

O let thy terrors and my anguish end!
Be thou my refuge and be thou my friend:
Receive the son thou didst so long reprove,
Thou that art the God of love!

Matthew Prior, 1664–1721

Lord, without thee I can do nothing; with thee I can do all. Help me   696
by thy grace, that I fall not; help me by thy strength, to resist mightily
the very first beginnings of evil, before it takes hold of me; help me to
cast myself at once at thy sacred feet, and lie still there, until the storm
be overpast; and, if I lose sight of thee, bring me back quickly to thee,
and grant me to love thee better, for thy tender mercy's sake.

Edward Bouverie Pusey, 1800–82

O my Saviour,   697
let me not fall by little and little,
or think myself able to bear
the indulgence of any known sin
because it seems so insignificant.
Keep me from sinful beginnings,
lest they lead me on
to sorrowful endings.

Charles Haddon Spurgeon, 1834–92

698   Give me, O Lord, a steadfast heart which no unworthy affection may drag downwards. Give me an unconquered heart which no tribulation can wear out. Give me an upright heart which no unworthy purpose may tempt aside. Bestow upon me also, O Lord my God, understanding to know thee, diligence to seek thee, wisdom to find thee, and a faithfulness that may finally embrace thee; through Jesus Christ our Lord.

Thomas Aquinas, c.1225–74

699   Blessed Lord, who wast tempted in all things like as we are, have mercy upon our frailty. Out of weakness give us strength. Grant to us thy fear, that we may fear thee only. Support us in time of temptation. Embolden us in the time of danger. Help us to do thy work with good courage, and to continue thy faithful soldiers and servants unto our life's end; through Jesus Christ our Lord.

Brooke Foss Westcott, 1825–1901

———✠———

THE PILGRIMAGE OF LIFE

———✠———

You show me the path of life.

In your presence there is fulness of joy;

in your right hand are pleasures for evermore.

Psalm 16.11

O Lord, support us all the day long of this troublous life, until the 700
shades lengthen and the evening comes, and the busy world is
hushed, the fever of life is over, and work done. Then, Lord, in thy
mercy, grant us safe lodging, and holy rest, and peace at the last;
through Jesus Christ our Lord.

Source unknown (Attributed to John Henry Newman, 1801–90)

My God,   701
  I pray that I may so know you and love you
  that I may rejoice in you.
And if I may not do so fully in this life,
  let me go steadily on
  to the day when I come to that fullness.
Let the knowledge of you increase in me here,
  and there let it come to its fullness.
Let your love grow in me here,
  and there let it be fulfilled
  so that here my joy may be in a great hope,
  and there in full reality.

Anselm, 1033–1109

O God, who hast brought us near to an innumerable company of 702
angels, and to the spirits of just men made perfect; grant us during
our earthly pilgrimage to abide in their fellowship, and in our
heavenly country to become partakers of their joy; through Jesus
Christ our Lord.

William Bright, 1824–1901

Gracious God, I need you more   703
now that I am growing older.

Help me do less talking
and more listening,
less complaining
and more exclaiming.
Please, no bossing now,
just watching over
and standing by,
but not telling how.

Keep me from moodiness
and self-pity;
from repetitious words
set me free.
Keep me in tune
with the young,
Let me be carefree
enough to have fun.

Let me not think the world
has changed so much
that I grow bitter
and out of touch.
Let me use my experience
in much living
as an incentive
for more giving.

Gracious God, I need you much more now.

Charlotte Carpenter

704 Alone with none but thee, my God,
I journey on my way.
What need I fear, when thou art near
O king of night and day?
More safe am I within thy hand
Than if a host did round me stand.

Columba, c.521–97

705 God of eternity,
God beyond time,
our refuge and hope
from one generation to another:
Before the mountains rose from the sea,
before the rivers carved the valleys,
before time itself began,
you are God, eternal.

From dust we came,
to dust we return.
'Be shaped from the clay,
be crumbled to earth.'
Creator of life, of death,
so did you order our ways.
A thousand years in your sight
are as yesterday.
As a watch in the night
comes quickly to an end,
so the years pass before you,
in a flicker of the eye.

The years are like the grass,
which in the morning is green,
and by evening is dried up and withered.
As the grass shrivels in the smoke,
so is our pride consumed in your fire:
we are afraid of the burning of the dross.

All our misdeeds and deceits
are brought to light before your eyes,
all our secret sins
made clear in the light of your truth.
When you are angry,
our days are as nothing:
our years come to an end,
vanishing with a sigh.

The decades soon pass,
no more than a handful.
Some show vigour in age,
yet even they are soon gone.
So much of our span is wearisome,
full of labour and sorrow.

O the speed of it all,
and the vanity of the years:
all I have done is like straw,
and most of it forgotten already.
Success crumbles into dust:
there is nothing to pay love's account.

Who is even aware
of the purging of your wrath?
Who pays a moment's attention
to the fierceness of your love?
Teach us to number our days,
and apply our hearts to wisdom.

Turn again, O God, do not delay:
give grace to your servants.
Satisfy us in the morning
with your lovingkindness.
So we shall rejoice and be glad
all the days of our life.

Give us days of gladness
to make up for those of affliction,
for the years of adversity.
Show your servants your deeds,
and your glory to our children.
May your grace be upon us:
fill us with the Spirit of love.
For in the evening of our days
when we come to be judged,
we shall be known only by love,
delivered only by love.

Jim Cotter (based on Psalm 90)

706 Lord God, our beginning and our end: you were with us at our birth,
be with us through our life: you are with us through our life, be with
us at our death: and because your love and mercy will not leave us
then, help us to pass through death and rise to everlasting life with
you.

Friends of Christ Church Moss Side

Our brother Jesus, you set our feet upon the way and sometimes 707
  where you lead we do not like or understand.
Bless us with courage where the way is fraught with dread or danger;
Bless us with graceful meetings where the way is lonely;
Bless us with good companions where the way demands a common
  cause;
Bless us with night vision where we travel in the dark, keen hearing
  where we have not sight, to hear the reassuring sounds of
  fellow travellers,
Bless us with humour – we cannot travel lightly weighed down with
  gravity;
Bless us with humility to learn from those around us;
Bless us with decisiveness where we must move with speed;
Bless us with lazy moments, to stretch and rest and savour;
Bless us with love, given and received;
And bless us with your presence, even when we know it in your
  absence.
Lead us into exile,
until we find that on the road
  is where you are,
and where you are is going home.
Bless us, lead us, love us, bring us home
  bearing the gospel of life.

Kathy Galloway (Iona Community)

Lord, be with my spirit, and dwell in my heart by faith. Oh, make me 708
such as I should be towards thee, and such as thou mayest take pleasure in me. Be with me everywhere and at all times, in all events and
circumstances of my life; to sanctify and sweeten to me whatever
befalls me; and never leave nor forsake me in my present pilgrimage
here, till thou hast brought me safe through all trials and dangers to
be ever with thee, there to live in thy sight and love, world without
end.

Benjamin Jenks, 1646–1724

709   We render unto thee our thanksgiving, O Lord our God, Father of our Lord and Saviour Jesus Christ, by all means, at all times, in all places; for that thou hast sheltered, assisted, supported, and led us on through the time past of our life and brought us to this hour. And we pray and beseech thee, O God and loving Lord, grant us to pass this day, this year, and all the time of our life without sin, with all joy, health and salvation.

Liturgy of St Mark, 2nd century

710   Almighty God, Creator:
In these last days storm has assailed us.
Greyness has enveloped and mist surrounded
our going out and our coming in.
Now again thy glory clarifies,
thy light lifts up our hearts to thee,
and night falls in peace.
But through mist and storm and sunshine,
the crops have ripened here
and vines of Spain have grown.
Thy constant care in all and everywhere is manifest.

Almighty God, Redeemer:
Even as with our bodies, so also with our souls.
Redeemer, Christ:
Sunshine and storm, mist and greyness
eddy round our inner lives.
But as we trace the pattern, looking back,
we know that both darkness and light have been of thine ordaining,
for our own soul's health.
Thy constant care in all, and everywhere,
is manifest.

Almighty God, Sustainer:
Sun behind all suns,
Soul behind all souls,
everlasting reconciler of our whole beings:
Show to us in everything we touch and in everyone we meet
    the continued assurance of thy presence round us:
lest ever we should think thee absent.
In all created things thou art there.
In every friend we have

the sunshine of thy presence is shown forth.
In every enemy that seems to cross our path,
thou art there within the cloud
to challenge us to love.
Show to us the glory in the grey.
Awake for us thy presence in the very storm
till all our joys are seen as thee
and all our trivial tasks emerge as priestly sacraments
in the universal temple of thy love.

Of ourselves we cannot see this. Sure physician give us sight.
Of ourselves we cannot act. Patient love give us love:
till every shower of rain speaks of thy forgiveness:
till every move of light and shadow speaks of grave and resurrection:
to assure us that we cannot die:
thou creating, redeeming and sustaining God.

George Macleod, 1895–1991

Lord Jesus Christ, the Way by which we travel: show me thyself, the   *711*
truth that we must walk in: and be in me the Life that lifts us up to
God, our journey's ending.

Frederick B. Macnutt, 1873–1949

O thou divine Spirit that, in all events of life, art knocking at the door   *712*
of my heart, help me to respond to thee. I would not be driven blindly
as the stars over their courses. I would not be made to work out thy
will unwillingly, to fulfil thy law unintelligently, to obey thy man-
dates unsympathetically. I would take the events of my life as good
and perfect gifts from thee; I would receive even the sorrows of life as
disguised gifts from thee. I would have my heart open at all times to
receive thee, at morning, noon, and night; in spring, and summer and
winter. Whether thou comest to me in sunshine or in rain, I would
take thee into my heart joyfully. Thou art thyself more than the sunshine, thou art thyself compensation for the rain; it is thee and not thy
gifts I crave; knock, and I shall open unto thee.

George Matheson, 1842–1906

713   My Lord God, I have no idea where I am going. I do not see the road ahead of me. I cannot know for certain where it will end. Nor do I really know myself, and the fact that I think I am following your will does not mean that I am actually doing so.

But I believe that the desire to please you does in fact please you, and I hope that I have that desire in all that I am doing. I hope that I never do anything apart from that desire. And I know that if I do this you will lead me by the right road though I may know nothing about it.

Therefore I will trust you always. Though I may seem to be lost and in the shadow of death I will not fear, for you are ever with me and you will never leave me to face my peril alone.

Thomas Merton

714   Thou art the Way
                    Hadst thou been nothing but the goal
                         I cannot say
                    If thou hadst ever met my soul.

                         I cannot see –
                    I, child of process – if there lies
                         An end for me
                    Full of repose, full of replies.

                         I'll not reproach
                    The road that winds, my feet that err.
                         Access, Approach
                    Art thou, Time, Way, and Wayfarer.

                    Alice Meynell, 1847–1922

715   O Lord, you have made us very small, and we bring our years to an end like a tale that is told; help us to remember that beyond our brief day is the eternity of your love.

Reinhold Niebuhr, 1892–1971

Through every minute of this day,   716
Be with me, Lord!
Through every day of all this week
Be with me, Lord!
Through every week of all this year
Be with me, Lord!
Through all the years of all this life,
Be with me, Lord!
So shall the days and weeks and years
Be threaded on a golden cord.
And all draw on with sweet accord
Unto thy fulness, Lord
That so, when time is past,
By grace I may at last,
Be with thee, Lord.

John Oxenham (William Arthur Dunkerley), 1862–1941

Before the beginning thou hast foreknown the end,   717
Before the birthday the death-bed was seen of thee:
Cleanse what I cannot cleanse, mend what I cannot mend,
O Lord all-merciful, be merciful to me.

While the end is drawing near I know not mine end;
Birth I recall not, my death I cannot foresee:
O God, wise to defend, wise to befriend,
O Lord all-merciful, be merciful to me.

Christina Rossetti, 1830–94

Give us grace, O Lord, to work while it is day, fulfilling diligently and   718
patiently whatever duty thou appointest us; doing small things in the
day of small things, and great labours if thou summon us to any; rising and working, sitting still and suffering, according to thy word. Go
with us, and we will go, but if thou go not with us, send us not; go
before us, if thou put us forth; let us hear thy voice when we follow.
Hear us, we beseech thee, for the glory of thy great name.

Christina Rossetti, 1830–94

719 Pilgrim God, there is an exodus going on in my life: desert stretches, a vast land of questions. Inside my head your promises tumble and turn. No pillar of cloud by day or fire by night that I can see. My heart hurts at leaving loved ones and so much of the security I have known. I try to give in to the stretching and the pain. It is hard, God, and I want to be settled, secure, safe and sure. And here I am feeling so full of pilgrim's fear and anxiety.

O God of the journey, lift me up, press me against your cheek. Let your great love hold me and create a deep trust in me. Then set me down, God of the journey; take my hand in yours, and guide me ever so gently across the new territory of my life.

Joyce Rupp

720   How easy, Lord, it is for me to live with you.
How easy it is for me to believe in you.
When my understanding is perplexed by doubts
or on the point of giving up,
when the most intelligent men see no further
than the coming evening, and know not
what they shall do tomorrow,
you send me a clear assurance
that you are there and that you will ensure
that not all the roads of goodness are barred.

From the heights of earthly fame I look back
in wonder at the road that led
through hopelessness
to this place whence I can send
mankind a reflection of your radiance.

And whatever I in this life may yet reflect,
that you will give me;
And whatever I shall not attain,
that, plainly, you have purposed for others.

Alexander Solzhenitsyn

721 Let us make our way together, Lord; wherever you go I must go: and through whatever you pass, there too I will pass.

Teresa of Avila, 1515–82

Fix thou our steps, O Lord, that we stagger not at the uneven motions 722
of the world, but steadily go on to our glorious home; neither censur-
ing our journey by the weather we meet with, nor turning out of the
way for anything that befalls us.

The winds are often rough, and our own weight presses us downwards. Reach forth, O Lord, thy hand, thy saving hand, and speedily
deliver us.

Teach us, O Lord, to use this transitory life as pilgrims returning to
their beloved home; that we may take what our journey requires, and
not think of settling in a foreign country.

John Wesley, 1703–91

Lord, let me not live to be useless. 723

John Wesley, 1703–91

GOD'S CARE AND GUIDANCE

As the rain hides the stars, as the autumn mist hides the hills, as the 724
clouds veil the blue of the sky, so the dark happenings of my lot hide
the shining of thy face from me. Yet, if I may hold thy hand in the
darkness, it is enough. Since I know that, though I may stumble in my
going, thou dost not fall.

Source unknown (Celtic).

725

Lord, hour by hour,
Be thou my Guide,
That, by thy power,
No step may slide.

Source unknown ('The Westminster Chimes')

726 The Lord is my pilot; I shall not drift, he lighteth me across the dark
waters; he steereth me in the deep channels: he keepeth my log. He
guideth me by the star of his holiness for his name's sake. Yea, though
I sail amid the hungers and tempests of life, I shall fear no danger, for
thou art near me; thy love and care, they shelter me. Thou preparest
a harbour before me in the homeland of eternity; thou anointest the
waves with oil; my ship rideth calmly. Surely sunlight and starlight
shall favour me in the voyage I take, and I shall rest in the port of my
God for ever.

Source unknown (based on Psalm 23)

727

Thou angel of God who hast charge of me
From the dear Father of mercifulness,
The shepherding kind of the fold of the saints
To make round about me this night;

Drive from me every temptation and danger,
Surround me on the sea of unrighteousness,
And in the narrows, crooks, and straits,
Keep thou my coracle, keep it always.

Be thou a bright flame before me;
Be thou a guiding star above me,
Be thou a smooth path below me,
And be a kindly shepherd behind me,
Today, tonight, and for ever.

I am tired and I am a stranger,
Lead thou me to the land of angels;
For me it is time to go home
To the court of Christ, to the peace of heaven.

Source unknown (Celtic)

Father, I am seeking: I am hesitant and uncertain, but will you, O 728
God, watch over each step of mine and guide me.

Augustine, 354–430

O Lord our God, teach us, we beseech thee, to ask thee aright for the 729
right things. Steer thou the vessel of our life towards thyself, thou
tranquil haven of all storm-tossed souls. Show us the course wherein
we should go. Renew a willing spirit within us. Let thy Spirit curb our
waywardness and guide and enable us unto that which is our true
good, to keep thy laws, and in all our works evermore to rejoice in thy
glorious and gladdening presence. For thine is the glory and praise
from all thy saints for ever and ever.

Basil the Great, c.330–379

O Lord Jesus Christ, who hast said that thou art the way, the truth, 730
and the life: suffer us not at any time to stray from thee, who art the
way; nor to distrust thy promises, who art the truth; nor to rest in any
other thing than thee, who art the life; beyond which there is nothing
to be desired, neither in heaven, nor in earth; for thy name's sake.

Christian Prayers, 1578 (based on Erasmus, 1467–1536)

Be kind to your little children, Lord. Be a gentle teacher, patient with 731
our weakness and stupidity. And give us the strength and discernment to do what you tell us, and so grow in your likeness.

May we all live in the peace that comes from you. May we journey
towards your city, sailing through the waters of sin untouched by the
waves, borne serenely along by the Holy Spirit. Night and day may
we give you praise and thanks, because you have shown us that all
things belong to you, and all blessings are gifts from you. To you, the
essence of wisdom, the foundation of truth, be glory for evermore.

Clement of Alexandria, c.150–c.215

May God Almighty direct our days in his peace, and grant us the gifts 732
of his blessing; may he deliver us in all our troubles, and establish our
minds in the tranquillity of his peace; may he so guide us through
things temporal that we finally lose not the things eternal.

Gregorian Sacramentary, 6th century

733   Lord,
you are the deepest wisdom,
the deepest truth,
the deepest love,
within me.
Lead me in your way.

Richard Harries

734 Lord, thou hast given us thy Word for a light to shine upon our path; grant us so to meditate on that Word, and to follow its teaching, that we may find in it the light that shines more and more until the perfect day; through Jesus Christ our Lord.

Jerome, c.342–420

735   The Lord is my shepherd;
I have everything I need.
He lets me see a country of justice and peace
   and directs my steps towards this land.
He gives me power.
He guides me in the paths of victory,
   as he has promised.
Even if a full-scale violent confrontation breaks out
   I will not be afraid, Lord,
   for you are with me.
Your shepherd's power and love protect me.
You prepare for me my freedom,
   where all my enemies can see it;
you welcome me as an honoured guest
   and fill my cup with righteousness and peace.
I know that your goodness and love will
   be with me all my life,
and your liberating love will be my home
   as long as I live.

Pastor Kameeta (based on Psalm 23)

736 Lord, I am blind and helpless, stupid and ignorant. Cause me to hear; cause me to know; teach me to do; lead me.

Henry Martyn, 1781–1812

I cannot dance, O Lord,   737
   unless you lead me.
If you will
   that I leap joyfully
   then you must be the first to dance
     and to sing!

Then, and only then,
   will I leap for love.
Then will I soar
   from love to knowledge,
   from knowledge to fruition
   from fruition to beyond
     all human sense.

And there
   I will remain
   and circle for evermore.

Mechthild of Magdeburg, c.1210–c.1280

Christ our companion,   738
you came not to humiliate the sinner
   but to disturb the righteous.
Welcome us when we are put to shame,
but challenge our smugness,
that we may truly turn from what is evil,
and be freed even from our virtues,
in your name.

Janet Morley

Lead, kindly light, amid the encircling gloom,   739
   Lead thou me on;
The night is dark, and I am far from home;
   Lead thou me on.
Keep thou my feet; I do not ask to see
The distant scene: one step enough for me.

John Henry Newman, 1801–90

740 God, I want thy guidance and direction in all I do. Let thy wisdom counsel me, thy hand lead me, and thine arm support me. I put myself into thy hands. Breathe into my soul holy and heavenly desires. Conform me to thine own image. Make me like my Saviour. Enable me in some measure to live here on earth as he lived, and to act in all things as he would have acted.

Ashton Oxenden, 1808–92

741   May the strength of God pilot us,
        May the power of God preserve us,
        May the wisdom of God instruct us,
        May the hand of God protect us,
        May the way of God direct us,
        May the shield of God defend us,
        May the host of God guard us against the snares of evil and
            the temptations of the world.

        Patrick, c.389–c.461

742   If I am right, thy Grace impart
            Still in the right to stay:
        If I am wrong, oh teach my heart
            To find that better way.

        Alexander Pope, 1688–1744

743 O Lord Jesus Christ, who art the very bright Sun of the world, ever rising, never going down: shine, we beseech thee, upon our spirit, that the night of sin and error being driven away by thy inward light, we may walk without stumbling, as in the day. Grant this, O Lord, who livest and reignest with the Father and the Holy Ghost for evermore.

Primer, 1559 (based on Erasmus, 1467–1536)

DELIVERANCE FROM EVIL

Fence me about, O Lord, with the power of thine honourable and   744
life-giving Cross, and preserve me from every evil.

Source unknown (Eastern Orthodox)

From witches, warlocks and wurricoes,   745
From ghoulies, ghosties and long-leggit beasties,
From all things that go bump in the night –
Good Lord, deliver us!

Source unknown (Early Cornish)

Circle me Lord   746
Keep protection near
And danger afar

Circle me Lord
Keep hope within
Keep doubt without

Circle me Lord
Keep light near
And darkness afar

Circle me Lord
Keep peace within
Keep evil out

David Adam

The right hand of the Lord preserve me always to old age! The grace   747
of Christ perpetually defend me from the enemy! Direct, Lord, my
heart into the way of peace. Lord God, haste thee to deliver me, make
haste to help me, O Lord.

Æthelwold, c.908–984

748   O God that art the only hope of the world,
the only refuge for unhappy men,
abiding in the faithfulness of heaven,
give me strong succour in this testing place.
O King, protect thy man from utter ruin
    lest the weak faith surrender to the tyrant,
facing innumerable blows alone.
Remember I am dust, and wind, and shadow,
and life as fleeting as the flower of grass.
But may the eternal mercy which hath shone from time of old
    rescue thy servant from the jaws of the lion.
Thou who didst come from on high in the cloak of flesh,
strike down the dragon with that two-edged sword,
whereby our mortal flesh can war with the winds
and beat down strongholds, with our Captain God.

Bede, c.673–725

749   We humbly beseech thee, O Father, mercifully to look upon our infirmities; and for the glory of thy name turn from us all those evils that we most righteously have deserved; and grant that in all our troubles we may put our whole trust and confidence in thy mercy, and evermore serve thee in holiness and pureness of living, to thy honour and glory; through our only Mediator and Advocate, Jesus Christ our Lord.

Church of England. Book of Common Prayer

750   Visit, we pray you, O Lord, this place, and drive from it all the snares of the enemy; let your holy angels dwell here to preserve us in peace; and may your blessing be upon us evermore; through Jesus Christ, our Lord.

Norman Goodacre

751   O Lamb of God, who takest away the sin of the world, look upon us and have mercy upon us; thou who art thyself both Victim and Priest, thyself both Reward and Redeemer, keep safe from all evil those whom thou hast redeemed, O Saviour of the world.

Irenaeus, c.130–c.200

It is a fearful thing to fall into the hands of the living God.   752
But it is a much more fearful thing to fall out of them.

Did Lucifer fall through knowledge?
oh then, pity him, pity him that plunge!

Save me, O God, from falling into the ungodly knowledge
of myself as I am without God.
Let me never know, O God
let me never know what I am or should be
when I have fallen out of your hands, the hands of the living God.

That awful and sickening endless sinking, sinking
through the slow, corruptive levels of disintegrative knowledge
when the self has fallen from the hands of God,
and sinks, seething and sinking, corrupt
and sinking still, in depth after depth of disintegrative consciousness
sinking in the endless undoing, the awful katabolism into the abyss!
Even of the soul, fallen from the hands of God!

Save me from that, O God!
Let me never know myself apart from the living God!
D. H. Lawrence, 1885–1930

Lord, in thine anger do not reprehend me,   753
  Nor in thy hot displeasure me correct;
Pity me, Lord, for I am much deject,
  Am very weak and faint; heal and amend me,
For all my bones, that even with anguish ache,
  Are troubled, yea, my soul is troubled sore:
And thou, O Lord, how long? turn, Lord, restore
  My soul, O save me for thy goodness' sake,
For in death no remembrance is of thee;
  Who in the grave can celebrate thy praise?
Wearied I am with sighing out my days,
  Nightly my couch I make a kind of sea;
My bed I water with my tears; mine eye
  Through grief consumes, is waxen old and dark
I' th' midst of all mine enemies that mark.
  Depart, all ye that work iniquity.
Depart from me, for the voice of my weeping
  The Lord hath heard; the Lord hath heard my prayer;

My supplication with acceptance fair
  The Lord will own, and have me in his keeping.
Mine enemies shall all be blank and dashed
  With much confusion; then grow red with shame;
They shall return in haste the way they came
  And in a moment shall be quite abashed.

John Milton, 1608–74 (based on Psalm 6)

754 Write thy blessed name, O Lord, upon my heart, there to remain so indelibly engraved, that no prosperity, no adversity shall ever move me from thy love. Be thou to me a strong tower of defence, a comforter in tribulation, a deliverer in distress, a very present help in trouble, and a guide to heaven through the many temptations and dangers of this life.

Thomas a Kempis, c.1380–1471

LONGING FOR SALVATION

755 Come, Lord Jesus!

Revelation 22.20

756 Lord God almighty, open my heart and enlighten by the grace of thy Holy Spirit, that I may seek what is well-pleasing to thy will; direct my thoughts and affections to think and to do such things as may make me worthy to attain to thine unending joys in heaven; and so order my doings after thy commandments that I may be ever diligent to fulfil them, and be found meet to be of thee everlastingly rewarded.

Bede, 675–735

O Saviour of the world, the Son, Lord Jesus: stir up thy strength and 757 help us, we humbly beseech thee.

By thy cross and precious blood thou hast redeemed us: save us and help us, we humbly beseech thee.

Thou didst save thy disciples when ready to perish: hear us and save us, we humbly beseech thee.

Let the pitifulness of thy great mercy loose us from our sins, we humbly beseech thee.

Make it appear that thou art our Saviour and mighty deliverer: O save us, that we may praise thee, we humbly beseech thee.

Draw near, according to thy promise from the throne of thy glory: look down and hear our crying, we humbly beseech thee.

Come again, and dwell with us, O Lord Christ Jesus: abide with us forever, we humbly beseech thee.

And when thou shalt appear with power and great glory: may we be made like unto thee in thy glorious kingdom.

Thanks be to thee, O Lord: Hallelujah.

Source unknown, 12th century

> I pray thee, merciful Jesus, 758
> that as thou hast graciously granted me
> to drink down sweetly from the Word
>   which tells of thee,
> so wilt thou kindly grant
> that I may come at length to thee,
> the fount of all wisdom,
> and stand before thy face for ever.
>
> *Bede, 675–735 (His Ecclesiastical History of the*
> *English People, 731, ended with this prayer)*

To thee, then O Jesus, do I turn my true and last end. Thou art the 759 river of life which alone can satisfy my thirst. Without thee all else is barren and void. Without all else thou alone art enough for me. Thou art the Redeemer of those that are lost; the sweet Consoler of the sorrowful; the crown of glory for the victors; the recompense of the blessed. One day I hope to receive of thy fullness, and to sing the song of praise in my true home. Give me only on earth some few drops of consolation, and I will patiently wait thy coming that I may enter into the joy of my Lord.

Bonaventure, 1221–74

760

How do I spin my time away
   In caring how to get
   Ungodly wealth, and fret
     My self to sweat,
As if thou Lord hadst meant this clay
No after life, no reckoning day.

What graceless fool would love his earth
   So, as with all his might
   To pamper with delight
     The same 'gainst right,
Forgetting his divine soul's birth
Was nobler, and of greater worth?

Thou Lord didst frame this soul of mine
   Only to honour thee,
   Not basely fond to be
     Of vanity,
Unflesh it then, and so refine
It Lord it may be all divine.

Quicken my dull-drooping spirit
   That it may praise thy name,
   Cleanse it from sin and blame,
     Take from it shame.
Grant that by my Saviour's merit
Eternity it may inherit.

Let it not grovelling lie pressed down
   With earth, but mount, and gain
   An everlasting reign,
     Let it retain
No dross, and when it shall have thrown
Its cover off, grant it a crown.

Henry Colman, 17th century

Bring us, O Lord, at our last awakening   761
into the house and gate of heaven,
to enter into that gate and dwell in that house
where shall be no darkness nor dazzling, but one equal light;
no noise nor silence, but one equal music;
no fears nor hopes, but one equal possession;
no ends nor beginnings, but one equal eternity
in the habitations of your glory and dominion,
world without end.

John Donne, 1573–1631

I know what must be done. Only now am I beginning to be a disciple.   762
May nothing of powers visible or invisible prevent me, that I may
attain unto Jesus Christ. Come fire and cross and grapplings with
wild beasts, the rending of my bones and body, come all the torments
of the wicked one upon me. Only let it be mine to attain unto Jesus
Christ.

Ignatius of Antioch, c.35–c.107

O merciful God, the Father of our Lord Jesus Christ, who is the resur-   763
rection and the life; in whom whosoever believeth shall live, though
he die; and whosoever liveth and believeth in him, shall not die eternally; we meekly beseech thee, O Father, to raise us from the death of
sin unto the life of righteousness; that when we shall depart this life,
we may be found acceptable in thy sight, and receive that blessing
which thy well-beloved Son shall pronounce to all that love and fear
thee, saying, 'Come ye blessed children of my Father, receive the
kingdom prepared for you from the beginning of the world.' Grant
this, we beseech thee, O merciful Father, through Jesus Christ, our
Mediator and Redeemer.

Methodist Church. Book of Offices

O Lord, who has taught us that to gain the whole world and to lose   764
our souls is great folly, grant us the grace so to lose ourselves that we
may truly find ourselves anew in the life of grace, and so to forget ourselves that we may be remembered in your kingdom.

Reinhold Niebuhr, 1892–1971

765

Jesus, receive my heart,
and bring me to thy love.
All my desire thou art.
Kindle fire within me,
that I may win to thy love,
and see thy face in bliss
which shall never cease,
in heaven with never an ending.

Richard Rolle, 1295–1349

———✠———

PRAYERS FOR EVERY DAY

———✠———

Every day I will bless you,

and praise your name for ever and ever.

Psalm 145.2

THE LORD'S PRAYER

Our Father in heaven,   766
may your name be hallowed;
your kingdom come,
your will be done,
on earth as in heaven.
Give us today our daily bread.
Forgive us the wrong we have done,
as we have forgiven those who have wronged us.
And do not put us to the test,
but deliver us from the evil one.

Matthew 6.9–13 (Revised English Bible)

Our Father   767
Who is in us here on earth,
Holy is your name
In the hungry who share their bread and their song.
Your Kingdom come,
A generous land where confidence and truth reign.
Let us do your will,
Bring a cool breeze for those who sweat.
You are giving us our daily bread
When we manage to get back our lands
Or to get a fairer wage.
Forgive us
For keeping silent in the face of injustice
And for burying our dreams.
Don't let us fall into the temptation
Of taking up the same arms as the enemy,
But deliver us from evil which disunites us.
And we shall have believed in humanity and life
And we shall have known your kingdom
Which is being built for ever and ever.

Source unknown (Central America)

768   Our Father,
      May all men honour you,
      May your rule be accepted and your purpose accomplished,
      As in heaven, so now on earth.
      Give us today the food we need.
      Forgive us the wrong we have done as we forgive those who have
         wronged us.
      Save us from losing our faith in you,
      And deliver us from the power of evil.

      Anglican Church of Canada. Experimental liturgy

769   Eternal Father, who didst all create,
      In whom we live, and to whose bosom move,
      To all men be thy name known, which is love,
      Till its loud praises sound at heaven's high gate.
      Perfect thy kingdom in our passing state,
      That here on earth thou may'st as well approve
      Our service, as thou ownest theirs above,
      Whose joy we echo and in pain await.

      Grant body and soul each day their daily bread:
      And should in spite of grace fresh woe begin,
      Even as our anger soon is past and dead
      Be thy remembrance mortal of our sin:
      By thee in paths of peace thy sheep be led,
      And in the vale of terror comforted.

      Robert Bridges, 1844–1930 (from 'The Growth of Love')

770   Our Father in heaven,
      holy be your Name,
      your kingdom come,
      Your will be done,
      on earth as in heaven.
      Give us today our daily bread.
      Forgive us our sins as we forgive those who sin against us.
      Do not bring us to the test but deliver us from evil.
      For the kingdom, the power and the glory are yours now and for ever.

      Church of England. Experimental services. Series III

Eternal Spirit,
Life-Giver, Pain-Bearer, Love-Maker,
Source of all that is and that shall be,
Father and Mother of us all,
Loving God, in whom is heaven:

771

The Hallowing of your Name
  echo through the universe!
The Way of your Justice
  be followed by the people of the world!
Your Heavenly Will
  be done by all created beings!
Your Commonwealth of Peace and Freedom
  sustain our hope and come on earth!

With the bread we need for today,
  feed us.
In the hurts we absorb from one another,
  forgive us.
In times of temptation and test,
  strengthen us.

From trials too great to endure,
  spare us.
From the grip of all that is evil,
  free us.

For you reign in the glory
  of the power that is love,
  now and for ever.

Jim Cotter

772 Loving Father of us all,
    transcendent in glory,
may all people honour your holy name
    and acknowledge your kingly rule,
that your purposes may be fulfilled on earth
    as truly as they are in heaven.
Give us today all things that we need
    for our material and bodily wants.
Forgive us the wrong we have done,
    and make us as ready to forgive others.
Save us from yielding to temptation
    and falling into sin;
and rescue us from the forces of evil
    at work around us and within us.
For you, O Lord, are sovereign over all things;
    your power is sufficient for all our need;
    to you be the glory now and for ever.

Frank Colquhoun

773 *Our Father.*
Our Creator, Redeemer, Comforter and Saviour.

Who art in heaven.
You are with the angels and the saints, bathing them in your light that they may be enlightened by your love, and dwelling within them that they may be filled with your joy. You are the supreme good, the eternal good, from whom comes all goodness, and without whom there is no goodness.

Hallowed be your name.
May our knowledge of you become ever clearer, that we may know the breadth of your blessings, the length of your promises, the height of your majesty, and the depth of your judgements.

Your kingdom come.
Rule in our hearts with your grace, that we may become fit subjects for your kingdom. We desire nothing more than to dwell in your kingdom, where we can watch you on your throne, and enjoy your perfect love.

Your will be done, on earth as it is in heaven.
May we love you with our whole heart by always thinking of you,

with our whole soul by always desiring you, with our whole mind by directing all our intentions to you, and with our whole strength by spending all our energies in your service. And may we love our neighbours as ourselves, drawing them to your love, rejoicing in their good fortunes, and caring for them in their misfortunes.

Give us this day our daily bread.
In memory and understanding and reverence of the love which our Lord Jesus Christ has for us, revealed by his sacrifice for us on the cross, we ask for the perfect bread of his body.

And forgive us our trespasses.
We know that you forgive us, through the suffering and death of your beloved Son.

As we forgive those who trespass against us.
Enable us to forgive perfectly and without reserve any wrong that has been committed against us. And strengthen our hearts truly to love our enemies, praying for them and striving to serve them.

And lead us not into temptation.
Save us not only from obvious and persistent temptations, but also those that are hidden or come suddenly when our guard is lowered.

But deliver us from evil.
Protect us from past evil, protect us against present evil, and free us from future evil.

Francis of Assisi, 1182–1226

God, lover of us all,   774
most holy one,
help us to respond to you,
to create what you want for us here on earth.
Give us today enough for our needs;
forgive our weak and deliberate offences,
just as we must forgive others
when they hurt us.
Help us to resist evil
and to do what is good;
for we are yours,
endowed with your power
to make our world whole.

Lala Winkley

775

Our Father, my Father,
   who art in heaven, and yet in me,
holy is thy name, holy thy purpose and thy work.
May thy holiness, thy wholeness,
   be more and more seen in me.
Thy kingdom is in heaven and on earth;
may it come with power and purpose in us all.
May thy will, for me and for all,
   which is perfect wholeness,
   be done in us, in soul and mind and body.

I ask, as a child asks, not for tomorrow's needs,
   but for those only of present concern;
and I ask, as a child asks,
   for daily sustenance for soul and body,
   knowing that it will be given,
   is being provided now, my daily bread.

Wash out my wrong-doings;
fill me with that knowledge of pardon
   which comes to those who forgive others,
   and enable me to be of a pardoning spirit.

Bring me not into any trial too great for my soul,
and keep me from thrusting myself
   or being thrust into occasions of sin,
but rather set me free from being a slave
   of any evil thing or thought.

All these things I ask with every confidence
   in thine answer,
for thy rule is sure,
   thy power unassailable,
   thy glory undimmed forever.

William Portsmouth

MORNING

All through this day, O Lord, may I touch as many lives as thou 776
wouldst have me touch for thee; and those whom I touch do thou
with thy Holy Spirit quicken, whether by the word I speak, the letter
I write, the prayer I breathe, or the life I live.

Source unknown

> I arise today 777
> Through the strength of heaven –
> Light of sun,
> Radiance of moon,
> Splendour of fire,
> Speed of lightning,
> Swiftness of wind,
> Depth of sea,
> Stability of earth,
> Firmness of rock.
>
> *Source unknown (Early Scottish)*

Into thy hands, O Lord, we commend ourselves this day. Let thy pres- 778
ence be with us to its close. Strengthen us to remember that in whatsoever good work we do we are serving thee. Give us a diligent and
watchful spirit, that we may seek in all things to know thy will, and
knowing it, gladly to perform it; to the honour of thy name.

Source unknown

We give thee hearty thanks, O God, for the rest of the past night and 779
for the gift of a new day with its opportunities of pleasing thee. Grant
that we so pass its hours in the perfect freedom of thy service, that at
eventide we may again give thanks unto thee; through Jesus Christ
our Lord.

Source unknown, 3rd century (Daybreak Office of the Eastern Church)

780

This new day you give to me
From your great eternity
This new day now enfold
Me in your loving hold

You are the star of the morn
You are the day newly born
You are the light of our night
You are the Saviour by your might

God be in me this day
God ever with me stay
God be in the night
Keep us by thy light
God be in my heart
God abide, never depart.

David Adam

781 Blessed art thou, O Lord our God, the God of our fathers, who turnest the shadow of death into the morning; who hast lightened mine eyes that I sleep not in death.

O Lord, blot out as a night-mist mine iniquities. Scatter my sins as a morning cloud. Grant that I may become a child of the light, and of the day. Vouchsafe to keep me this day without sin. Uphold me when I am falling, and lift me up when I am down. Preserve this day from any evil of mine, and me from the evils of this day. Let this day add some knowledge, or good deed, to yesterday.

Oh, let me hear thy loving-kindness in the morning, for in thee is my trust. Teach me to do the thing that pleaseth thee, for thou art my God. Let thy loving Spirit lead me forth into the land of righteousness.

Lancelot Andrewes, 1555–1626

782 O Lord our God, as thou hast in mercy preserved us to the beginning of another day, enable us by thy grace to live to thee, and to set our affections on things above, not on things upon the earth. Pour into our minds the light of thy truth and cause us to rejoice in thy word. Shed abroad thy love in our hearts, and bestow upon us abundantly the peace and comfort of thy Holy Spirit; for the sake of Jesus Christ our Lord.

Isaac Ashe, 19th century

Lord, let us learn from the experience of today the lessons which thou *783*
meanest today to teach.

Clement Bailhache, 1856–1924

O God, our Father, help us all through this day so to live that we may *784*
bring help to others, credit to ourselves and to the name we bear, and
joy to those that love us, and to you.
 Cheerful when things go wrong;
 Persevering when things are difficult;
 Serene when things are irritating.
Enable us to be:
 Helpful to those in difficulties;
 Kind to those in need;
 Sympathetic to those whose hearts are sore and sad.
Grant that:
 Nothing may make us lose our tempers;
 Nothing may take away our joy;
 Nothing may ruffle our peace;
 Nothing may make us bitter towards anyone.
So grant that through all this day all those with whom we work, and
all those whom we meet, may see in us the reflection of the master,
whose we are, and whom we seek to serve. This we ask for your love's
sake.

William Barclay

O God, by whom the world is governed and preserved, we thine *785*
unworthy servants draw nigh unto thee to offer our morning sacrifice
of prayer and praise. May we remember that every day is thy gift, to
be used in thy service. Enable us to resist all evil, and dispose us to follow the guidance of thy good Spirit, not trusting to our own strength
or wisdom, but looking to thee to establish us in every good word and
work; through Jesus Christ our Lord.

Charles James Blomfield, 1786–1857

 Lord, whatever this day may bring, *786*
 Thy name be praised.

 Dietrich Bonhoeffer (Written while awaiting execution in a Nazi prison)

787   O Holy Spirit of God –
come into my heart and fill me:
I open the windows of my soul to let thee in.
I surrender my whole life to thee:
come and possess me, fill me with light and truth.
I offer to thee the one thing I really possess,
my capacity for being filled by thee.
Of myself I am an unprofitable servant,
an empty vessel.
Fill me so that I may live the life of the Spirit:
The life of truth and goodness, the life of beauty and love,
the life of wisdom and strength.
And guide me today in all things:
guide me to the people I should meet or help:
to the circumstances in which I can best serve thee,
whether by my action, or by my sufferings.
But, above all, make Christ to be formed in me,
that I may dethrone self in my heart
   and make him king.
Bind and cement me to Christ by all thy ways
   known and unknown:
by holy thoughts, and unseen graces,
and sacramental ties:
so that he is in me, and I in him,
today, and for ever.

W. J. Carey

788   Be thou a bright flame before me,
Be thou a guiding star above me,
Be thou a smooth path below me,
Be thou a kindly shepherd behind me,
Today – tonight – and forever.

Columba, c.521–97

O thou most holy and everloving God, 789
we thank thee once more
for the quiet rest of the night that has gone by,
for the new promise that has come with this fresh morning,
and for the hope of this day.
While we have slept,
the world in which we live has swept on in its awful space,
great fires have burned under us,
great waters have been all about us,
and great storms above us;
but thou hast held them back by thy strong hand,
and we have rested under the shadow of thy love.
The bird sat on the spray out in the darkness,
the flower nestled in the grass,
we lay down in our home, and all slept in the arms of God.
The bird will trust thee this day to give its morsel of meat,
and the flower will trust thee for its fresh raiment;
so may we trust thee this day for all the needs
of the body, the soul, and the spirit.
Give us this day our daily bread.

Robert Collyer, 1823–1912

i thank You God for most this amazing 790
day: for the leaping greenly spirits of trees
and a blue true dream of sky; and for everything
which is natural which is infinite which is yes

(i who have died am alive again today,
and this is the sun's birthday; this is the birth
day of life and of love and wings: and of the gay
great happening illimitably earth)

how should tasting touching hearing seeing
breathing any – lifted from the no
of all nothing – human merely being
doubt unimaginable You?

(now the ears of my ears awake and
now the eyes of my eyes are opened)

E. E. Cummings, 1894–1962

791   You big, bright, beautiful God,
       this is my day for flying!
       I reach out to the bigness of you.
       I touch the brightness of you
       and I feel the beauty of you
       in the centre of my living.
       Today you bear me up, up,
       past my doubts about both of us,
       to the certainty of your love.
       Today, God, I know you.
       All those words I learned
       are burnt up in your fire.
       You are sun to my Icarus,
       candle to my moth.
       Today I fly
       and am dissolved in you!

       And if tomorrow I am grounded
       by a weight of anxieties,
       if my feet are heavy and there are clouds
       between me and the sun,
       then let me keep hold of the warm place in my heart
       reminding me that today I flew
       and was kissed by God.

       Joy Cowley

792   As we rejoice in the gift of this new day, so may the light of your pre-
       sence, O God, set our hearts on fire with love for you; now and for
       ever.

       The Daily Office

793   Lord, help us to use honestly and well this day all the talents which
       you have given us, that the gain may not be ours only, but yours, and
       your kingdom's; through Jesus Christ, our Lord.

       Daily Prayer

O Lord our God, who hast chased the slumber from our eyes, and   794
once more assembled us to lift up our hands unto thee and to praise
thy just judgements, accept our prayers and supplications, and give
us faith and love. Bless our coming in and our going out, our
thoughts, words, and works, and let us begin this day with the praise
of the unspeakable sweetness of thy mercy. Hallowed be thy name.
Thy kingdom come; through Jesus Christ our Lord.

Greek Liturgy, 3rd century

O God, who hast folded back the mantle of the night to clothe us in   795
the golden glory of the day, chase from our hearts all gloomy
thoughts, and make us glad with the brightness of hope, that we may
effectively aspire to unwon virtues, through Jesus Christ our Lord.

Gregorian Sacramentary, 6th century

Lo, fainter now lie spread the shades of night,   796
    and upward spread the trembling gleams of morn,
suppliant we bend before the Lord of Light,
    and pray at early dawn,
that this sweet charity may all our sin
    forgive, and make our miseries to cease;
may grant us health, grant us the gift divine
    of everlasting peace.
Father Supreme, this grace on us confer;
    and thou, O Son by an eternal birth!
with thee, coequal Spirit, comforter!
    whose glory fills the earth.

(Pope) Gregory I, c.540–604

O Lord, prepare us for all the events of the day; for we know not what   797
a day may bring forth. Give us grace to deny ourselves; to take up our
cross daily, and to follow in the steps of our Lord and Master.

Matthew Henry, 1662–1714

798   Cold, slow, silent, but returning, after so many hours.
The sight of something outside me, the day is breaking.
May salt, this one day, be sharp upon my tongue;
May I sleep, this one night, without waking.

Randall Jarrell

799   Make us to remember, O God, that every day is thy gift, and ought to
be used according to thy command; through Jesus Christ our Lord.

Samuel Johnson, 1709–84

800   To thee, O Master that lovest all men, I hasten on rising from sleep;
by thy mercy I go forth to do thy work, and I pray to thee: help me at
all time, in everything; deliver me from every evil thing of this world
and from every attack of the devil; save me and bring me to thine eternal Kingdom. For thou art my Creator, the Giver and Provider of
everything good; in thee is all my hope, and to thee I ascribe glory,
now and ever, and to the ages of ages.

Macarius of Egypt, c.300–c.390 (attributed)

801   Lord, we offer you ourselves this day
for the work you want accomplished,
for the people you want us to meet,
for the word you want to be uttered,
for the silence you want to be kept,
for the places you want us to enter,
for the new ways you want pioneered.
Go with us along the way, Lord,
and enable us to realize your presence,
at all times and in all places,
our loving Lord Jesus Christ.

Morris Maddocks

Eternal God, who committest to us the swift and solemn trust of life; 802
since we know not what a day may bring forth, but only that the hour
for serving thee is always present, may we wake to the instant claims
of thy holy will; not waiting for tomorrow, but yielding today. In all
things draw us to the mind of Christ, that thy lost image may be
traced again, and thou mayest own us as at one with him and thee.

James Martineau, 1805–1900

O sweet and loving God, 803
When I stay asleep too long,
Oblivious to all your many blessings,
Then, please, wake me up,
And sing to me your joyful song.
It is a song without noise or notes.
It is a song of love beyond words,
Of faith beyond the power of human telling.
I can hear it in my soul,
When you awaken me to your presence.

Mechthild of Magdeburg, c.1210–c.1280

O my God, make me happy this day in thy service. Let me do nothing, 804
say nothing, desire nothing, which is contrary to thy will. Give me a
thankful spirit, and a heart full of praise for all that thou hast given
me, and for all thou hast withheld from me.

Ashton Oxenden, 1808–92

Lord, be with us this day, 805
Within us to purify us;
Above us to draw us up;
Beneath us to sustain us;
Before us to lead us;
Behind us to restrain us;
Around us to protect us.

Patrick, c.389–c.461

806

I bind unto myself today
  The power of God to hold and lead,
His eye to watch, his might to stay,
  His ear to hearken to my need,
The wisdom of my God to teach,
  His hand to guide, his shield to ward,
The Word of God to give me speech,
  His heavenly host to be my guard.

Christ be with me, Christ within me,
Christ behind me, Christ before me,
Christ beside me, Christ to win me,
Christ to comfort and restore me,
Christ beneath me, Christ above me,
Christ in quiet, Christ in danger,
Christ in hearts of all that love me,
Christ in mouth of friend and stranger.

Patrick, c.389–c.461 (attributed)

807   O Lord, grant me to greet the coming day in peace. Help me in all things to rely upon thy holy will. In every hour of the day reveal thy will to me. Bless my dealings with all who surround me. Teach me to treat all that comes to me throughout the day with peace of soul, and with firm conviction that thy will governs all. In all my deeds and words guide my thoughts and feelings. In unforeseen events let me not forget that all are sent by thee. Teach me to act firmly and wisely, without embittering and embarrassing others. Give me strength to bear the fatigue of thy coming day with all that it shall bring. Direct my will, teach me to pray, pray thou thyself in me.

Drizdov Philaret, 1782–1867

808

May we accept this day at your hand, O Lord,
  as a gift to be treasured,
  a life to be enjoyed,
  a trust to be kept,
  and a hope to be fulfilled;
  and all for your glory.

Stanley Pritchard

Teach me, O Father, how to ask thee each moment, silently, for thy help. If I fail, teach me at once to ask thee to forgive me. If I am disquieted, enable me, by thy grace, quickly to turn to thee. May nothing this day come between me and thee. May I will, do, and say, just what thou, my loving and tender Father, willest me to will, do, and say. Work thy holy will in me and through me this day. Protect me, guide me, bless me, within and without, that I may do something this day for love of thee; something which shall please thee; and that I may, this evening, be nearer to thee, though I see it not, nor know it. Lead me, O Lord, in a straight way unto thyself, and keep me in thy grace unto the end. 809

Edward Bouverie Pusey, 1800–82

Today, my Father, let me be like a tree planted by the river, bringing forth fruit in its season. Let the sap of your Holy Spirit rise within me. Let me not become dry and barren but rich in abundance and fertility. May many weary ones find refreshment in the shadow of my branches. 810

(Brother) Ramon

Here, Lord, is my life. I place it on the altar today. Use it as you will. 811

Albert Schweitzer, 1875–1965

All this day, O Lord, 812
let me touch as many lives as possible for thee;
and every life I touch, do thou by thy Spirit quicken,
whether through the word I speak,
the prayer I breathe, or the life I live.

Mary Sumner, 1828–1921

My life is an instant, 813
An hour which passes by;
My life is a moment
Which I have no power to stay.
You know, O my God,
That to love you here on earth –
I have only today.

Thérèse of Lisieux, 1873–97

814 My soul hath desired thee all night, O eternal wisdom! and in the early morning I turn to thee from the depths of my heart. May thy holy presence remove all dangers from my soul and body. May thy many graces fill the inmost recesses of my heart, and inflame it with thy divine love.

O most sweet Jesus! turn thy face towards me, for this morning with all the power of my soul I fly to thee and salute thee, beseeching thee that the thousand times a thousand angels who minister to thee may praise thee for me, and that the thousand times ten thousand blessed spirits who surround thy throne may glorify thee for me today.

May all that is beautiful and amiable in creatures praise thee for me, and may all creation bless thy holy name, our consoling protection in time and in eternity.

(Brother) Henry Suso, c. 1295–1366

815   Stand by us, Lord,
       Give us peace,
       courage and bright hopes,
       This day and all our days.

       Angela Tilby (BBC)

816   Lord, that which we have prayed against this morning,
       suffer us not to have done before the evening.

       Charles John Vaughan, 1816–97

MEALTIMES

Bless, O Lord, this food to our use and bless us to your service, and 817
make us ever mindful of the needs of others; through Jesus Christ our
Lord.
Source unknown

Lord, may our fellowship be the revelation of your presence and turn 818
our daily bread into bread of life.
Anglican Church of Canada. Alternative Service Book

Creator of the universe, you give us this gift of food to nourish us and 819
give us life. Bless this food that you have made and human hands have
prepared. May it satisfy our hunger, and in sharing it together may
we come closer to one another.
Anglican Church of Canada. Alternative Service Book

Blessed are you, O Lord God, King of the Universe, for you give us 820
food to sustain our lives and make our hearts glad; through Jesus
Christ our Lord.
Episcopal Church of the United States of America. Book of Common Prayer

Bless, O Lord, thy gifts to our use and us to thy service; for Christ's 821
sake.
Episcopal Church of the United States of America. Book of Common Prayer

Come Lord Jesus be our guest, 822
And may our meal by thee be blest.
Martin Luther, 1483–1546 (attributed)

823   To God who gives our daily bread
A thankful song we raise,
And pray that he who sends us food
May fill our hearts with praise.

Thomas Tallis, 1510–85

824   O Lord:

In a world where many are lonely:
We thank you for our friendships.

In a world where many are captive:
We thank you for our freedom.

In a world where many are hungry:
We thank you for your provision.

We pray that you will:
Enlarge our sympathy,
Deepen our compassion,
And give us grateful hearts.

In Christ's name.

Terry Waite

825   Bless me, O Lord, and let my food strengthen me to serve thee,
for Jesus Christ's sake.

Isaac Watts, 1674–1748

826   Be present at our table, Lord;
Be here and everywhere adored.
Thy creatures bless, and grant that we
May feast in paradise with thee.

John Wesley, 1703–91

DAILY WORK

Almighty God, you have so linked our lives one with another that all   827
we do affects, for good or ill, all other lives: so guide us in the work
we do, that we may do it not for self alone, but for the common good;
and, as we seek a proper return for our own labour, make us mindful
of the rightful aspirations of other workers, and arouse our concern
for those who are out of work; through Jesus Christ our Lord, who
lives and reigns with you and the Holy Spirit, one God, for ever and
ever.

Source unknown

> God give me work   828
> Till my life shall end,
> And life
> Till my work is done.
>
> *Source unknown (Found on the grave of Winifred Holtby, 1898–1935)*

> The sacred Three be over me   829
> With my working hands this day
> With the people on my way
> With the labour and the toil
> With the land and with the soil
> With the tools that I take
> With the things that I make
> With the thoughts of my mind
> With the sharing with mankind
> With the love of my heart
> With each one who plays a part
> The sacred Three be over me
> The blessing of the Trinity
>
> *David Adam*

830　O God, grant unto us that we be not unwise, but understanding thy will: not slothful, but diligent in thy work: that we run not as uncertainly, nor fight thy battles as those that beat the air. Whatsoever our hand findeth to do, may we do it with our might: that when thou shalt call thy labourers to give them their reward, we may so have run that we may obtain; so have fought the good fight, as to receive the crown of eternal life; through Jesus Christ our Lord.

Henry Alford, 1810–71

831　Jesus, you knew rejection and disappointment;
help us if our work seems distasteful;
help us to decide what best to do,
what next to do,
or what to do at all.
Give us courage and cheerfulness to go the second mile,
and all the miles ahead.

Anglican Church in Aotearoa, New Zealand and Polynesia.
A New Zealand Prayer Book

832　Lord, thou knowest how busy I must be this day. If I forget thee, do not thou forget me.

Jacob Astley, 1579–1652 (Prayed before commanding troops at the battle of Edgehill, 23 October 1642, first battle of English Civil War)

833　This day, O Lord:
give me courtesy;
give me meekness of bearing, with decision of character;
give me long-suffering;
give me charity;
give me chastity;
give me sincerity of speech;
give me diligence in my allotted task.

John Baillie, 1886–1960

O God, your Word tells me that,   *834*
whatever my hand finds to do, I must do it with my might.
Help me today to concentrate with my whole attention on whatever
    I am doing, and keep my thoughts from wandering and my mind
    from straying.
When I am studying, help me to study with my whole mind.
When I am playing, help me to play with my whole heart.
Help me to do one thing at a time, and to do it well.
This I ask for Jesus' sake.

William Barclay

O God, from whom we have received life, and all earthly blessings,   *835*
vouchsafe to give unto us each day what we need. Give unto all of us
strength to perform faithfully our appointed tasks; bless the work of
our hands and of our minds. Grant that we may ever serve thee, in
sickness and in health, in necessity and in abundance; sanctify our
joys and our trials, and give us grace to seek first thy kingdom and its
righteousness, in the sure and certain faith that all else shall be added
unto us; through Jesus Christ, thy Son, our Lord and Saviour.

Eugene Bersier, 1831–89

O Lord, I do not pray for tasks equal to my strength: I ask for strength   *836*
equal to my tasks.

Phillips Brooks, 1835–93

Grant, O Lord, that as we go forth once more to our daily labour we   *837*
may remember the truths that we learnt, and may carry out the resolutions we made on thy holy day. Keep us from our besetting sins, and
strengthen us to do thy holy will, that we may never forget whose we
are and whom we serve; through Jesus Christ our Lord.

William Walsham How, 1823–97

838 Almighty God, the giver of all good things, without whose help all labour is ineffectual, and without whose grace all wisdom folly, grant, we beseech thee, that in all our undertakings, thy Holy Spirit may not be withheld from us: but that we may promote thy glory, and the salvation both of ourselves and others. Grant this, O Lord, for the sake of Jesus Christ our Lord.

Samuel Johnson, 1709–84

839
That which I give my energy to;
  which I love
  hate
  find challenging
  demanding
  frustrating
  rewarding:
This is my work –
  that which I must do
  on a daily basis
  in order to live
  and to prove
  that I am fully alive.

Lord, thank you that as we work in the world
  engaging our best energies
  in that which is before us,
  you work within us
  through that same struggle,
  the fabric of our redemption.

Kathy Keay

840 O my God, since thou art with me, and I must now, in obedience to thy commands, apply my mind to these outward things, I beseech thee to grant me the grace to continue in thy presence; and to this end do thou prosper me with thy assistance, receive all my work and possess all my affections.

(Brother) Lawrence, 1611–91

If this day I should get lost amid the perplexities of life and the rush of 841 many duties, do thou search me out, gracious Lord, and bring me back into the quiet of thy presence.

F. B. Meyer

O Lord Jesus Christ, who at the carpenter's bench didst manifest the 842 dignity of honest labour, and dost give to each of us our tasks to perform, help us to do our weekday work with readiness of mind and singleness of heart, not with eye-service as men-pleasers, but as thy servants, labouring heartily as unto thee and not unto men, so that whatever we do, great or small, may be to the glory of thy holy name.

John R. W. Stott

Lord, a lot of the work I have to do is dull – deadly dull. Sometimes 843 I'm so bored, and sometimes I'm depressed. It goes on day after day. God, sometimes I hate work. And then I remember two things, and take heart. I ask your help to keep them more in mind. I remember the carpenter's shop at Nazareth. That can't always have been all joy and sunshine. People can be very rude to others who work for them. So I know that you understand – and I'm thankful. I remember, too, that my work is linked through the work of others to the work of all men, just as I am linked through others to all men. They depend on me and I depend on them. Lord, keep me faithful.

(Brother) John Charles Vockler

EVENING

844　Stay with us, Lord:
　　　the day is almost over and it is getting dark.

　　　Luke 24.29 (Good News Bible, adapted)

845　Almighty God, we confess that it is by the Spirit of thy Son in our
　　　hearts that we cry, 'Abba, Father,' to thee. We thank thee that we are
　　　united to Christ by faith, and that it is no longer we who live, but
　　　Christ who lives in us. Hear us, for his sake.

　　　　Our Father, forgive us wherein we have not lived by faith in Christ
　　　today. Forgive the actions that have not been Christlike, the speech
　　　that has not been seasoned with his Spirit, and those things within
　　　our hearts which have defiled us in his sight.

　　　Source unknown

846　Come, Lord, and cover me with the night. Spread your grace over us
　　　　as you assured us you would do.
　　　Your promises are more than all the stars in the sky;
　　　Your mercy is deeper than the night.
　　　Lord, it will be cold.
　　　The night comes with its breath of death.
　　　Night comes, the end comes,
　　　but Jesus Christ comes also.
　　　Lord, we wait for him day and night.

　　　Source unknown (West Africa)

Ere thou sleepest, gently lay 847
Every troubled thought away.
Put off worry and distress
As thou puttest off thy dress.
Drop thy worry and thy care
In the quiet arms of prayer.
Lord, thou knowest how I live;
All I've done amiss, forgive;
All the good I've tried to do
Hallow, bless, and carry through.
All I love in safety keep,
While, in thee, I fall asleep.

Source unknown

Give me this night, O Father, the peace of mind 848
   which is truly rest.
Take from me
  All envy of anyone else
  All resentment for anything which has been
    withheld from me
  All bitterness against anyone who has hurt
    or wronged me
  All anger against the apparent injustices of life
  All foolish worry about the future
    and all futile regret about the past.
Help me to be
  At peace with myself
  At peace with my fellow human beings
  At peace with you
So indeed may I lay myself down to rest in peace,
   through Jesus Christ my Lord.

Source unknown

O Lord Jesus Christ, who received the children who came to you, 849
receive also from me, your child, this evening prayer. Shelter me
under the shadow of your wings, that in peace I may lie down and
sleep; and waken me in due time, that I may glorify you, for you alone
are righteous and merciful.

Source unknown

850

O God of life, this night
O darken not to me thy light,
O God of life, this night
Close not thy gladness of my sight,
O God of life, this night
Thy door to me do shut not tight,
O God of life, this night
Refuse not mercy to my plight,
O God of life, this night
Quell unto me thy grieving slight,
O God of life, this night
Crown thou to me thy joy's delight,
O crown to me thy joy's delight,
O God of life, this night

Source unknown (Early Scottish)

851 That this evening may be holy, good and peaceful:
We pray to you, O Lord.

That your holy angels may lead us in the paths of peace and goodwill:
We pray to you, O Lord.

That we may be pardoned and forgiven for our sins and offences:
We pray to you, O Lord.

That there may be peace in your Church and for the whole world:
We pray to you, O Lord.

That we may be bound together by your Holy Spirit, in communion with (— and with) all your saints, entrusting one another and all our life to Christ:
We pray to you, O Lord.

Source unknown (Orthodox Litany for the evening)

The sacred Three   852
To save,
To shield,
To surround
The hearth,
The house,
The household,
This eve,
This night,
Oh! this eve,
This night,
And every night,
Each single night.

Source unknown (Celtic)

Protecting me   853
The Father be
Over me
The Saviour be
Under me
The Spirit be
About me
The Holy Three
Defending me
As evening come
Bless my home
Holy Three
Watching me
As shadows fall
Hear my call
Sacred Three
Encircle me
So it may be
Amen to Thee
Holy Three
About me

David Adam

854   Take us, we pray thee, O Lord of our life, into thy keeping this night and for ever. O thou light of lights, keep us from inward darkness; grant us so to sleep in peace, that we may arise to work according to thy will; through Jesus Christ our Lord.

Lancelot Andrewes, 1555–1626

855   Glory be to thee, my God, for all the blessings of the past day, for thy presence ever with me, for the love of family and friends, for every kindness shown me by others, for the satisfaction of my work and for the knowledge that I am held safe in thy hand whatever happens. I lift my heart in love and gratitude to thee, dear Father, praising thee that thou hast made me thy child through Jesus Christ.

George Appleton

856   Before we go to rest, we would commit ourselves to God's care through Christ, beseeching him to forgive us for all our sins of this day past, and to keep alive his grace in our hearts, and to cleanse us from all sin, pride, harshness, and selfishness, and to give us the spirit of meekness, humility, firmness, and love. O Lord, keep thyself present to us ever, and perfect thy strength in our weakness. Take us and ours under thy blessed care, this night and evermore; through Jesus Christ our Lord.

Thomas Arnold, 1795–1842

857   Watch, dear Lord, with those who wake, or watch, or weep tonight, and give your angels charge over those who sleep. Tend your sick ones, O Lord Christ, rest your weary ones. Bless your dying ones. Soothe your suffering ones. Pity your afflicted ones. Shield your joyous ones. And all for your love's sake.

Augustine, 354–430

858   Abide with us, O good Lord, through the night, guarding, keeping, guiding, sustaining, sanctifying, and with thy love gladdening us, that in thee we may ever live, and in thee may die; through Jesus Christ our Lord.

Edward White Benson, 1829–96

As I take off my dusty, dirty clothes, let me also be stripped of the sins 859
I have committed this day. I confess, dear Lord, that in so many ways
my thoughts and actions have been impure. Now I come before you,
naked in body and bare in soul, to be washed clean. Let me rest
tonight in your arms, and so may the dreams that pass through my
mind be holy. And let me awake tomorrow, strong and eager to serve
you.

Jakob Boehme, 1575–1624

O Lord my God, thank you for bringing this day to a close; thank you 860
for giving me rest in body and soul. Your hand has been over me and
has guarded and preserved me. Forgive my lack of faith and any
wrong that I have done today, and help me to forgive all who have
wronged me.

Let me sleep in peace under your protection, and keep me from all
the temptations of darkness.

Into your hands I commend my loved ones and all who dwell in this
house; I commend to you my body and soul. O God, your holy name
be praised.

Dietrich Bonhoeffer

O Lord Jesus Christ, our watchman and keeper, take us into thy care, 861
and grant that, our bodies sleeping, our minds may watch in thee and
be made merry by some sight of that celestial and heavenly life
wherein thou art the King and Prince, together with the Father and
the Holy Ghost, where thy angels and holy souls be most happy citizens. O purify our souls, keep clean our bodies, that in both we may
please thee, sleeping and waking, for ever.

Christian Prayers, 1566

Be present, Spirit of God, within us, 862
   your dwelling place and home,
that this house may be one where
all darkness is penetrated by your light,
all troubles calmed by your peace,
all evil redeemed by your love,
all pain transformed in your suffering,
and all dying glorified in your risen life.

Jim Cotter

863

Ere I sleep, for every favour
   This day showed
   By my God
I will bless my Saviour.

O my Lord, what shall I render
   To thy name,
   Still the same,
Merciful and tender?

Thou hast ordered all my goings
   In thy way,
   Heard me pray,
Sanctified my doings.

Leave me not, but ever love me:
   Let thy peace
   Be my bliss,
Till thou hence remove me.
Thou my rock, my guard, my tower,
   Safely keep,
   While I sleep,
Me, with all thy power.

So, whene'er in death I slumber,
   Let me rise
   With the wise,
Counted in their number.

John Cennick, 1718–55

864 Keep us, Lord, so awake in the duties of our calling that we may sleep
in thy peace and wake in thy glory.

John Donne, 1573–1631

O merciful God, eternal light, shining in darkness, thou who dispellest the night of sin and all blindness of heart, since thou hast appointed the night for rest and the day for labour, we beseech thee grant that our bodies may rest in peace and quietness, that afterward they may be able to endure the labour they must bear. 865

Temper our sleep that it be not disorderly, that we may remain spotless both in body and soul, yea that our sleep itself may be to thy glory.

Enlighten the eyes of our understanding that we may not sleep in death, but always look for deliverance from this misery.

Defend us against all assaults of the devil and take us into thy holy protection.

And although we have not passed this day without greatly sinning against thee, we beseech thee to hide our sins with thy mercy, as thou hidest all things on earth with the darkness of the night, that we may not be cast out from thy presence.

Relieve and comfort all those who are afflicted in mind, body, or estate. Through Jesus Christ our Lord.

John Calvin, 1509–64

O God, your unfailing providence sustains the world we live in and the life we live: watch over those, both night and day, who work while others sleep, and grant that we may never forget that our common life depends upon each other's toil; through Jesus Christ our Lord. 866

Episcopal Church of the United States of America. Book of Common Prayer

We thank thee, O Lord and master, for teaching us how to pray simply and sincerely to thee, and for hearing us when we so call upon thee. We thank thee for saving us from our sins and sorrows, and for directing all our ways this day. Lead us ever onwards to thyself; for the sake of Jesus Christ our Lord and Saviour. 867

(Father) John of the Russian Church, 1829–1909

Be present, O merciful God, and protect us through the silent hours of this night, so that we who are fatigued by the changes and chances of this fleeting world, may repose upon thy eternal changelessness; through Jesus Christ, the same yesterday, today and forever. 868

Leonine Sacramentary

869   We thank thee, our heavenly Father, through Jesus Christ, thy dear Son, that thou hast graciously kept us this day; and we pray thee that thou wouldst forgive us all our sins where we have done wrong, and graciously keep us this night. For into thy hands we commend ourselves, our bodies and souls, and all things. Let thy holy angel be with us, that the wicked foe may have no power over us.

Martin Luther, 1483–1546

870   O eternal God, King of all creation, who hast brought me to this hour, forgive me the sins which I have committed this day in thought, word, and deed, and cleanse, O Lord, my humble soul from every stain of flesh and spirit.

    Grant me, O Lord, to pass through the sleep of this night in peace, to rise from my lowly bed, to please thy holy name all the days of my life, and to vanquish the enemies both bodily and spiritual that contend against me.

    Deliver me, O Lord, from the vain thoughts that stain me, and from evil desires. For thine is the kingdom and the power, and the glory, of the Father, and the Son, and the Holy Ghost, now and for ever and unto the ages of ages.

Macarius of Egypt, c.300–c.390

871   O Lord God, the life of mortals, the light of the faithful, the strength of those who labour, the repose of the dead; grant us a tranquil night, free from all disturbances; that after an interval of quiet sleep, we may, by thy bounty, at the return of light, be endued with activity from the Holy Spirit, and enabled in security to render thanks to thee, through Jesus Christ our Lord.

Mozarabic Liturgy, 7th century

O Jesus, King of the poor, 872
shield this night
those who are imprisoned without charge,
those who have 'disappeared'.
Cast a halo of your presence around those
who groan in sorrow or pain.

Protect those whose livelihoods are threatened.
Encourage those forbidden to worship.
Encompass your little ones
gone hungry to sleep,
cold and fitfully waking.
Guide your witnesses for peace.
Safeguard your workers for justice.

Encircle us with your power,
compass us with your grace,
embrace your dying ones,
support your weary ones,
calm your frightened ones –

and as the sun scatters the mist on the hills,
bring us to a new dawn,
when all shall freely
sit at table in your kingdom,
rejoicing in a God who saves them.

Kate McIlhagga

Into thine arms we now commend ourselves this night. We will lay us 873
down in peace, if thou speak peace to us through Jesus Christ. May
our last thoughts be of thee. And when we awake, may thy Spirit
bring heavenly things to our mind. Pardon the imperfections of our
prayers. Supply what we have omitted to ask for, and do for us
exceeding abundantly above all that we ask or think; for the merits of
Jesus Christ our Lord.

Fielding Ould, 19th century

874   Holy God,
> Creator and Father,
> thank you for our family,
> thank you for your loving care of all of us,
> all through the day,
> in everything and everywhere,
> and while we sleep.

> Help me to remember that you are always with me, Lord.
> Help me to remember you in the good times,
> Not just to call for help when things go wrong.

> Thank you, God, for everything you have made in your world,
> and bless all who live in it
> especially —,

> For all the wrong things I have said and done, forgive me, Lord.
> And help me to be able to say sorry to those I hurt.

> Thank you, God, for being with me always.

Mothers' Union (A prayer that may be used by children)

875   When the day returns, call us with morning faces, and with morning hearts, eager to labour, happy if happiness be our portion, and if the day is marked for sorrow, strong to endure.

Robert Louis Stevenson, 1850–94 (Written and read to his family on the eve of his unanticipated death)

876   God, my Father, you know all that has made up today:
> its joys and perplexities; its promises broken; its opportunities not seized.

O God, forgive me for my share in these things today:
> for my slowness to respond; for my dullness of mind; for my eyes lifted afar when beauty was all about me.

O God, strengthen me with a greater dependence:
> only in your way of life is satisfaction; you have made me for yourself; you have set me in this wonderful world to love and serve.

God, bless my coming-in this night as you blessed my going-out at the day's beginning.

Rita Snowden

Into thy hands, most blessed Jesus, I commend my soul and body, for thou hast redeemed both by thy most precious blood. So bless and sanctify my sleep to me, that it may be temperate, holy, and safe, a refreshment to my weary body, to enable it so to serve my soul, that both may serve thee with never-failing duty. Visit, I beseech thee, O Lord, this habitation with thy mercy, and me with thy grace and favour. Teach me to number my days, that I may apply my heart unto wisdom, and ever be mindful of my last end.   877

Jeremy Taylor, 1613–67

Send thy peace into our hearts, O Lord, at the evening hour, that we may be contented with thy mercies of this day, and confident of thy protection for this night; and now, having forgiven others, even as thou dost forgive us, may we have a pure comfort and a healthful rest within the shelter of this home; through Jesus Christ our Saviour.   878

Henry van Dyke, 1852–1933

And now, O blessed Redeemer, our rock, our hope, and only sure defence, to thee do we cheerfully commit both our soul and body. If thy wise providence see fit, grant that we may rise in the morning, refreshed with sleep, and with a spirit of activity for the duties of the day, but whether we wake here or in eternity grant that our trust in thee may remain sure, and our hope unshaken, through Jesus Christ our Lord.   879

Henry Kirke White, 1785–1806

PRAYERS FOR

SPECIAL OCCASIONS

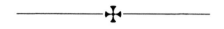

This is the day that the Lord has made;

let us rejoice and be glad in it .

Psalm 118.24

BEFORE WORSHIP

Prepare us, O God, for the worship of your house, and give us grace   *880*
to serve you with reverence, joy, and thanksgiving; through Jesus
Christ our Lord.

Source unknown

Father, help us to worship you in spirit and in truth,   *881*
that our consciences may be quickened by your holiness,
   our minds nourished by your truth,
   our imagination purified by your beauty,
   our hearts opened by your love,
   our wills surrendered to your purpose;
and may all this be gathered up in adoration,
as we ascribe glory, praise and honour to you alone,
through Jesus Christ our Lord.

Howard Booth

Give us, our Father, a sense of your presence   *882*
   as we gather now for worship.
Grant us gratitude as we remember your goodness,
   penitence as we remember our sins,
   and joy as we remember your love;
and enable us to lift up our hearts
   in humble prayer and fervent praise;
through Jesus Christ our Lord.

Frank Colquhoun

883 Almighty God, who hast given us grace at this time with one accord to make our common supplications unto thee; and dost promise that when two or three are gathered together in thy name thou wilt grant their requests: fulfil now, O Lord, the desires and petitions of thy servants, as may be most expedient for them; granting us in this world knowledge of thy truth, and in the world to come life everlasting.

John Chrysostom, c.347–407

884 Heavenly Father, we are here to worship you, but first we ask you to forgive us all our sins: so many wrong things we ought not to have done, we have done; so many right things we ought to have done we have not done. In your mercy forgive us – help us to do right, and to reject what is wrong; through Jesus Christ our Lord.

Guy King

885 Lord our God, help us to give our minds to you in our worship, so that we may listen to what you have to say to us, and know your will. Help us to give our hearts to you in our worship, so that we may really want to do what you require from us. Help us to give our strength to you in our worship, so that through us your will may be done. In the name of Jesus Christ our Lord.

Caryl Micklem

886 O almighty God, the searcher of all hearts, who hast declared that all such as shall draw nigh to thee with their lips when their hearts are far from thee are an abomination unto thee: cleanse, we beseech thee, the thoughts of our hearts by the inspiration of thy Holy Spirit, that no wandering, vain, nor idle thoughts may put out of our minds that reverence and godly fear that becomes all those who come into thy presence.

Jonathan Swift, 1667–1745

Grant, O Lord, that through our worship this day we may be *887*
awakened to the wonder of thy love for us; that familiar words may
shine with new meaning and that the habit of worship may be
cleansed of all stale formality and mere ceremonial observance. Open
our eyes to see thy loveliness and make our hearts to burn within us as
thou dost speak thy word to us in this hour, so that in wondering awe
we may know ourselves forgiven, energized with new life and throbbing with new power. Through Jesus Christ our Lord.

Leslie D. Weatherhead, 1883–1975

AFTER WORSHIP

Accept, O God, the worship of our hearts and of our lips, and give us *888*
grace to glorify you in our lives, for the sake of Jesus Christ our Lord.

Source unknown

O God, whose nature is ever to have mercy and to forgive, receive our *889*
humble petitions; and though we be tied and bound with the chain of
our sins, yet let the pitifulness of thy great mercy loose us; for the honour of Jesus Christ, our Mediator and Advocate.

Church of England. Book of Common Prayer

Heavenly Father, you have promised to hear us when we ask in the *890*
name of your Son: accept and fulfil our petitions, we pray, not as we
ask in our ignorance, nor as we deserve in our sinfulness, but as you
know and love us in your Son Jesus Christ our Lord.

Episcopal Church of the United States of America

891 Grant, we beseech thee, almighty God, that the words which we have heard this day with our outward ears may, through thy grace, be so grafted inwardly in our hearts that they may bring forth in us the fruit of good living, to the honour and praise of thy name, through Jesus Christ our Lord.

Gelasian Sacramentary, 5th century

892 O gracious Lord, since thou hast promised that, where two or three are gathered together in thy name, thou wilt be in the midst of them to grant their requests: grant to us who are met in thy name that those requests which in the utmost sincerity of our hearts we have now made, may effectually be answered; through the merits of Jesus Christ our Lord.

Jonathan Swift, 1667–1745

BAPTISM

893   May the Lord of his great mercy bless you,
and give you understanding of his wisdom and grace.
May he nourish you with the riches of the catholic faith,
and make you persevere in all good works.
May he keep your steps from wandering,
and direct you into the paths of love and peace.

Source unknown

Thou Being who inhabitest the heights   894
Imprint thy blessing betimes,
Remember thou the child of my body,
In name of the Father of peace;
When the priest of the King
On him puts the water of meaning,
Grant him the blessing of the Three
    Who fill the heights.
  The blessing of the Three
    Who fill the heights.

Sprinkle down upon him thy grace,
Give thou to him virtue and growth,
Give thou to him strength and guidance,
Give thou to him flocks and possessions,
Sense and reason void of guile,
Angel wisdom in his day,
That he may stand without reproach
    In thy presence.
  He may stand without reproach
    In thy presence.

Source unknown (Welsh)

Yours be the blessing of God and the Lord,   895
The perfect Spirit his blessing afford,
The Trinity's blessing on you outpoured
With gentle and gen'rous shedding abroad,
So gently gen'rously for you unstored.

Source unknown (Celtic)

God our Creator, thank you for the waiting and the joy, thank you 896
for new life and for parenthood, thank you for the gift of —,
entrusted to our care. May we be patient and understanding, ready to
guide and forgive, that in our love — may know your love. May he
learn to love your world and the whole family of your children;
through Christ our life.

Anglican Church of Canada. Alternative Service Book

897   Lord God, our Father,
you have given your Son, Jesus Christ, to us
as the good shepherd
who knows all by name.
   We thank you
for your grace and your faithfulness,
for the new life that you have created,
for this child who has been born among us
and whom you have entrusted to us.
   You have given him/her ears to hear with
and eyes to see with.
Bless too this child's mouth,
so that he/she may learn how to laugh
and to speak the language of men.
   Bless also his/her hands and feet
and may he/she learn from his/her own experience
that everything that you have made
is good.
   We ask you to shelter this child
and keep him/her safe in this rough world.
Keep everything that is bad and inhuman away from him/her,
protect him/her from evil influences
and never let him/her be perverted.
   May he/she be secure with his/her parents
and may we who are mature and responsible
never give scandal to this child,
but lead him/her to the truth.
If, however, sin should ever have power over him/her,
be merciful to him/her, Lord God –
you make good all human guilt and shortcomings
and are yourself, even before this child is able to sin,
the forgiveness of all sins,
through Jesus Christ, our Lord.

Huub Oosterhuis

CONFIRMATION

We ask our God to make you worthy of the life he has called you to 898
live. May he fulfil by his power all your desire for goodness and complete your work of faith. In this way the name of our Lord Jesus will receive glory from you, and you from him, by the grace of our God and of the Lord Jesus Christ.

2 Thessalonians 1.11–12 (Good News Bible)

O God, the God of all goodness and of all grace, who art worthy of a 899
greater love than we either give or understand, fill our hearts, we beseech thee, with such love toward thee, that nothing may seem too hard for us to do or to suffer in obedience to thy will; and grant that thus loving thee we may become daily more like unto thee, and finally obtain the crown of life which thou hast promised to those that love thee; through Jesus Christ our Lord.

Source unknown, 19th century

Defend, O Lord, this thy child [or this thy servant] with thy heavenly 900
grace, that he may continue thine for ever; and daily increase in thy Holy Spirit, more and more, until he come unto thy everlasting kingdom.

Church of England. Book of Common Prayer

May God stride out before you on your journey through life 901
and through prayer.

May Jesus, your playful brother,
pace you in his holy way to the end.

May the Holy Spirit greet you at
each corner and cwch you to her breast.

Siân Swain Taylor ('cwch' is a Welsh word meaning 'cuddle')

347

902 Lord,
I can only see a little of the road ahead.
I can't see my final destination.
I can't even see over the next hill,
and I know there'll be other ups and downs beyond it –
high points from which one can see quite a long view,
valleys where the hills shut one in.
And some of those clouds may mean storms.
But the great thing is to have got started!

Lord,
thank you for calling me,
and setting my feet on the way.

Thank you for the map of the way,
which is yourself.

Lord,
help me to persevere.

Margaret Dewey (USPG)

COMMUNION

903 Lord Christ, who said, 'Do this in remembrance of me': help us at every communion service to look back, and remember your death for us on the cross; to look up, and know that you are the risen saviour among us; to look around, and rejoice in our fellowship with one another; and to look forward in hope to the coming of your kingdom and the heavenly banquet. For your name's sake.

Llewellyn Cumings

We give you thanks, holy Father,   904
for your holy name,
which you planted in our hearts;
and for the knowledge, faith and immortality
which you sent us through Jesus Christ, your child.

Glory to you throughout the ages.

You created everything, sovereign Lord,
for the glory of your name.
You gave food and drink to men
for their enjoyment,
and as a cause for thanksgiving.
And to us you have given
spiritual food and spiritual drink,
bestowing on us the promise of eternal life.
Above all we thank you
for the power of your love.

Glory to you throughout the ages.

Deliver your Church, Lord, from all evil
and teach it to love you perfectly.
You have made it holy.
Build it up from the four winds
And gather it into the kingdom
for which you have destined it.

Power and glory to you throughout the ages.

The Didache, 1st or 2nd century

We pray thee, Lord, let thy Spirit purify our hearts, lest we come   905
unworthily to the heavenly feast, that thou being shed abroad in our
hearts, we may grow up into thee, and become strong in spiritual
growth, so that we may persevere in the blessed society of thy mystical body, which it is thy will should be so one with thee as thou art
one with the Father in the unity of the Holy Ghost, to whom be praise
and thanksgiving for ever.

Desiderius Erasmus, 1467–1536

906 Blessed be God! and the Father of all mercy! who continueth to pour his benefits upon us. Thou hast elected us, thou hast called us, thou hast justified us, sanctified us, and glorified us; thou wast born for us, and thou livedst and diedst for us: thou hast given us the blessings of this life, and of a better. Oh Lord! thy blessings hang in clusters, they come trooping upon us! they break forth like mighty waters on every side.

And now, Lord, thou hast fed us with the bread of life: so man did eat Angels' food: Oh Lord, bless it: Oh Lord, make it health and strength unto us; still striving and prospering so long within us, until our obedience reach the measure of thy love, who hast done for us as much as may be.

Grant this, dear Father, for thy Son's sake, our only Saviour: to whom with thee, and the Holy Ghost, three Persons, but one most glorious, incomprehensible God, be ascribed all Honour, and Glory, and Praise, ever.

George Herbert, 1593–1633

907   Whether I kneel or stand or sit in prayer,
I am not caught in time nor held in space,
but thrust beyond this posture I am where
time and eternity come face to face;
infinity and space meet in this place
where crossbar and high upright hold the one
in agony and in all Love's embrace.
The power in helplessness that was begun
when all the brilliance of the flaming sun
contained itself in the small confines of a child
now comes to me in this strange action done
in mystery. Break me, break space, O wild
and lovely power. Break me: thus am I dead,
am resurrected now in wine and bread.

Madeleine L'Engle

Glory be to thee, O Jesus, my Lord and my God, for thus feeding my 908
soul with thy most blessed body and blood. Oh, let thy heavenly food
transfuse new life and new vigour into my soul, and into the souls of
all that communicate with me, that our faith may daily increase; that
we may all grow more humble and contrite for our sins; that we may
all love thee and serve thee, and delight in thee, and praise thee more
fervently, more incessantly, then ever we have done heretofore.

Thomas Ken, 1637–1711

Strengthen for service, Lord, the hands that have taken holy things; 909
may the ears which have heard your word be deaf to clamour and dispute; may the tongues which have sung your praise be free from
deceit; may the eyes which have seen the tokens of your love shine
with the light of hope; and may the bodies which have been fed with
your body be refreshed with the fulness of your life; glory to you for
ever.

Malabar Liturgy

O Christ who holds the open gate, 910
O Christ who drives the furrow straight,
O Christ, the plough, O Christ, the laughter
Of holy white birds flying after,
Lo, all my heart's field red and torn,
And Thou wilt bring the young green corn
The young green corn divinely springing,
The young green corn forever singing,
And when the field is fresh and fair
Thy blessed feet shall glitter there
And we will walk the weeded field,
And tell the golden harvest's yield,
The corn that makes the holy bread
By which the soul of man is fed,
The holy bread, the food unpriced,
Thy everlasting mercy, Christ.

John Masefield, 1878–1967

911   Lord, this is thy feast,
        prepared by thy longing,
        spread at thy command,
        attended at thine invitation,
        blessed by thine own Word,
        distributed by thine own hand,
        the undying memorial of thy sacrifice upon the cross,
        the full gift of thine everlasting love,
        and its perpetuation till time shall end.

    Lord, this is Bread of heaven, Bread of life,
        that, whoso eateth, never shall hunger more.
        And this the Cup of pardon, healing, gladness, strength,
        that, whoso drinketh, thirsteth not again.

    So may we come, O Lord, to thy Table;
        Lord Jesus, come to us.
    Eric Milner-White, 1884–1963

912 Just as a grain of wheat must die in the earth in order to bring forth a rich harvest, so your Son died on the cross to bring a rich harvest of love. Just as the harvest of wheat must be ground into flour to make bread, so the suffering of your Son brings us the bread of life. Just as bread gives our bodies strength for our daily work, so the risen body of your Son gives us strength to obey your laws.
    Thomas Münzer, c.1490–1525

913 Come, Lord, in the fullness of your risen presence, and make yourself known to your people again through the breaking of the bread, and the sharing of the cup.
    Robert Runcie

914 Grant, O Lord, we beseech thee, unto thy servants who shall this day commemorate in the holy sacrament the precious death of thy dear Son, and receive the blessed communion of his body and blood, that they may approach thy holy table with true repentance, faith, thankfulness and charity; and being filled with thy grace, and heavenly benediction, may obtain remission of their sins and all other benefits of his passion, through the same Jesus Christ our Lord.
    W. E. Scudamore, 1813–81

In this Holy Sacrifice,   915
may we be redeemed
by the precious Body and Blood
of our Saviour Jesus Christ:
may our lives be made new in him.

In this Holy Eucharist,
in humble thanksgiving
for the life, suffering and resurrection
of our Lord,
may we offer to him
ourselves, our souls and bodies.

In this Holy Communion,
may we be one in the mystical Body of Christ,
united in loving fellowship
with our Lord,
his saints in heaven,
and our fellow Christians everywhere.

In this Holy Communion,
may we be one with all humanity;
may we offer the joy and sorrow,
the good and evil
of all creation.

In this Holy Memorial of the Last Supper,
may we remember with penitence and joy
his great love for us sinners;
may we offer to him our sacrifice
of praise and thanksgiving.

In this Holy Mystery,
may we abide in him
and he in us.

Peter Nott

916

With my heart I worship,
O hidden deity.
Thou dost hide thyself
Beneath these images
In full reality.

My heart submits to thee,
Yea, all my thought:
For contemplating thee,
All else is naught.

I cannot touch, I cannot taste, I cannot see.
All sense is cheated of thee, but the ear.
The Son of God hath spoken: I believe:
For naught hath truth beyond the word I hear.

Upon the cross thy deity was hid,
And here is hidden thy humanity:
Yet here I do acknowledge both and cry,
As the thief cried to thee on Calvary.

I do not gaze, like Thomas, on thy wounds,
But I confess thee God.
Give me a stronger faith, a surer hope,
More love to thee, my Lord.

O thou memorial of the dying Lord,
O living Bread that givest life to men,
Make strong my soul that it may live by thee,
And for all sweetness turn to thee again.

O Christ that gave thy heart to feed thy young,
Cleanse thou my foulness in thy blood was spilt.
One single drop of it would save a world,
A whole world from its guilt.

The veil is on thy face: I cannot see.
I cry to thee for grace,
That I may see thee with thy face unveiled,
And in that vision rest.

Thomas Aquinas, c.1225–74 (attributed)

Almighty, everlasting God, I draw near to the sacrament of your   917
only-begotten Son, our Lord Jesus Christ. I who am sick approach
the physician of life. I who am unclean come to the fountain of mercy;
blind, to the light of eternal brightness; poor and needy to the Lord of
heaven and earth. Therefore, I implore you, in your boundless mercy,
to heal my sickness, cleanse my defilement, enlighten my blindness,
enrich my poverty, and clothe my nakedness.

Then shall I dare to receive the bread of angels, the King of kings
and Lord of lords, with reverence and humility, contrition and love,
purity and faith, with the purpose and intention necessary for the
good of my soul. Grant, I beseech you, that I may receive not only the
Body and Blood of the Lord, but also the grace and power of the sacrament. Most merciful God, enable me so to receive the Body of your
only-begotten Son, our Lord Jesus Christ, which he took from the
Virgin Mary, that I may be found worthy to be incorporated into his
mystical Body, and counted among his members.

Most loving Father, grant that I may one day see face to face your
beloved Son, whom I now intend to receive under the veil of the sacrament, and who with you and the Holy Spirit, lives and reigns for
ever, one God, world without end.

Thomas Aquinas, c.1225–74

Blessed Jesus, who art about to come to us thy unworthy servants in   918
the blessed sacrament of thy body and blood, prepare our hearts, we
beseech thee, for thyself. Grant us that repentance for our past sins,
that faith in the atonement made for them by thee upon the cross, that
full purpose of amendment of life, that perfect love to thee and to all
men, which shall fit us to receive thee. Lord, we are not worthy that
thou shouldest come under our roof, much less that we should receive
thee into ourselves; but since thou didst not disdain to be laid in a
manger amidst unclean beasts, so vouchsafe to enter into our souls and
bodies, unclean though they be through many sins and defilements.

Lord, come to us that thou mayest cleanse us.

Lord, come to us that thou mayest heal us.

Lord, come to us that thou mayest strengthen us.

And grant that having received thee, we may never be separated
from thee by our sins, but may continue thine for ever, till we see thee
face to face in thy heavenly kingdom, where, with the Father and the
Holy Ghost, thou livest and reignest, ever one God, world without end.

Treasury of Devotion, 1869

WEDDINGS

919   Almighty God, in whom we live and move and have our being, look graciously upon the world which you have made and for which your Son gave his life, and especially on all whom you make to be one flesh in holy marriage. May their lives together be a sacrament of your love to this broken world, so that unity may overcome estrangement, forgiveness heal guilt, and joy overcome despair.

Anglican Church of Canada. Alternative Service Book

920
> All praise and glory to you most gracious God,
> for in the beginning you created us men and women.
> Grant your blessing then, we pray, to — and —,
> so that in marriage they may be a source of blessing
> to each other and to all,
> and live together in holy love until their lives' end.

Anglican Church in Aotearoa, New Zealand and Polynesia.
A New Zealand Prayer Book

921
> O God, our Father,
>   whose greatest gift is love,
> bless those, we ask you,
>   who today within your presence
> will take each other in marriage.
>
> We thank you that they have
>   found such love and faith
>   and trust in each other
> that they wish to take each other
>   to have and to hold
>   all the days of their life.
> Let nothing ever come between them,
>   but throughout all the chances
>   and changes of life,

keep them for ever loving
and for ever true.

Keep them from illness,
    from poverty,
    and from all the trouble
    which would hurt them in any way.
But if any trial does come to them,
    grant that it may only drive them
    closer together, and closer to you.

Grant to them through all their days
    the perfect love which many waters
    cannot quench and which is stronger
    than death itself;
through Jesus Christ our Lord.

William Barclay

O God, by whom, in the Gospel, we are all invited to the marriage 922
supper of your Son, so incline the hearts of these your servants that
they may give obedience to your call. Bring them, at the end of their
days, to your banqueting house, and may your banner over them be
always love; through Jesus Christ our Lord.

Worship Now

Most holy and merciful God, by whom the solitary are set in families, 923
we pray that your blessing may remain with — and —, now joined in
your name. May their marriage be for them a source of great and lasting good. Spare them long to each other, and keep them faithful, tender and true, so that they may live together in peace and holiness. In
prosperity may they be grateful to you, the giver of all good; in trouble may they find that you are their refuge and their strength. So lead
them through this life, we pray, that when they have fully served you
in their generation, they may be received into the presence of your
glory; through Jesus Christ our Lord.

Worship Now

924   May peace be yours and peace be yours.
May all that is good and makes for happiness
come upon both of you.
May peace be with you all
and in the whole world.

If you, there in your inaccessible light,
you who are God,
if you see and hear us here,
if we exist for you,
accept then our words of thanksgiving,
this song of great surprise,
on this day which you have made.

We who are simply people
and whose lives are short,
have never seen you,
but we venture to sing your name

and in the words of people
we call you, with the names of centuries
we look for you,
O eternal, living God.
You said, 'Let there be light,'
and the light was born;
you saw that it was good,
the land of the morning,
earth and heaven
and all the vaults of water and fire;
you saw that the trees were good
and all the beasts very good
and all the birds perfect;
then you said, 'O man,'
and man was born;
but you saw man
and that he was lonely
and could not be comforted,
and so created him man and woman;
you changed and directed all paths
so that these two might find each other –
we thank you, God,

for having done it like this
and in no other way.

I ask you, God, complete them and bless them,
make them become more and more human
and let them experience in their bodies
that they are called
to be as good as God to each other,
that they may become more and more
like him who is your image, your Son.

O God, who are greater than all sin, all death,
and who made the sons of men rise again,
you will also never let these two be lost.

Let nothing in them be lost,
because of today.
Keep them alive and let death,
which separates and makes everything dark and empty,
never come upon them.
Let them never tire of each other,
so that they may not falter,
for this world passes,
but love does not pass –
it is like the sea,
flashing like fire and stronger than death.

Keep them together in love,
write their names in the palm of your hand,
write them in your heart,
because of their friends, ourselves,
because of your son, the son of men,
who now lives with you
now and for ever.

Huub Oosterhuis

BIRTHS

925   O Lord God, in whose hands are the issues of life, we thank thee for thy gifts to us at this time. We thank thee for the life given, and the life preserved. And as thou hast knit together life and love in one fellowship, so we pray thee to grant that with this fresh gift of life to us, there may be given an increase of love one to another; through Jesus Christ our Lord.

William Boyd Carpenter, 1841–1918

926   Heavenly Father, how good you are!
How wonderful are your works!
We praise you for all your gifts
and especially for your gift to us
      of this dear child.
We take him/her to our hearts
and welcome him/her to our home
      as a token of your love;
and gratefully we give him/her back to you,
to love and serve you all his/her days,
      in the name of Jesus our Lord.

Frank Colquhoun

927   Heavenly Father, creator and giver of life, there is such joy in our hearts at the news of a baby's birth,
      a most special and complete gift of your love,
      a new being and a wonder of creation.
  Be with the mother and father of this little baby in their happiness, and accept their praise and ours as we give thanks to you, through Jesus Christ our Lord.

Mothers' Union

God our Father, 928
author of eternity,
creator of the highest heaven,
when your Son took our flesh
and was born among us,
the heavens opened and the angels sang.
We now join with them rejoicing in the birth of this child.
We give thanks for his/her safe delivery
and for the beginning of this new life.
We pray that the love which created him/her
may continue to nurture him/her
in home and family.
As he/she grows in stature,
may he/she also grow in grace
and in the knowledge of that love
which you have made known to us
in the person of your son, Jesus Christ our Lord.

Neville Smith

ANNIVERSARIES

Gracious God, on this our special day we remember with thanks- 929
giving our vows of love and commitment to you and to each other in
marriage. We pray for your continued blessing. May we learn from
both our joys and sorrows, and discover new riches in our life
together in you. We ask this in the name of Jesus Christ our Lord.

Anglican Church of Canada. Alternative Service Book

930 God our Father, the birth of your son Jesus Christ brought great joy to Mary and Joseph. We give thanks to you for —, whose birthday we celebrate today. May he/she ever grow in your faith, hope, and love. We ask this in the name of our Lord Jesus Christ.

Anglican Church of Canada. Alternative Service Book

931 O God, our times are in your hands: Look with favour, we pray, on your servant — as he begins another year. Grant that he may grow in wisdom and grace, and strengthen his trust in your goodness all the days of his life; through Jesus Christ our Lord.

Episcopal Church of the United States of America. Book of Common Prayer

932   God's child in Christ adopted, – Christ my all, –
       What that earth boasts were not lost cheaply, rather
       Than forfeit that blest name, by which I call
       The Holy One, the Almighty God, my Father? –
       Father! in Christ we live, and Christ in thee –
       Eternal thou, and everlasting we.
       The heir of heaven, henceforth I fear not death:
       In Christ I live! in Christ I draw the breath
       Of the true life! – Let, then, earth, sea, and sky
       Make war against me! On my front I show
       Their mighty Master's sea. In vain they try
       To end my life, that can but end its woe. –
       Is that a deathbed where a Christian lies? –
       Yes! but not his – 'tis Death itself that dies.

       Samuel Taylor Coleridge, 1772–1834

NEW YEAR

God of all time,
who makes all things new,
we bring before you the year now ending.
For life full and good,
for opportunities recognized and taken,
for love known and shared,
we thank you.

Where we have fallen short,
forgive us.
When we worry over what is past,
free us.

As we begin again
and take our first few steps into the future,
where nothing is safe and certain,
except you,
we ask for the courage of the wise men
who simply went and followed a star.
We ask for their wisdom,
in choosing to pursue the deepest truth,
not knowing where they would be led.
In the year to come, God of all time,
be our help and company.
Hold our hands as we journey onwards
and may your dream of shalom,
where all will be at peace,
be our guiding star.

Francis Brienen

934   Almighty God, who alone art without variableness or shadow of turning, and hast safely brought us through the changes of time to the beginning of another year: we beseech thee to pardon the sins that we have committed in the year which is past; and give us grace that we may spend the remainder of our days to thy honour and glory; through Jesus Christ our Lord.

Church of Ireland. Book of Common Prayer

935   Lord! Father of the Universe
        And Father of all Creatures
        Spirit and Matter
        Today hear if she asks
        The least of your children
        Who loves you from the depths of her heart
        Her happiness to live for ever
        Before you like a child before his father
        With neither pain nor suspicion
        I start a new year
        In the beginning of the springtime.
        What will I be? I am in your hands.
        Respectful? . . . Yes. Obedient? Hardly . . .
        But may your will be done
        And may a morsel of wisdom descend on my old age
        So that my time will not be empty or vain
        Give me love and enlightenment
        Sufficient to share with others who
        Stumble and grope on the Way
        The Way so narrow that leads to eternity . . .

        Anjela Duval

936   Almighty God, by whose mercy my life has been yet prolonged to another year, grant that thy mercy may not be vain. Let not my years be multiplied to increase my guilt, but as age advances, let me become more pure in my thoughts, more regular in my desires, and more obedient to thy laws. Let not the cares of the world distract me, nor the evils of age overwhelm me. But continue and increase thy loving kindness towards me, and when thou shalt call me hence, receive me to everlasting happiness, for the sake of Jesus Christ, our Lord.

Samuel Johnson, 1709–84

My heart for very joy doth leap,   937
My lips no more their silence keep;
I too must sing with joyful tongue
That sweetest ancient cradle-song:

Glory to God in highest heaven,
Who unto man his Son hath given;
While angels sing with pious mirth
A glad new year to all the earth.

Martin Luther, 1483–1546

For all the possibilities ahead in this new year make us thankful, O 938
Lord. Give us wisdom, courage, and discernment in the face of so
much chaos, despair, and fear. Help us to see how, in our circumstances, we can contribute towards peace, faith and love. And give us
the will to translate our desires into actions.

(Brother) John Charles Vockler

O God who changest not with changing years, we, creatures of time, 939
look back along the road we have come. We thank thee for all thy loving kindness and tender mercies along the way. When the road has
been dark thou hast not failed us, though we have often failed thee.
Forgive us and help us to do better.

We look forward, knowing not what may befall in the year that has
just begun. Help us to live a day at a time, to trust thee as much in the
shadow as in the sunshine and to find our way by the light of thy will.

O thou who art both guide and goal, whose companionship is our
stay and strength, go with us, we pray thee, into the New Year and
bring us at last to our journey's end in peace. Through Jesus Christ
our Lord.

Leslie D. Weatherhead, 1883–1975

TIMES OF RETREAT

940   O Lord Jesu Christ, who didst say to thine apostles, come ye apart into a desert place and rest awhile, for there were many coming and going; grant, we beseech thee, to thy servants here gathered together, that they may rest awhile at this present time with thee. May they so seek thee, whom their souls desire to love, that they may both find thee, and be found of thee.

And grant such love and such wisdom to accompany the words which shall be spoken in thy name, that they may not fall to the ground, but may be helpful in leading them onward through the toils of their pilgrimage, to that rest which remaineth to the people of God; where, nevertheless, they rest not day and night from thy perfect service; who with the Father and the Holy Spirit, livest and reignest ever one God, world without end.

Richard Meux Benson, 1824–1915

941   Loving God, look with mercy on your servants who seek in solitude and silence refreshment of soul and strengthening for service; grant them your abundant blessing in the peace of Christ our Lord.

The Daily Office

FUNERALS

May Christ give you rest in the land of the living and open for you the 942
gates of Paradise; may he receive you as a citizen of the kingdom, and
grant you forgiveness of your sins: for you were his friend.

Source unknown (Orthodox funeral rite)

May his soul and the souls of all the departed, through the mercy of 943
God, rest in peace.

Source unknown

O God, whose beloved Son took children into his arms and blessed 944
them, give us grace to entrust — to your never-failing care and love,
and bring us all to your heavenly kingdom; through Jesus Christ our
Lord, who lives and reigns with you and the Holy Spirit, one God,
now and for ever.

Anglican Church of Canada. Alternative Service Book

Depart, O Christian soul, out of this world; 945
In the name of God the Father Almighty who created you;
In the name of Jesus Christ who redeemed you;
In the name of the Holy Spirit who sanctifies you.
May your rest be this day in peace,
and your dwelling place in the Paradise of God.

Episcopal Church of the United States of America. Book of Common Prayer

Deliver your servant, —, O Sovereign Lord Christ, from all evil, and 946
set him/her free from every bond; that he/she may rest with all your
saints in the eternal habitations; where with the Father and the Holy
Spirit you live and reign, one God, for ever and ever.

Episcopal Church of the United States of America. Book of Common Prayer

947 Into your hands, O merciful Saviour, we commend your servant —. Acknowledge, we humbly beseech you, a sheep of your own fold, a lamb of your own flock, a sinner of your own redeeming. Receive him/her into the arms of your mercy, into the blessed rest of everlasting peace, and into the glorious company of the saints in light.

Episcopal Church of the United States of America. Book of Common Prayer

948 O thou Lord of all worlds, we bless thy name for all those who have entered into their rest, and reached the promised land where thou art seen face to face. Give us grace to follow in their footsteps, as they followed in the footsteps of thy holy Son. Keep alive in us the memory of those dear to ourselves whom thou hast called to thyself; and grant that every remembrance which turns our hearts from things seen to things unseen may lead us always upwards to thee, till we come to our eternal rest; through Jesus Christ our Lord.

Fenton John Anthony Hort, 1828–92

949 Almighty God, giver of every good and perfect gift, we praise thee for little children, in whom thou dost come to visit us anew. Receive our humble thanksgiving for the life of him/her whom we this day lay to rest. We bless thee for the gentle appeal of his helplessness and innocence, and for all the love and tenderness he has inspired. And now that, in thine inscrutable wisdom, thou hast called him/her from our side, help us to trust him to thy care in the quiet confidence that knows no fear; through Jesus Christ our Lord.

Methodist Church. Book of Offices

950 Give rest, O Christ, to your servant with your saints: where sorrow and pain are no more; neither sighing, but life everlasting.

You alone are immortal, the creator and maker of man; and we are mortal, formed from the earth, and to the earth we shall return; for you so ordained when you created us, saying, 'Dust you are, and to dust you shall return'; we shall all go down to the dust; and, weeping over the grave, we sing alleluia, alleluia, alleluia.

Give rest, O Christ, to your servant with your saints: where sorrow and pain are no more; neither sighing, but life everlasting.

Russian Liturgy, 6th century

O God, the maker and redeemer of all believers: grant to the soul of   951
thy servant — all the unsearchable benefits of thy Son's passion; that
in the day of his appearing he/she, and all the faithful departed, may
be manifested as thy children; through the same Jesus Christ our
Lord, who liveth and reigneth with thee and the Holy Ghost, one God
world without end.

A Book of Common Prayer, South Africa

We thank thee for all thou givest – for the love that has been ours, of   952
which even death does not deprive us. Teach us to thank thee even for
all thou takest away, and evermore to cry, with Christ, 'Thy will, O
God, be done.'

   Touch us, too, as we stand beside our dead, with thought of all
who are by dying beds or open graves of any dear to their souls. Lift
their hearts and ours to the light above all earth's darkness, to the life
of peace and gladness where thou art. Go with us. Guard and guide,
strengthen and save us through thy love, O Christ. Let us not faint or
fall in following after thee.

Lauchlan Maclean Watt, 1867–1957

---✠---

THE CHRISTIAN YEAR

---✠---

For everything there is a season,

and a time for every matter under heaven.

Ecclesiastes 3.1

ADVENT

You are our eternal salvation, 953
the unfailing life of the world.
Light everlasting,
you are truly our redemption.

Grieving that the human race was perishing
through the tempter's power,
without leaving the heights
you came to the depths in your loving kindness.

Readily taking our humanity by your own gracious will,
you saved all earthly creatures, long since lost,
restoring joy to the world.

Redeem our souls and bodies, O Christ,
and so possess us as your shining dwellings.

By your first coming, make us righteous;
at your second coming, set us free:
so that, when the world is filled with light
and you judge all things,
we may be clad in spotless robes
and follow in your steps, O King,
into the heavenly hall.

Source unknown, 10th century

Keep us, O Lord, while we tarry on this earth, in a serious seeking 954
after thee, and in an affectionate walking with thee, every day of our
lives; that when thou comest, we may be found not hiding our talent,
nor serving the flesh, nor yet asleep with our lamp unfurnished, but
waiting and longing for our Lord, our glorious King, for ever and
ever.

Richard Baxter, 1615–91

955 Wilderness is the place of Moses,
a place of no longer captive and not yet free,
of letting go and learning new living.

Wilderness is the place of Elijah,
a place of silence and loneliness,
of awaiting the voice of God and finding clarity.

Wilderness is the place of John,
a place of repenting,
of taking first steps on the path of peace.

Wilderness is the place of Jesus,
a place of preparation,
of getting ready for the reckless life of faith.

> We thank you, God, for the wilderness.
> Wilderness is our place.
> As we wait for the land of promise,
> teach us the ways of new living,
> lead us to where we hear your word most clearly,
> renew us and clear out the wastelands of our lives,
> prepare us for life in the awareness of Christ's coming
> when the desert will sing
> and the wilderness will blossom as the rose.

Francis Brienen

956 O God our Father, we are preparing to celebrate the birthday of your Son Jesus Christ. While we recall his coming as a tiny baby in weakness and humility, may we be reminded that one day he will come in power and glory.

We make this prayer to you through the same Jesus Christ your Son, who lives and reigns with you in the unity of the Holy Spirit, for ever and ever.

A Catholic Prayer Book

Almighty God, who in many and various ways didst speak to thy cho- 957
sen people by the prophets, and hast given us, in thy Son our Saviour
Jesus Christ, the fulfilment of the hope of Israel: hasten, we beseech
thee, the coming of the day when all things shall be subject to him,
who liveth and reigneth with thee and the Holy Spirit, ever one God,
world without end.

Church of South India

Most gracious Lord, by whose direction this time is appointed for 958
renewing the memory of thy infinite mercy to man in the incarnation
of thy only Son; grant that we may live, this holy time, in the spirit of
thanksgiving, and every day raise up our hearts to thee in the grateful
acknowledgement of what thou hast done for us.

Besides this, we ask thy grace, O God, that we may make a due use
of this holy time, for preparing our souls to receive Christ our Lord
coming into the world at the approaching solemnity of Christmas.

Christ came into the world to do good to all. Grant, O God, we
may thus prepare to meet him. Grant we may be watchful at this time
above all others, in avoiding every thing that can be injurious to our
neighbour, whether in afflicting him, or giving him scandal, or drawing him into sin, or casting any blemish on his reputation; but in all
things, O God, may we follow the spirit of charity, being forward in
bringing comfort and relief to all, as far as their circumstances shall
require, and ours permit.

Grant, O Lord, that we may prepare to meet our redeemer.

John Goter, 17th century

May God the Father, who loved the world so much that he sent his 959
   only Son, give you grace to prepare for eternal life.
May God the Son, who comes to us as Redeemed and Judge, reveal
   to you the path from darkness to light.
May God the Holy Spirit, by whose working the Virgin Mary
   conceived the Christ, help you bear the fruits of holiness.

Michael Perham

CHRISTMAS

960 Let your goodness, Lord, appear to us, that we, made in your image, conform ourselves to it. In our own strength we cannot imitate your majesty, power and wonder; nor is it fitting for us to try. But your mercy reaches from the heavens, through the clouds, to the earth below. You have come to us as a small child, but you have brought us the greatest of all gifts, the gift of eternal love. Caress us with your tiny hands, embrace us with your tiny arms, and pierce our hearts with your soft, sweet cries.

Bernard of Clairvaux, 1090–1153

961 O God the Son, highest and holiest, who didst humble thyself to share our birth and our death: Bring us with the shepherds and wise men to kneel before thy lowly cradle, that we may come to sing with thine angels thy glorious praises in heaven; where with the Father and the Holy Spirit thou livest and reignest God, world without end.

Frank Colquhoun

962 Lord Jesus, this Christmas as we sing the familiar carols, hear the familiar readings and ponder on familiar mysteries, give to us the gift of pure worship – that ability which Mary had of attributing to you your true worth, your full value, your inestimable greatness.

Teach us to be reverent; yet teach us how to express the love that burns within our hearts as we think of your goodness to us – that you have come to be our light in darkness, our hope in despair, our strength in weakness, our shelter in the storm – yes, and our eternal Saviour.

Joyce Huggett

The feast day of your birth resembles you, Lord,   963
Because it brings joy to all humanity.
Old people and infants alike enjoy your day.
Your day is celebrated from generation to generation.
Kings and emperors may pass away,
And the festivals to commemorate them soon lapse.
But your festival will be remembered till the end of time.
Your day is a means and a pledge of peace.
At your birth heaven and earth were reconciled,
Since you came from heaven to earth on that day
You forgave our sins and wiped away our guilt.
You gave us so many gifts on your birthday:
A treasure chest of spiritual medicines for the sick;
Spiritual light for those that are blind;
The cup of salvation for the thirsty;
The bread of life for the hungry.
In the winter when trees are bare,
You give us the most succulent spiritual fruit.
In the frost when the earth is barren,
You bring new hope to our souls.
In December when seeds are hidden in the soil,
The staff of life springs forth from the virgin womb.

Ephraim the Syrian, c.306–373

Sweet Child of Bethlehem, grant that we may share with all our   964
hearts in this profound mystery of Christmas. Pour into the hearts of
men the peace which they sometimes seek so desperately, and which
you alone can give them. Help them to know one another better and
to live as brothers, children of the same Father. Awaken in their
hearts love and gratitude for your infinite goodness; join them
together in your love; and give us all your heavenly peace.

(Pope) John XXIII, 1881–1963

965   Glory be to God in the highest, and on earth peace, goodwill towards men; for unto us is born a Saviour, who is Christ the Lord.

We praise thee, we bless thee, we glorify thee, we give thanks unto thee for this greatest of thy mercies, O Lord God, heavenly king, God the Father almighty.

O Lord, the only-begotten Son, Jesus Christ. O Lord God, Lamb of God, Son of the Father, who wast made man to take away the sins of the world, have mercy upon us by turning us from our iniquities. Thou, who wast made manifest to destroy the works of the devil, have mercy upon us by enabling us to renounce and forsake them. Thou who art the great advocate with the Father, receive our prayer we humbly beseech thee.

Thomas Ken, 1637–1711

966   We thought we knew where to find you;
we hardly needed a star to guide the way,
just perseverance and common sense;
why do you hide yourself away from the powerful
and join the refugees and outcasts,
calling us to follow you there?
   Wise God, give us wisdom.

We thought we had laid you safe in the manger;
we wrapped you in the thickest sentiment we could find,
and stressed how long ago you came to us;
why do you break upon us in our daily life
with messages of peace and goodwill,
demanding that we do something about it?
   Just and righteous God, give us justice and righteousness.

So where else would we expect to find you
but in the ordinary place with the faithful people,
turning the world to your purpose through them.
Bring us to that manger, to that true rejoicing,
which will make wisdom, justice and righteousness alive in us.

Stephen Orchard

Merciful and most loving God, by whose will and bountiful gift thine 967
eternal Son humbled himself that he might exalt mankind, and
became flesh that he might renew in us the divine image: perfect us in
thy likeness, and bring us at last to rejoice in beholding thy beauty,
and, with all thy saints, to glorify thy grace; through the same Jesus
Christ our Lord.

Prayers for the Christian Year

May the joy of the angels, 968
the eagerness of the shepherds,
the perseverance of the wise men,
the obedience of Joseph and Mary,
and the peace of the Christ child
   be yours this Christmas.
And the blessing of God almighty, the Father, the Son and the Holy
Spirit, be upon you and remain with you always.

The Promise of His Glory

Almighty and everlasting God, you have stooped to raise fallen 969
humanity by the child-bearing of blessed Mary; grant that we who
have seen your glory revealed in our human nature, and your love
made perfect in our weakness, may daily be renewed in your image,
and conformed to the pattern of your Son, Jesus Christ our Lord.

David Silk

O Lord our God, as we celebrate again the festival of Christmas, we 970
ask you to make us humble and loving like Jesus, who did not come to
be served but to serve, and who said that it is better to give than to
receive; so that, in his name, we may devote ourselves to the care and
service of all those who are in need. We ask this through the same
Jesus Christ, our Lord.

Stephen S. Smalley

971 O God, our loving Father, help us rightly to remember the birth of Jesus, that we may share in the songs of the angels, the gladness of the shepherds, and the worship of the wise men. May the Christmas morning make us happy to be thy children, and the Christmas evening bring us to our beds with grateful thoughts, forgiving and forgiven, for Jesus' sake.

Robert Louis Stevenson, 1850–94

972 We pray thee, O Lord, to purify our hearts that they may be worthy to become thy dwelling place. Let us never fail to find room for thee, but come and abide in us that we also may abide in thee, who as at this time wast born into the world for us, and dost live and reign, King of kings and Lord of lords, now and for evermore.

William Temple, 1881–1944

973 Into this holy place at this happy time, O Lord, we come to worship that little child whose nature revealed thine own and what ours might become. We ask that the lovely things in his nature may grow in us and that all things hostile to his spirit may die. For his name's sake.

Leslie D. Weatherhead, 1883–1975

974 God of love, open the hearts and minds of many this Christmas time to the good and saving news of Jesus Christ; that those whose lives are insecure, or empty, or aimless, may find in the one born at Bethlehem all that they need today, and much more besides. For his name's sake.

Worship Now

EPIPHANY

God of gold, we seek your glory: 975
    the richness that transforms our drabness into colour,
    and brightens our dullness with vibrant light;
your wonder and joy at the heart of all life.

God of incense, we offer you our prayer:
    our spoken and unspeakable longings, our questioning of truth,
    our search for your mystery deep within.

God of myrrh, we cry out to you in our suffering:
    the pain of all our rejections and bereavements,
    our baffled despair at undeserved suffering,
    our rage at continuing injustice;
and we embrace you, God-with-us,
    in our wealth, in our yearning, in our anger and loss.

Jan Berry

O God, our Father, Creator of the universe, whose Son, Jesus Christ, 976
came to our world, pour your Holy Spirit upon your Church, that all
the people of our world, being led through the knowledge of your
truth to worship you, may offer the gold of intellect, the frankincense
of devotion and the myrrh of discipline to him who is with you and
the Holy Spirit who liveth and reigneth forever one God, world without end.

Church of Ceylon (Sri Lanka)

O God, who by a star guided the wise men to the worship of your 977
Son; we pray you to lead to yourself the wise and the great of every
land, that unto you every knee may bow, and every thought be
brought into captivity through Jesus Christ our Lord.

Church in Jerusalem and Middle East

978 Almighty God, who hast manifested thy Son Jesus Christ to be a light to mankind: grant that we thy people, being nourished by thy Word and sacraments, may be strengthened to show forth to all men the unsearchable riches of Christ, so that he may be known, adored and obeyed, to the ends of the earth; who liveth and reigneth with thee and the Holy Spirit, one God, world without end.

Church of South India

979
       Lord Jesus, may your light shine upon our way,
       as once it guided the steps of the magi:
       that we too may be led into your presence
       and worship you,
          the Child of Mary,
          the Word of the Father,
          the King of nations,
          the Saviour of mankind;
       to whom be glory for ever.

Frank Colquhoun

980 O God, by the leading of a star you manifested your only Son to the peoples of the earth. Lead us, who know you now by faith, to your holy presence, where we may see your glory face to face; through Jesus Christ our Lord.

Episcopal Church in the United States of America. Book of Common Prayer

981 O God, who by the shining of a star didst guide the wise men to behold thy Son, our Lord: show us thy heavenly light, and give us grace to follow until we find him, and, finding him, rejoice. And grant that as they presented gold, frankincense, and myrrh, we now may bring him the offering of a loving heart, an adoring spirit, and an obedient will; for his honour, and for thy glory, O God most high.

Prayers for the Christian Year

ASH WEDNESDAY

Lord, for our sake you fought and overcame the temptations in the   982
wilderness. We pray that we may have the strength to fight against
our enemy the devil. Be with us today in our thoughts and plans to
spread your word to all lands, through Jesus Christ our Lord.

Anglican Church of Papua New Guinea

O Lord of grace, lead us and guide us from a life of self-centredness   983
and satisfaction for what we are and what we do to a life of dependence on you. Inspire our hearts that we rise beyond the daily trifles
of our existence and join with you in love and concern of the whole
creation, that we may always remind ourselves that we are the disciples of one who did not help himself but was a man for others.
Grant that we may, through our life and example, work for a world
where God is praised and we all live like salt and leaven in the midst
of this mass of humanity and in a bond of charity. O God the Holy
Spirit, inspire, hallow and guide us in this vocation of wholeness and
healing, through Jesus Christ our Lord.

Church of Bangladesh

Almighty and everlasting God,   984
you hate nothing that you have made
and forgive the sins of all those who are penitent.
Create and make in us new and contrite hearts,
that, lamenting our sins
and acknowledging our wretchedness,
we may receive from you, the God of all mercy,
perfect forgiveness and peace;
through Jesus Christ our Lord.

Church of England. The Alternative Service Book 1980
(adapted from the Book of Common Prayer)

985   O God,
        you have made us for yourself,
        and against your longing there is no defence.
        Mark us with your love,
        and release in us a passion for your justice
        in our disfigured world;
        that we may turn from our guilt and face you,
        our heart's desire.

        Janet Morley

986   May God the Father, who does not despise the broken spirit,
            give to you a contrite heart.
        May Christ, who bore our sins in his body on the tree,
            heal you by his wounds.
        May the Holy Spirit, who leads us into all truth,
            speak to you words of pardon and peace.

        Michael Perham

LENT

987   Lord God almighty, grant your people grace to withstand the tempta-
        tions of the world, the flesh, and the devil, and with pure hearts and
        minds to follow you, the only God; through Jesus Christ, our Lord.

        Church of England. The Alternative Service Book 1980
        (adapted from the Book of Common Prayer)

988   Joy with peace, amendment of life, time for true repentance, the grace
        and comfort of the Holy Spirit, and perseverance in good works,
        grant us, O almighty and merciful Lord.

        Enriching the Christian Year

Grant, we beseech thee, O Lord, that by the observance of this Lent 989
we may advance in the knowledge of the mystery of Christ, and show
forth his mind in conduct worthy of our calling; through Jesus Christ
our Lord.

Gelasian Sacramentary, 5th century

You, Lord Jesus, knew great power, 990
to heal, to transform,
to proclaim the reign of God.
So you met great temptations.
The wrong way, glittering and possible, was open;
you could rule if you chose,
in majesty and wonder,
more victorious than Alexander,
more imperial than Caesar.
But you said No,
simply, decisively, for ever, for us.

We pray for the Church, tempted like its Head.
When the Church seeks political power,
Jesus, stay with us.
When the Church longs to become wealthy,
Jesus, speak to us.
When the Church strives to impress with splendour,
Jesus, give us simplicity.
When the Church wanders from the way of sacrifice,
Jesus, hold us.
When the Church listens to the call for cheap grace,
Jesus, keep us always in your way.

Holy Spirit of God, enable us to respond to temptation
with the strength of your Word within us,
so that we may hold firm to our calling
and take your better way in faithfulness.

Bernard Thorogood

991   O Lord and heavenly Father, who hast given unto us thy people the true bread that cometh down from heaven, even thy Son Jesus Christ: grant that throughout this Lent our souls may so be fed by him that we may continually live in him and he in us; and that day by day we may be renewed in the spirit by the power of his endless life, who gave himself for us, and now liveth and reigneth with thee and the Holy Spirit, one God, for ever and ever.

Frederick B. Macnutt, 1873–1949

992   As the days lengthen and the earth spends longer in the light of day, grant that I may spend longer in the light of your presence, O Lord, and may those seeds of your Word, which have been long-buried within me, grow, like everything around us, into love for you, and love for people; to become a visible declaration of your Lordship in my life. Grant, Father, that this Lent there may be a springtime for my life in Christ.

Dick Williams

MOTHERING SUNDAY

993   Thank you, Lord, for our mothers. We remember today their loving care, and their ceaseless love for us. May we show them by our gifts, our words and our actions that we love them and care about them too.

Father, we thank you for the family of the Church. May they know your blessing and strength as they care for others.

Mary Batchelor

May we obey like Mary and work hard like Joseph, and may the 994
childlike joy and devotion and love of Jesus be with us as we continue
to grow in the grace and knowledge of our Lord and Saviour, to
whom be glory now and for all eternity.

Trevor Lloyd

God our mother, 995
you hold our life within you,
nourish us at your breast,
and teach us to walk alone.
Help us so to receive your tenderness
and respond to your challenge
that others may draw life from us,
in your name.

Janet Morley

Motherhood was never easy, 996
not for Mary, not for us.
There's longing in it, waiting, pain,
hard work and tight budgets.
But you, creating God, come that way,
lighting with glory the bond of trust
    and humble devotion.
Speak to us, God, through our mothers
    that we may know your steadfast love.

Bernard Thorogood

PALM SUNDAY

997 Jesus, King of the universe,
ride on in humble majesty:

Lord, this Palm Sunday may I recognize in you the Lord who comes
to his world, and join with full heart in the children's 'hosanna'.

Ride on, through conflict and debate,
ride on through sweaty prayer and betrayal of friends:

Lord, this Palm Sunday forgive me my evasions of truth, my carelessness of your honour; my weakness which leave me sleeping even
while in others you suffer and are anguished; my cowardice that does
not risk the consequences of publicly acknowledging you as Lord.

Ride on to the empty tomb and your rising in triumph,
Ride on to raise up your Church, a new body for your service;
Ride on, King Jesus, to renew the whole earth in your image,
in compassion come to help us.

Source unknown (India)

998 Let the mountains and all the hills
Break out into great rejoicing at the mercy of God,
And let the trees of the forest clap their hands.
Give praise to Christ, all nations,
Magnify him, all peoples, crying:
Glory to thy power, O Lord.

Seated in heaven upon thy throne
And on earth upon a foal, O Christ our God,
Thou hast accepted the praise of the angels
And the songs of the children who cried out to thee:
Blessed art thou that comest to call back Adam.

Source unknown (Eastern Orthodox)

O Christ, the King of glory, who didst enter the holy city in meekness 999
to be made perfect through the suffering of death: give us grace, we
beseech thee, in all our life here to take up our cross daily and follow
thee, that hereafter we may rejoice with thee in thy heavenly kingdom; who livest and reignest with the Father and the Holy Spirit,
God, world without end.

Church of South India

As on this day we keep the special memory of our redeemer's entry 1000
into the city, so grant, O Lord, that now and ever he may triumph in
our hearts. Let the king of grace and glory enter in, and let us lay ourselves and all we are in full joyful homage before him; through the
same Jesus Christ our Lord.

Handley C. G. Moule, 1841–1920

MAUNDY THURSDAY

Lord Jesus Christ, who when thou wast able to institute thy holy sac- 1001
rament at the Last Supper, didst wash the feet of the apostles, and
teach us by thy example the grace of humility: cleanse us, we beseech
thee, from all stain of sin, that we may be worthy partakers of thy
holy mysteries; who livest and reignest with the Father and the Holy
Ghost, one God, world without end.

Church of England (Office of the Royal Maundy in Westminster Abbey, adapted)

1002
Servant Jesus,
    what love you showed to your disciples
      and what humility in your service.
You are the Lord of life, Son of God,
    yet you stooped down
      to take off the grimy sandals
      and to wash their dusty feet.
With loving care you dried them with the towel
    making them fresh and cool.
Since you, our Lord and Saviour,
    did such lowly service for us,
    ought we not humbly to serve others also?

Lord God,
    it is not easy to walk in your way
      when we seek peace among the nations.
We find there are many who hate peace
    and prefer to seek the victory in war.
Even amongst our neighbours and friends
    are those who want to prepare for war.
I am for peace;
    but when I speak, they are for war.
In my distress I call to you, O Lord;
    give me the courage and the faith
      to speak for peace.

Spirit of God,
    you call your people to patient endurance
      that we might not fail in time of testing,
      that we might not grow weary in well-doing,
      that we should not abandon our first love.
Help us to find our constant inspiration in you
    that the lamp may be kept burning
      as we witness by your grace.

John Johansen-Berg

1003   Lord Christ, our Servant and Saviour, on earth you washed the feet of
your disciples, and now through your cross and resurrection you
always live to make intercession for us: give us grace to be your faithful disciples and servants to our lives' end; for your name's sake.

Stephen S. Smalley

GOOD FRIDAY

Lord Jesus, who on this holy day of thy passion didst stretch out thine   *1004*
arms upon the hard wood of the cross, that all men might be brought
within their saving embrace; draw us unto thyself with the bands of
thy love, that we may be found of thee and find thee; and grant that,
evermore being bound unto thee as thy faithful servants, we may take
up our cross daily and follow thee, and at last attain to thine eternal
joy; who livest and reignest with the Father and the Holy Spirit,
world without end.

Source unknown

Walking alone, Lord, you go to your sacrifice,   *1005*
victim of death, and our death's mighty conqueror.
What can we say to you, knowing our poverty,
you, who have freed us from sin and from slavery?

Ours are the sins, Lord, and we are the guilty ones,
you, in your innocence, take on our punishment;
grant that our spirits may share in your suffering,
may our compassion respond to your pardoning.

Three sacred days are the time of our sorrowing,
as we endure now the night of our heaviness,
until the morning restores to us joyfulness;
Christ, newly risen, brings gladness for tearfulness.

Grant us, O Lord, to take part in your suffering,
that we may share in your heavenly victory;
through these sad days living humbly and patiently,
may we at Eastertide see you smile graciously.

Peter Abelard, 1079–1142

1006
From the foot of the cross I look up to thee
O Jesus Lord bow down to me.
For I stand in the faith of my God today
Put love in my heart and hope alway.

Source unknown (Early Scottish)

1007 We adore thee, O Christ, and we bless thee, because by thy cross thou
hast redeemed the world.

Source unknown

1008 Thou whose eternal love for our weak and struggling race was most
perfectly shown forth in the blessed life and death of Jesus Christ our
Lord, enable me now so to meditate upon my Lord's passion that,
having fellowship with him in his sorrow, I may also learn the secret
of his strength and peace.

John Baillie, 1886–1960

1009
May the Lord be my friend,
Who once on earth endured on the gallows-tree
Suffered here for the sins of men.
He has redeemed us, he has given us life
And a home in Heaven. Hope was renewed
With bliss and blessing for those who had been
   through burning.
The Son was successful in that expedition,
Mighty in victory, when with a mass,
A great crowd of souls, came to God's kingdom
The Almighty Ruler, to joy among the angels
And all the saints, who in heaven already
Lived in glory, then the Lord,
Almighty God, came home to his own land.

The Dream of the Rood, 8th century

By your wounded hands: 1010
  teach us diligence and generosity.
By your wounded feet:
  teach us steadfastness and perseverance.
By your wounded and insulted head
  teach us patience, clarity and self-mastery.
By your wounded heart:
  teach us love, teach us love, teach us love,
    O Master and Saviour.

Daphne Fraser

Lord Jesus Christ, Son of the living God, who for our redemption wil- 1011
ledst to be born, and on the cross to die the most shameful of deaths,
do thou by thy death and passion deliver us from all sins and penal-
ties, and by thy holy cross bring us, miserable sinners, to that place
where thou livest and reignest with the Father and the Holy Spirit,
ever one God, world without end.

(Pope) Innocent III, c.1161–1216

Great God, our Father: as we call to mind the scene of Christ's suffer- 1012
ing in Gethsemane, our hearts are filled with penitence and shame
that we foolishly waste our time in idleness and that we make no progress in the Christian life from day to day . . . We are ashamed that
war and lust flourish and grow more rampant every day. Forgive us
for our cruel indifference to the cross, and pardon us that, like the
bystanders of old, we merely stand and gaze in idle curiosity upon the
piteous scene. O teach us, we beseech thee, the good news of thy forgiveness. Cause humanity, degenerate as it is, to live anew, and hasten the day when the whole world shall be born again.

Toyohiko Kagawa, 1888–1960

Let us pray to the Father, who loved the world so much that he sent 1013
  his only Son to give us life.

Simon from Cyrene was forced to carry the cross for your Son.
Give us grace to lift heavy loads off those we meet and to put
  ourselves with those condemned to die.

Lord, hear us.
Lord, graciously hear us.

Your Son watched the soldiers gamble to share his clothes.
Look with your forgiveness on those who make a profit from their
victims, and on those whose hearts may be hardened by their work.

Lord, hear us.
Lord, graciously hear us.

The thief looked for a part in the coming of your kingdom, and
received your Son's words of hope and comfort.
Give hope and reconciliation, healing and peace to all who look
death in the face today.

Lord, hear us.
Lord, graciously hear us.

In Mary and John your Son created a new family at the cross.
Fill our relationships, and those of new families today, with mutual
care and responsibility, and give us a secure hope for the future.

Lord, hear us.
Lord, graciously hear us.

The centurion was astonished to see your glory in the crucified
Messiah.
Open the eyes of those who are not yet your people to see in your Son
the meaning of life and death.

Lord, hear us.
Lord, graciously hear us.

Nicodemus came to take your Son's body away.
Give gentleness, hope and faith to all who minister to the dying and
bereaved, and courage to those whose faith is secret.

Lord, hear us.
Lord, graciously hear us.

Simon and Nicodemus, Mary and John became part of your Church
in Jerusalem.
May your Church today be filled with such different people, united
by the cross, and celebrating our unity in your Son with all your
saints in glory.

Lord of the Church,
*Hear our prayer, and make us one in heart and mind to serve you in
Christ our Lord.*

Trevor Lloyd

Let us recall the words Jesus spoke from the cross.
Father, forgive them: for they know not what they do.
We thank you, Father, that Jesus did as he told others to do, and forgave those who wronged him. Help us to forgive others from our
heart. And forgive our world for still committing acts of great cruelty.

Truly, I say to you, today you will be with me in Paradise.
We thank you, Father, that Jesus gave this assurance to a man con-
vinced he deserved to die. Awaken us and all siners to a true understanding of what we are and what we have done. But give us, too, the
same assurance, that whatever we have done nothing can separate us
from your love.

Woman, behold your son. Behold your mother.
We thank you, Father, that Jesus thought of others even when dying.
Deliver us from self-pity, from brooding on our own wrongs and misfortunes. Help us to be like Christ to our neighbour, acting as Jesus
would act, mediating your love.

My God, my God, why have you forsaken me?
We thank you, Father, that Jesus was fully human, and no stranger to
the anguish of despair. Help us also through the dark times, so that
we may emerge with faith strengthened.

I am thirsty.
We thank you, Father, that someone answered this cry. Help us to
answer the cry of those in our world who are hungry.

It is finished.
We thank you, Father, that Jesus died believing he had done your will
and accomplished your work. May we too be single-minded, and when
we die not need to regret that we have squandered your gift of life.

Father, into your hands I commit my spirit.
We thank you, Father, that Jesus died trusting fully in you. May all
Christians have the same confidence in the hour of death. May we
know that Jesus has conquered death for us all.

Caryl Micklem

1015

Thou art my God, sole object of my love;
Not for hope of endless joys above;
Not for the fear of endless pains below,
Which they who love thee must not undergo.
For me, and such as me, thou deignst to bear
An ignominious cross, the nails, the spear;
A thorny crown transpierced thy sacred brow,
While bloody sweats from every member flow.
For me in tortures thou resignst thy breath,
Embraced me on the cross, and saved me by death.
And can these sufferings fail my heart to move?
Such as then was, and is, thy love to me,
Such is, and shall be still, my love to thee –
To thee, Redeemer! mercy's sacred spring!
My God, my Father, Maker, and my King!

Alexander Pope, 1688–1744

1016

Tell Us

We have had names for you:
The Thunderer, the Almighty
Hunter, Lord of the snowflake
and the sabre-toothed tiger.
One name we have held back
unable to reconcile it
with the mosquito, the tidal wave,
the black hole into which
time will fall. You have answered
us with the image of yourself
on a hewn tree, suffering
injustice, pardoning it;
pointing as though in either
direction; horrifying us
with the possibility of dislocation.
Ah, love, with your arms out
wide, tell us how much more
they must still be stretched
to embrace a universe drawing
away from us at the speed of light.

R. S. Thomas

The Way of the Cross

First station: Jesus is condemned to death

O innocent Jesus, who with wonderful submission wast for our sakes condemned to die. Grant that we may bear in mind that our sins were the false-witnesses; our blasphemies, backbitings, and evil speakings were the cause of thy accepting with gladness the sentence of the impious judge. O may this thought touch our hearts and make us hate those sins which caused thy death.

Second station: Jesus receives his cross

O blessed Jesus, grant us by virtue of thy cross and bitter passion, cheerfully to submit to and willingly to embrace all the trials and difficulties of this our earthly pilgrimage, and may we be always ready to take up our cross daily and follow thee.

Third station: Jesus falls under the weight of the cross

O Jesus, who for our sins didst bear the heavy burden of the cross and didst fall under its weight, may the thought of thy sufferings, make us watchful against temptation, and do thou stretch out thy sacred hand to help us lest we fall into any grievous sin.

Fourth station: The cross is laid upon Simon of Cyrene

O Jesus! I thank thee, that thou hast permitted me to suffer with thee, may it be my privilege to bear my cross, may I glory in nothing else; by it may the world be crucified unto me, and I unto the world, may I never shrink from suffering, but rather rejoice, if I be counted worthy to suffer for thy name's sake.

Fifth station: Jesus speaks to the women of Jerusalem

O Lord Jesus, we mourn and will mourn both for thee and for ourselves; for thy sufferings, and for our sins which caused them. Oh, teach us so to mourn, that we may be comforted, and escape those dreadful judgments prepared for all those who reject or neglect thee.

Sixth station: Jesus is stripped of his garments

O Lord Jesus! Thou didst suffer shame for our most shameful deeds. Take from us, we beseech thee, all false shame, conceit, and pride, and make us so to humble ourselves in this life, that we may escape everlasting shame in the life to come.

Seventh station: Jesus is nailed to the cross
O Jesus! Crucified for me, subdue my heart with thy holy fear and love, and since my sins were the cruel nails that pierced thee, grant that in sorrow for my past life I may pierce and nail to thy cross all that offends thee.

Eighth station: Jesus hangs on the cross
O Jesus! we devoutly embrace that honoured cross, where thou didst love us even unto death. In thy death is all our hope. Henceforth let us live only unto thee, so that whether we live or die we may be thine.

Ninth station: Jesus is taken down from the cross
O Lord Jesus, grant that we may never refuse that cross, which thou hast laid upon us: who willed not to be taken down from the cross, until thou hadst accomplished the work which thou camest to do.

Tenth station: Jesus is laid in the sepulchre
O Jesus, most compassionate Lord, we adore thee dead and enclosed in the holy sepulchre. We desire to enclose thee within our hearts, that, united to thee, we may rise to newness of life, and by the gift of final perseverance die in thy grace.

Treasury of Devotion, 1869

1018　O Jesus, poor and abject, unknown and despised, have mercy upon me, and let me not be ashamed to follow thee.

　　O Jesus, hated, calumniated, and persecuted, have mercy upon me, and make me content to be as my master.

　　O Jesus, blasphemed, accused, and wrongfully condemned, have mercy upon me, and teach me to endure the contradiction of sinners.

　　O Jesus, clothed with a habit of reproach and shame, have mercy upon me, and let me not seek my own glory.

　　O Jesus, insulted, mocked, and spit upon, have mercy upon me, and let me not faint in the fiery trial.

　　O Jesus, crowned with thorns and hailed in derision;

　　O Jesus, burdened with our sins and the curses of the people;

　　O Jesus, affronted, outraged, buffeted, overwhelmed with injuries, griefs and humiliations;

　　O Jesus, hanging on the accursed tree, bowing the head, giving up the ghost, have mercy upon me, and conform my whole soul to thy holy, humble, suffering Spirit.

John Wesley, 1703–91

Lord! when thou didst thy self undress   *1019*
Laying by thy robes of glory,
To make us more, thou wouldst be less,
And becamest a woeful story.

To put on clouds instead of light,
And clothe the morning-star with dust,
Was a translation of such height
As, but in thee, was ne'r expressed;

Brave worms, and earth! that thus could have
A God enclosed within your cell,
Your maker pent up in a grave,
Life locked in death, heaven in a shell;

Ah, my dear Lord! what couldst thou spy
In this impure, rebellious clay,
That made thee thus resolve to die
For those that kill thee every day?

O what strange wonders could thee move
To slight thy precious blood, and breath!
Sure it was love, my Lord; for love
Is only stronger far than death.

Henry Vaughan, 1621–1695

O God, as on this solemn day we bow at the foot of the cross, may the   *1020*
love that was manifested there stream into our hearts, challenging
and subduing them and winning from us that response which is thy
will for us. Through Jesus Christ our Lord.

Leslie D. Weatherhead, 1883–1975

1021 *At 9 o'clock*

O Lord Jesus Christ, Son of the living God, who from the bosom of the Father didst descend from the heavens to the earth, and on the wood of the cross didst suffer five wounds, and shed thy precious blood for the remission of our sins: we meekly beseech thee that, in the day of judgment, we may be set on thy right hand, and hear thy joyful sentence, 'Come, ye blessed of my Father, enjoy ye the kingdom prepared for you from the foundation of the world'; where with the Father and the Holy Ghost thou livest and reignest, God, for ever and ever.

John Hilsey, Prymer, 1539

1022 *At noon*

O Lord Jesus Christ, Son of the living God, who, at the sixth hour of the day, didst with great tumult ascend on Golgotha the Cross of pain; whereon, thirsting for our salvation, thou didst permit gall and vinegar to be given thee to drink: we beseech thee that thou wouldest kindle and inflame our hearts with the love of thy Passion, and make us to find our delight in thee alone, our crucified Lord; who livest and reignest God, world without end.

John Hilsey, Prymer, 1539

1023 *At 3 o'clock*

Hear us, O merciful Lord Jesus Christ, and remember now the hour in which thou didst commend thy blessed spirit into the hands of thy heavenly Father; and so assist us by this thy most precious death, that, being dead unto the world, we may live only unto thee; and that, at the hour of our departing from this mortal life, we may be received into thine everlasting kingdom, there to reign with thee, world without end.

John Cosin, 1594–1672

EASTER

O Lord God, our Father. You are the light that can never be put out; 1024 and now you give us a light that shall drive away all darkness. You are love without coldness, and you have given us such warmth in our hearts that we can love all when we meet. You are the life that defies death, and you have opened for us the way that leads to eternal life.

None of us is a great Christian; we are all humble and ordinary. But your grace is enough for us. Arouse in us that small degree of joy and thankfulness of which we are capable, to the timid faith which we can muster, to the cautious obedience which we cannot refuse, and thus to the wholeness of life which you have prepared for all of us through the death and resurrection of your Son. Do not allow any of us to remain apathetic or indifferent to the wondrous glory of Easter, but let the light of our risen Lord reach every corner of our dull hearts.

Karl Barth, 1886–1968

Christ is now risen again 1025
From his death and all his pain:
Therefore will we merry be,
And rejoice with him gladly.
> *Kyrieleison.*

Had he not risen again,
We had been lost, this is plain:
But since he is risen in deed,
Let us love him all with speed.
> *Kyrieleison.*

Now is a time of gladness,
To sing of the Lord's goodness:
Therefore glad now will we be,
And rejoice in him only.
> *Kyrieleison.*

Miles Coverdale, 1488–1568

1026   O Lord, who by triumphing over the power of darkness, didst prepare our place in the New Jerusalem, grant us who have this day given thanks for thy resurrection to praise thee in that city whereof thou art the light, where with the Father and the Holy Spirit thou livest and reigneth, world without end.

William Bright, 1824–1901

1027   Almighty God, our Father, you have redeemed us by the death and resurrection of your only Son Jesus Christ and given us your Holy Spirit that we may be your witnesses in the world: banish the powers of darkness and sin from the minds of those who refuse to believe in your name and open their hearts to your gospel that they may believe in you and become temples of your Holy Spirit. Grant also that we who believe in you may be effective ministers of your Word to those whose lives have not been touched by your saving grace. We make this prayer through our Lord Jesus Christ who reigns with you and the Holy Spirit, one God for ever and ever.

Church in Korea

1028

Christ is risen:
    The world below lies desolate.
Christ is risen:
    The spirits of evil are fallen.
Christ is risen:
    The angels of God are rejoicing.
Christ is risen:
    The tombs of the dead are empty.
Christ is risen indeed from the dead,
    The first of the sleepers.
Glory and power are his forever and ever.

Hippolytus of Rome, c.190–c.236

1029   God Almighty, we praise your holy name in this joyful Eastertide. We thank you, Lord, because through your death and resurrection we have won the victory and your redeeming grace and love. Loving Father God, fill us with new life so that we may love one another and do what you want us to do in sharing your love with those who don't know you. In Jesus' name we pray.

Mothers' Union

Christ our life,

you are alive
> in the beauty of the earth
> in the rhythm of the seasons
> in the mystery of time and space
> *Alleluia*

Christ our life,
you are alive
> in the tenderness of touch
> in the heartbeat of intimacy
> in the insights of solitude
> *Alleluia*

Christ our life,
you are alive
> in the creative possibility
> of the dullest conversation
> the dreariest task
> the most threatening event
> *Alleluia*

Christ our life,
you are alive
> to offer re-creation
> to every unhealed hurt
> to every deadened place
> to every damaged heart
> *Alleluia*

You set before us a great choice.
Therefore we choose life.
The dance of resurrection soars and surges
  through the whole creation.
It sets gifts of bread and wine upon our table.
This is grace, dying we live.
So let us live.

Kathy Galloway (Iona Community)

1031

Listen to the sounds of earth's resurrection,
as a solitary blackbird heralds the dawn
calling his fellows to sing out a chorus
in glad celebration of light and life reborn.

The sun has risen. Let us greet the day. Alleluia!

Listen to the sounds of Christ's Resurrection,
as the earth trembles and the stone is rolled away,
as women take courage to tell their good news
no longer fearful of what anyone might say.

Christ has risen. The stone is rolled away. Alleluia!

Listen to the sounds of faith's resurrection,
in the thud of racing heartbeats and running feet.
In word tumbling over word in their eagerness
to announce love's vindication and death's defeat.

Christ has risen. He has given us the victory. Alleluia!

Celebrate today the sounds of resurrection
in early morning worship and breaking bread.
Sing with glad thanksgiving the church's dawn chorus,
'Christ is alive! He has risen from the dead.'

Christ is alive. He has risen from the dead. Alleluia!

Celebrate today the sounds of resurrection
where truth is mocked and violence glorified.
Shout out for joy, an Easter song of freedom
in every place where love is crucified.

Christ is risen. He is risen indeed. Alleluia!

Jean Mortimer

1032 Lord Jesus, risen from the dead and alive for evermore: stand in our
midst tonight as in the upper room; show us thy hands and thy side;
speak thy peace to our hearts and minds; and send us forth into the
world as thy witnesses; for the glory of thy name.

John R. W. Stott

Most glorious Lord of Life! that, on this day,   1033
Didst make thy triumph over death and sin;
And, having harrowed hell, didst bring away
Captivity thence captive, us to win:
This joyous day, dear Lord, with joy begin;
And grant that we, for whom thou diddest dye,
Being with thy dear blood clean washed from sin,
May live for ever in felicity!
And that thy love we weighing worthily,
May likewise love thee for the same again;
And for thy sake, that all like dear didst buy,
With love may one another entertain!
So let us love, dear Love, like as we ought,
Love is the lesson which the Lord us taught.

Edmund Spenser, 1552–99

O God, by whose power Christ was raised from the dead, so that the   1034
worst that men could do had no dominion over him, lay thy hand in
loving tenderness on all who need this message most. Because the Son
of Man came to seek and to save that which was lost, we pray –

For those who have lost their dear ones and whose hearts are sad;
For those who have lost their health and vitality;
For those who have lost their youth;
For those who have lost their livelihood;
For those who have lost opportunities;
For those who have lost patience;
For those who have lost their faith;
For all, we pray, who are wounded in the battle of life and are nigh
    unto despair.

Give to us all such a vision of Christ's risen glory that we, too, may
trust his power; that we, too may know that nothing can separate us
from thy loving purposes or finally defeat thy will.

So may we rise up from all our distress and despair and take heart
again; walk with Christ, the companion of our souls, to whatever lies
in store for us, to find at last that faith has its own reward, that we
have not missed our way, that the Son of Man came to seek and to
save that which seemed lost for ever.

We ask it through Jesus Christ our Lord.

Leslie D. Weatherhead, 1883–1975

ASCENSION

1035 O Almighty God, who by thy holy apostle hast taught us to set our affection on things above: grant us so to labour in this life as ever to be mindful of our citizenship in those heavenly places whither our Saviour Christ is gone before; to whom with thee, O Father, and thee, O Holy Ghost, be all honour and glory, world without end.

A Book of Common Prayer, South Africa

1036 You are not only risen and alive, you are Lord.
This is your ascension, your ascendancy over the whole universe.
You stand over and above all that is best in life as its source.
You stand above all that is worst as ultimate victor.
You stand above all powers and authorities as judge.
You stand above all failure and weakness and sin as forgiveness and love.
You alone are worthy of total allegiance, total commitment.
You are Lord,
'My Lord and my God.'

Rex Chapman

1037 O God, the king of glory, who hast exalted thine only Son Jesus Christ with great triumph unto thy kingdom in heaven, we beseech thee leave us not comfortless, but send to us thine Holy Ghost to comfort us, and exalt us unto the same place whither our Saviour Christ is gone before; who livest and reignest with thee and the Holy Ghost, one God, world without end.

Church of England. Book of Common Prayer

O God, whose blessed Son, our great High Priest, has entered once 1038
for all into the holy place, and ever liveth to intercede on our behalf:
grant that we, sanctified by the offering of his body, may draw near
with full assurance of faith by the way which he has dedicated for us,
and evermore serve thee, the living God; through the same thy Son
our Lord Jesus Christ, who liveth and reigneth with thee, O Father,
and the Holy Spirit, one God, world without end.

Church of South India

Blessed art thou, O Lord God Almighty, the Ancient of Days, who 1039
hast set thy Son Jesus Christ our Lord upon the glorious throne of thy
kingdom, exalted far above all peoples, all places, all times, eternally;
that he who hath worn our flesh, and borne our manhood into the
holy of holies, should henceforth pour down heavenly gifts upon his
brethren, and be both our righteous judge and most merciful interces-
sor; to whom with thee, O Father, and thee, O Holy Spirit, one God,
be ascribed all might, majesty, dominion, and praise, now and for
ever.

Frank Colquhoun

PENTECOST

Spirit of the living Christ, come upon us in the glory of your risen 1040
power; Spirit of the Living Christ, come upon us in all the humility of
your wondrous love; Spirit of the Living Christ, come upon us that
new life may course within our veins, new love bind us together in
one family, a new vision of the kingdom of God spur us on to serve
you with fearless passion.

Source unknown

1041

Come, Holy Ghost, our souls inspire,
And lighten with celestial fire.
Thou the anointing Spirit art,
Who dost thy seven-fold gifts impart.

Thy blessed unction from above
Is comfort, life, and fire of love.
Enable with perpetual light
The dullness of our blinded sight.

Anoint and cheer our soiled face
With the abundance of thy grace.
Keep far our foes, give peace at home:
Where thou art guide, no ill can come.

Teach us to know the Father, Son,
And thee, of both, to be but one.
That, through the ages all along,
This may be our endless song;

Praise to thy eternal merit,
Father, Son, and Holy Spirit.

Source unknown

1042 Come, Holy Spirit, creator, and renew the face of the earth.
Come, Holy Spirit, come.

Come, Holy Spirit, counsellor, and touch our lips that we may
proclaim your word.
Come, Holy Spirit, come.

Come, Holy Spirit, power from on high: make us agents of peace and
ministers of wholeness.
Come, Holy Spirit, come.

Come, Holy Spirit, breath of God, give life to the dry bones of this
exiled age, and make us a living people, holy and free.
Come, Holy Spirit, come.

Come, Holy Spirit, wisdom and truth: strengthen us in the risk of
faith.
Come, Holy Spirit, come.

Anglican Church of Canada. Alternative Service Book

Father, pour out your Spirit upon your people, 1043
and grant to us
    a new vision of your glory;
    a new faithfulness to your Word;
    a new consecration to your service;
that your life may grow among us,
and your kingdom come;
through Jesus Christ our Lord.

Anglican Church in Australia

Almighty God, our heavenly Father, the privilege is ours to be called 1044
to share in the loving, healing and reconciling mission of your Son
Jesus Christ our Lord in this age and wherever we are. Since without
you we can do no good thing,
    may your Spirit make us wise;
    may your Spirit guide us;
    may your Spirit renew us;
    may your Spirit strengthen us
so that we will be
    strong in faith;
    discerning in proclamation;
    courageous in witness;
    persistent in good deeds.
This we ask through the same Jesus Christ our Lord.

Anglican Church of the West Indies

Almighty God, we thank you for having renewed your Church, at 1045
various times and in various ways, by rekindling the fire of love for
you through the work of your Holy Spirit. Rekindle your love in our
hearts and renew us to fulfil the Great Commission which your Son
committed to us; so that, individually and collectively, as members of
your Church we may help many to know Jesus Christ as their Lord
and Saviour. Empower us by your Spirit to share, with our
neighbours and friends, our human stories in the context of your
divine story; through Jesus Christ our Lord.

Anglican Church of West Malaysia

1046   Exuberant Spirit of God,
bursting with the brightness of flame
into the coldness of our lives
to warm us with a passion for justice and beauty
we praise you.

Exuberant Spirit of God,
sweeping us out of the dusty corners of our apathy
to breathe vitality into our struggles for change,
we praise you.

Exuberant Spirit of God,
speaking words that leap over barriers of mistrust
to convey messages of truth and new understanding,
we praise you.

Exuberant Spirit of God,
flame
      wind
           speech,
burn, breathe, speak in us;
fill your world with justice and with joy.

Jan Berry

1047 We praise you, O God, because you gave the Holy Spirit to the first Christians, making Jesus real to them, teaching them the truth and giving them the power to witness boldly: fill us with the same Spirit that we may know their experience and follow their example, in the service of your Son Jesus, our Lord and saviour.

Michael Botting

1048 O Spirit of the living God, who dwellest in us; who art holy, who art good: come thou, and fill the hearts of thy faithful people, and kindle within them the fire of thy love: through Jesus Christ our Lord.

Catholic Apostolic Church Liturgy

410

O Lord, who hast taught us that all our doings without love are noth-   *1049*
ing worth, send thy Holy Ghost, and pour into our hearts that most
excellent gift of love, the very bond of peace and all virtues, without
which whosoever liveth is counted dead before thee; grant us this for
thy Son Jesus Christ's sake.

Thomas Cranmer, 1489–1556

Wind of God, keep on blowing.   *1050*
Sail over the barriers that we build
to divide ourselves from each other.
Pick up your seeds of freedom and truth wherever they flourish,
carry them across frontiers to be planted in other soil,
to begin fresh growth and new forms.
Blow from the South
to the ears of Northern peoples.
Blow away the blinkers
which keep our eyes focused only on the past,
repeating its violence, deepening its divisions
and adding to its despair.
Reveal the new future you have in mind for us.

Fire of God, keep on burning,
smoulder in the hearts of people
where oppression keeps them in chains,
where unemployment and poverty devalue their humanity
and where hunger weakens the spirit.
Burn in them, like Moses' bush,
and do not let them be destroyed.

Tongue of God, keep on speaking
so that the peoples of earth
can speak your language to each other
and all can hear you in their own.

Speak peace where nations meet,
justice where ideas clash,
mercy where power reigns,
healing where minds and bodies hurt,
and love where churches seek your unity,
and wherever else Babel drowns out the sound of Pentecost.

Graham Cook

1051
Creator Spirit, by whose aid
The world's foundations first were laid,
Come visit every pious mind;
Come pour thy joys on humankind;
From sin and sorrow set us free,
And make thy temples worthy thee . . .

Plenteous of grace, descend from high,
Rich in thy sevenfold energy,
Thou strength of his almighty hand,
Whose power does heaven and earth command!
Proceeding Spirit, our defence,
Who dost the gift of tongues dispense,
And crown'st thy gift with eloquence!

Refine and purge our earthy parts;
But, O, inflame and fire our hearts!
Our frailties help, our vice control,
Submit the senses to the soul;
And when rebellious they are grown,
Then lay thy hand and hold them down.

Chase from our minds the infernal foe,
And peace, the fruit of love, bestow;
And lest our feet should step astray,
Protect and guide us in the way.

Make us eternal truths receive,
And practise all that we believe:
Give us thyself that we may see
The Father and the Son, by thee.

Immortal honour, endless fame,
Attend the Almighty Father's Name:
The Saviour Son be glorified,
Who for lost man's redemption died;
And equal adoration be,
Eternal Paraclete, to thee.

John Dryden, 1631–1700 (based on the Veni Creator Spiritus)

Come, free, abundant Spirit of God; fill this place with the wonder of   *1052*
your presence; fill our hearts with your love; fill the whole Church
with the power of Christ. Come in all the mystery signified by wind
and fire, beyond human definition, not held in the grasp of anyone, or
any thought, or any programme. Come, sovereign Spirit, and move
our hearts to awe and wonder.

Michael Fooler

O Holy Ghost, O faithful Paraclete,   *1053*
Love of the Father and the Son.
In whom Begetter and Begotten meet . . .
Bond that holdeth God to man.
Power that welds in one
Humanity and Deity.
God making all that is
Before our day,
God guiding all that's made
Throughout our day,
Gift that abides through an eternity
Of giving, and is made no less.
Thy going forth preceded Time,
Thy pouring forth took place in Time.
The one, the well-spring of power and the river of grace,
The other, the flowing, the giving, the light on our face.
Thou camest forth from thy transcendent day,
To make for us this shining feasting day.
Thou who alone
Art worthily adored
With Father and with Son.
To Thee in heart and word
Be honour, worship, grace,
Here and in every place,
World without end.

Hildebert of Lavardin, 1056–1133

1054   Enter my heart, O Holy Spirit,
        come in blessed mercy and set me free.
    Throw open, O Lord, the locked doors of my mind;
        cleanse the chambers of my thought for thy dwelling:
        light there the fires of thine own holy brightness in new
          understandings of truth,
    O Holy Spirit, very God, whose presence is liberty,
        grant me the perfect freedom
          to be thy servant
        today, tomorrow, evermore.

Eric Milner-White, 1884–1963

1055   O God the Holy Ghost
        who art light unto thine elect,
    Evermore enlighten us.
    Thou who art fire of love,
    Evermore enkindle us.
    Thou who art Lord and giver of life,
    Evermore live in us.
    Thou who bestowest sevenfold grace,
    Evermore replenish us.
    As the wind is thy symbol,
    So forward our goings.
    As the dove,
    So launch us heavenwards.
    As water,
    So purify our spirits.
    As a cloud,
    So abate our temptations.
    As dew,
    So revive our languor.
    As fire,
    So purge out our dross.

Christina Rossetti, 1830–94

We do not understand, eternal God,
the ways of your Spirit in the lives
of women and men.
She comes along secret paths
to take us unawares.
She touches us in joy and sorrow
to make us whole.
She hides behind coincidence
to lead us forward,
and uses our human accidents
as occasions for influence.
We do not understand
but we welcome her presence
and rejoice in her power.

St Hilda Community

O living God, come and make our souls temples of thy Spirit.
Sanctify us, O Lord!

Baptize thy whole Church with fire, that the divisions soon may cease, and that it may stand before the world as a pillar and buttress of thy truth.
Sanctify us, O Lord!

Grant us all the fruits of thy Holy Spirit: brotherly love, joy, peace, patience, goodwill and faithfulness.
Sanctify us, O Lord!

May the Holy Spirit speak by the voice of thy servants, here and everywhere, as they preach thy word.
Sanctify us, O Lord!

Send thy Holy Spirit, the comforter, to all who face adversity, or who are the victims of men's wickedness.
Sanctify us, O Lord!

Preserve all nations and their leaders from hatred and war, and build up a true community among nations, through the power of thy Spirit.
Sanctify us, O Lord!

Holy Spirit, Lord and source of life, giver of the seven gifts,
Sanctify us, O Comforter.

Spirit of wisdom and understanding, Spirit of counsel and strength,
Sanctify us, O Comforter.

Spirit of knowledge and devotion, Spirit of obedience to the Lord.
Sanctify us, O Comforter.

Taizé Community

1058   O Holy Spirit, who so many centuries ago didst come in creative power, and, brooding upon the face of the waters, didst from chaos bring calm, brood over us.

O Holy Spirit, who didst speak through the prophets and the saints inspiring men with the power to speak for God and to live for God, breathe upon us.

O Holy Spirit, who in the hush of an upper room didst fall upon men and women like a rushing, mighty wind, purifying them as with flame, sending them out with a power beyond themselves, knit us in a close and loving fellowship that we too may receive thee. Through Jesus Christ our Lord.

Leslie D. Weatherhead, 1883–1975

TRINITY SUNDAY

1059   Receive, O Holy Trinity, these oblations which I, a sinner, offer, both for myself and for the whole Christian people, for our brothers and sisters and for those who remember us regularly in their prayers, so that in this present world we may deserve to receive forgiveness of all our sins, and in the next may deserve to attain to eternal rest, through you, Jesus Christ, the redeemer of the world, who with the Father and the Holy Spirit lives and reigns for ever and ever.

Source unknown, 11th century

God the Father, God beyond us, we adore you.　　　　　　　　1060
　　You are the depth of all that is.
　　You are the ground of our being.
　　We can never grasp you, yet you grasp us;
　　the universe speaks of you to us, and your love comes to us through
　　　　Jesus.
God the Son, God beside us, we adore you.
　　You are the perfection of humanity.
　　You have shown us what human life should be like.
　　In you we see divine love and human greatness combined.
God the Spirit, God around us, we adore you.
　　You draw us to Jesus and the Father.
　　You are power within us.
　　You give us abundant life and can make us the men and women we
　　　　are meant to be.
Father, Son, and Spirit;
God, beyond, beside and around us;
We adore you.

Caryl Micklem

Giver of life,　　　　　　　　1061
Infinite God,
penetrating and containing,
gestating and birthing,
open our being to yours.

Bearer of pain,
Gracious Beloved,
seeded with Truth,
yearning, dying for new life,
open our being to yours.

Maker of love,
hungry and passionate,
refining and enlivening,
open our being to yours.

Holy Trinity, looking at one another,
earthing and impregnating,
evoking life between you,
open our being to yours.

Mary Robins

1062

O God, the source of our being
and the goal of all our longing,
we believe and trust in you.
The whole earth is alive with your glory,
and all that has life is sustained by you.
We commit ourselves to cherish your world,
and to seek your face.

O God, embodied in a human life,
we believe and trust in you.
Jesus our brother, born of the woman Mary,
you confronted the proud and the powerful,
and welcomed as your friends
those of no account.
Holy Wisdom of God, firstborn of creation,
you emptied yourself of power,
and became foolishness for our sake.
Your laboured with us upon the cross,
and have brought us forth
to the hope of resurrection.
We commit ourselves to struggle against evil,
and to choose life.

O God, life-giving Spirit,
Spirit of healing and comfort,
of integrity and truth
we believe and trust in you.
Warm-winged Spirit, brooding over creation,
rushing wind and Pentecostal fire,
we commit ourselves to work with you,
and renew our world.

Janet Morley

Almighty God, most blessed and most holy, before the brightness of   *1063*
whose presence the angels veil their faces: with lowly reverence and
adoring love we acknowledge thine infinite glory, and worship thee,
Father, Son, and Holy Spirit, eternal Trinity. Blessing, and honour,
and glory, and power be unto our God, for ever and ever.

Church of Scotland. Book of Common Order

Living Love,   *1064*
beginning and end,
giver of food and drink,
clothing and warmth,
love and hope:
life in all its goodness –
We praise and adore you.

Jesus, Wisdom and Word;
lover of outcasts,
friend of the poor;
one of us yet one with God;
crucified and risen:
life in the midst of death –
We praise and adore you.

Holy Spirit, storm and breath of love;
bridge-builder, eye-opener,
waker of the oppressed,
unseen and unexpected,
untameable energy of life –
We praise and adore you.

Holy Trinity, forever one,
whose nature is community;
source of all sharing,
in whom we love, and meet, and know our neighbour:
life in all its fullness, making all things new:
We praise and adore you.

Brian Wren

HARVEST

1065 Almighty God, Lord of heaven and earth, in whom we live and move and have our being; who doest good unto all men, making thy sun to rise on the evil and on the good, and sending rain on the just and on the unjust: favourably behold us thy servants, who call upon thy name, and send us thy blessing from heaven, in giving us fruitful seasons, and satisfying us with food and gladness; that both our hearts and mouths shall be continually filled with thy praise, giving thanks to thee in thy holy church; through Jesus Christ our Lord.

John Cosin, 1594–1672

1066
We dare not ask you bless our harvest feast
Till it is spread for poorest and for least.
We dare not bring our harvest gifts to you
Unless our hungry brothers share them too.

Not only at this time, Lord; every day
Those whom you love are dying while we pray.
Teach us to do with less, and so to share
From our abundance more than we can spare.

Now with this harvest plenty round us piled,
Show us the Christ in every starving child;
Speak, as you spoke of old in Galilee,
'You feed, or you refuse, not them but me!'

Lilian Cox

Lord, your harvest is the harvest of love; 1067
love sown in the hearts of people;
love that spreads out
like the branches of a great tree
covering all who seek its shelter;
love that inspires and recreates;
love that is planted in the weak and the weary,
the sick and the dying.
The harvest of your love is the life that reaches
through the weeds of sin and death
to the sunlight of resurrection.
Lord, nurture my days with your love,
water my soul with the dew of forgiveness,
that the harvest of my life might be your joy.

Frank Topping

Creator God, we thank you for your promise that while the earth 1068
endures seed-time and harvest, summer and winter, day and night,
shall not fail. We thank you for the reliability of this good earth, for
the variety of the seasons and for all the unity and contrasts of creation. We thank you for this world's agenda for the labours of men
and for permitting us to be partners to the earth's activity. We thank
you that we can nourish the miracle of life upon the miracle of harvest
and we praise you for the dignity of sharing in the work of your
almighty hands, O God our Father, blessed for ever.

Dick Williams

REMEMBRANCE DAY

1069

Almighty God, from whose love in Christ
    we cannot be parted, by death or by life:
hear our prayers and thanksgivings
    for those whom we remember this day.
Fulfil in them the purpose of your love;
and bring us, with them, to your eternal joy;
through Jesus Christ our Lord.

We give thanks this day, O Lord of hosts,
    for all that makes our common life secure;
    for the peace and freedom we enjoy;
    and for the opportunity that is ours
        of building a better order of society
        for the generation to come.

We remember with pride and gratitude
    those who fought and died to make this possible;
and we pray that the memory of their sacrifice
    may inspire in us the resolve to seek your kingdom
    and to do your will for the world of our day;
    through Jesus Christ our Lord.

Source unknown

Let us pray for all who suffer as a result of war: 1070
    for the injured and the disabled,
    for the mentally distressed,
    and for those whose faith in God and in man has been weakened
      or destroyed . . .
    for the homeless and refugees,
    for those who are hungry,
    and for all who have lost their livelihood and security . . .
    for those who mourn their dead,
    those who have lost husband or wife, children or parents,
    and especially for those who have no hope in Christ to sustain them
      in their grief . . .
Almighty God, our heavenly Father, infinite in wisdom, love and
power: have compassion on those for whom we pray; and help us to
use all suffering in the cause of your kingdom, through him who gave
himself for us on the cross, Jesus Christ your Son our Lord.

Source unknown

Gracious Father, 1071
we pray for peace in our world:
for all national leaders,
that they may have wisdom to know and courage to do what is right;
for all men and women,
that their hearts may be turned to yourself in the search for
    righteousness and truth;
for those who are working to improve international relationships,
that they may find the true way of reconciliation;
for those who suffer as a result of war:
    the injured and disabled,
    the mentally distressed,
    the homeless and hungry,
    those who mourn their dead,
    and especially for those who are without hope or friend to sustain
      them in their grief.

Baptist Peace Fellowship

1072   God our Father, as on this day we look back and remember with
gratitude those who died in time of war, so also we look around and
remember with compassion those who still suffer as the result of war:
the bereaved, the lonely, the disabled, and the mentally ill.

O God of love, comfort their hearts, uphold their faith, and give
them peace, for Jesus Christ's sake.

Frank Colquhoun

1073   Father of mercies and God of all comfort, whose Son ministered to
those in need: remember for good all who suffer through war, by loss
of home or faculties, by loss of friends and loved ones, by loss of security or freedom.

Look upon our world, still torn apart by violence and fighting, and
grant success to those who work for peace; through him who reconciled men with God, and men with men, the Lord Jesus Christ.

Christopher Idle

1074   Grant peace and eternal rest to all the departed, but especially the
millions known and unknown who died as prisoners in many lands,
victims of the hatred and cruelty of man. May the example of their
suffering and courage draw us closer to thee through thine own
agony and passion, and thus strengthen us in our desire to serve thee
in the sick, the unwanted and the dying wherever we may find them.
Give us the grace so to spend ourselves for those who are still alive,
that we may prove most truly that we have not forgotten those who
died.

Sue Ryder and Leonard Cheshire

1075   On this Remembrance Day we come, O Lord, in gratitude for all who
have died that we may live, for all who endured pain that we might
know joy, for all who suffered imprisonment that we might know
freedom. Turn our deep feeling now into determination, and our
determination into deed, that as men died for peace, we may live for
peace for the sake of the Prince of Peace, even Jesus Christ our Lord.

Leslie D. Weatherhead, 1883–1975

ALL SAINTS

How shining and splendid are your gifts, O Lord, 1076
which you give us for our eternal well-being!

Your glory shines radiantly in your saints, O God,
in the honour and noble victory of the martyrs.

The white-robed company follow you, bright with their abundant
    faith;
they scorned the wicked words of those with this world's power.

For you they sustained fierce beatings, chains, and torments,
they were drained by cruel punishments.
they bore their holy witness to you, who were grounded deep within
    their hearts;
they were sustained by patience and constancy.

Endowed with your everlasting grace,
may we rejoice for ever with the martyrs in our bright fatherland.
O Christ, in your goodness,
grant to us the gracious heavenly realms of eternal life.

Source unknown, 10th century

We give you thanks, our God and Father, for all those who have died 1077
in the faith of Christ; for the memory of their words and deeds and all
they accomplished in their time; for the joyful hope of reunion with
them in the world to come; and for our communion with them now in
your Son, Jesus Christ our Lord.

Source unknown

1078 O Almighty God, who hast knit together thine elect in one communion and fellowship, in the mystical body of thy Son Jesus Christ our
Lord: grant us grace so to follow thy blessed saints in all virtuous and
godly living, that we may come to those unspeakable joys, which
thou hast prepared for them that unfeignedly love thee; through Jesus
Christ our Lord.

Church of England. Book of Common Prayer

1079 Almighty God, we offer unto thee most high praise and hearty thanks
for the wonderful graces and virtues which thou has manifested in all
thy saints and in all other holy persons upon earth, who by their lives
and labours have shined forth as lights in the world, whom we
remember with honour and commemorate with joy. For these and
for all thy other servants who have departed this life with the seal of
faith, we praise and magnify thy holy name; through Jesus Christ our
Lord.

Church of Scotland. Book of Common Order

1080 Almighty and everlasting God, who dost enkindle the flame of thy
love in the hearts of the saints, grant unto us the same faith and power
of love; that, as we rejoice in their triumphs, we may profit by their
examples, through Jesus Christ our Lord.

Gothic missal

1081 Almighty and ever-living God, we offer thee most hearty thanks for
the grace and virtue made manifest in all thy saints, who have been
chosen vessels of thy favour and lights of the world in their several
generations: and we most humbly beseech thee to give us grace so to
follow their good examples that with them we may be partakers of
thy heavenly kingdom; through Jesus Christ our Lord.

Methodist Church. Book of Offices

——————✠——————

PRAYERS FOR

THE CHURCH

——————✠——————

For as in one body we have many

members, and not all the members

have the same function, so we, who are

many, are one body in Christ.

Romans 12.4-5

Eternal Father, who wouldst make the Church of thy dear Son a city *1082* great and fair, the joy of the whole earth: we beseech thee, by the sending of thy Holy Spirit, to direct its counsels now in all manner of wisdom, love, and might; remove perplexity, establish concord, kindle flame, and gather a people single and strong in faith; to the praise of him who with thee and the same Spirit liveth and reigneth, one God, world without end.

Anglican Church. Lambeth Conference, 1930

Grant more of thy Spirit to all thy churches and servants in the world: *1083* that as their darkness and selfishness and imperfections have defiled and divided and weakened them, and made them scandalous and harsh toward unbelievers, so may their knowledge, self-denial and impartial love truly reform, unite and strengthen them: that the glory of their holiness may win an unbelieving world to Christ.

Richard Baxter, 1615–91

Most gracious Father, we humbly beseech thee for thy holy catholic *1084* Church. Fill it with all truth; in all truth with all peace. Where it is corrupt, purify it; where it is in error, direct it; where anything is amiss, reform it; where it is right, strengthen and confirm it; where it is in want, furnish it; where it is divided and rent asunder, make up the breeches of it, O thou holy one of Israel.

(Archbishop) Bull, 1571–1645

O Lord Jesus Christ, prince of peace, break down the barriers which *1085* separate us from each other and from God. Teach Christians to love each other across the walls of colour, class and creed; forgive us, too, the excuses we make for our own prejudice. And lead us captive in your cause of peace and goodwill on earth; for your name's sake.

Ian Bunting

1086 Almighty and everlasting God, who didst form thy Church to be of one heart and soul in the power of the resurrection and the fellowship of the Holy Spirit: renew her evermore in her first love; and grant to thy people such a measure of thy grace that their life may be hallowed, their way directed, and their work made fruitful to the good of thy Church and the glory of thy holy name; through the same Jesus Christ our Lord.

Community of the Resurrection

1087 Every history of ours, O Lord, is the history of all. For no church is an island, entire to itself. For the fire of thy servants in far centuries, thy name be praised, O Lord; for ancient stones and liturgies, for ripened learning and long disciplines of prayer and peace, thy name be blessed, O Lord, and every saint, O Lord, preserve, renew and multiply, in the eternal Christ.

Kenneth Cragg

1088 O Lord of the lovers of mankind who, for your sake, break the alabaster box of life, quicken your Church today with the ardour of the saints, so that by prayer and scholarship, by discipline and sacrifice, your name may be made truly known.

Kenneth Cragg

1089 God, our Shepherd, give to the Church a new vision and a new charity, new wisdom and fresh understanding, the revival of her brightness and the renewal of her unity; that the eternal message of thy Son, undefiled by the traditions of men, may be hailed as the good news of the new age; through him who maketh all things new, Jesus Christ our Lord.

Percy Dearmer, 1867–1936

1090 We pray you, Lord, to direct and guide your Church with your unfailing care, that it may be vigilant in times of quiet, and daring in times of trouble; through Jesus Christ our Lord.

Franciscan Breviary

O God of unchangeable power and eternal light, look favourably 1091
upon thy whole Church, that wonderful and sacred mystery; and by
the tranquil operation of thy perpetual providence carry out the work
of man's salvation; and let the whole world feel and see that things
which were cast down are being raised up; that those which had
grown old are being made new; and that all things are returning into
unity through him by whom all things were made, even thy Son Jesus
Christ our Lord.

Gelasian Sacramentary, 5th century

O God, make the door of this house wide enough to receive all who 1092
need human love and fellowship; narrow enough to shut out all
envy, pride and strife. Make its threshold smooth enough to be no
stumbling-block to children, nor to straying feet, but rugged and
strong enough to turn back the tempter's power. God make the door
of this house the gateway to thine eternal kingdom.

Thomas Ken, 1637–1711 (on St Stephen's Walbrook, London)

O God of all power, who hast called from death the great pastor of 1093
the sheep, our Lord Jesus: comfort and defend the flock which he
hath redeemed by the blood of the eternal testament. Increase the
number of true preachers; lighten the hearts of the ignorant; relieve
the pains of such as be afflicted, especially of those that suffer for the
testimony of the truth; by the power of our Lord Jesus Christ.

John Knox, 1505–72

We thank you, Lord Jesus Christ, King of Glory, that you have called 1094
us to be your people. Help us to know the greatness of our calling, so
that we, having one spirit of faith and love, may live in the world as a
new and holy generation. May your eternal and righteous will be
always before our eyes, so that in soberness and vigilance we may
await your time, and witness to your promises, until your kingdom
comes.

Lutheran Liturgy

1095   Let us pray for all those, throughout the world, who believe in the
      Gospel:
That they may grow in grace and humanity.
Let us also pray for all churches, that they may not lay up treasures
      on earth or become monuments to a past age,
Clinging to what is already dead and remote from people of today,
But that they may be converted and receive the spirit of Jesus, our
      Lord, who is the light and life, hope and peace of this world, for
      ever and ever.

Huub Oosterhuis

1096   Lord of the Church, enable your people to be the Church – a
redeemed people, a holy people, a united people, a missionary
people, and in all things a people gladly submissive to the truth you
have shown us in yourself, Jesus Christ our Lord.

Michael Saward

1097   Remember, O Lord, thy Church, to deliver it from all evil and to perfect it in thy love. Strengthen and preserve it by thy Word and Sacraments. Enlarge its borders, that so thy gospel may be preached to all
nations; and gather the faithful from all the ends of the earth into the
kingdom which thou hast prepared.

Swedish Liturgy

1098   Hasten thou, O Christ, that day when every heart shall know and
love thee, the Lord. Bless thy holy Church throughout the earth. Free
her from narrowness, bigotry, and pride of self. Throw her doors
wide to the wall, deepen her thought, broaden her sympathies, till she
shall be as thou art, shelter and home, and shield and dwelling-place,
of all the weary and the wandering that are seeking rest.

Lauchlan MacLean Watt, 1867–1957

THE CHURCH'S MISSION
AND MINISTRY

O Lord, convert the world – and begin with me.   *1099*
Source unknown (China)

God our Father, you sent your Son to us: grant that filled with your   *1100*
Spirit we may be renewed in faith, and inspired in hope and love, to
spread the gospel of your kingdom to all humankind; through Christ
our Lord.

Anglican Province of Central Africa

For a clearer vision of the work you have set before us and for a better   *1101*
understanding of your gospel,
    Lord, direct us.
For a deeper commitment in your service and a greater love for all
your children,
    Lord, direct us.
For a fresh understanding of the task before us and for a sense of
urgency in our proclamation,
    Lord, direct us.
For a greater respect and acceptance among Christians of different
traditions and for a common goal in evangelism,
    Lord, direct us.

Anglican Province of the Indian Ocean

1102 Lord Jesus, who didst stretch out thine arms of love on the hard wood of the cross, that all men might come within the reach of thy saving embrace, clothe us in thy Spirit, that we, stretching forth our hands in loving labour for others, may bring those who know thee not, to the knowledge and love of thee, who with the Father and the Holy Ghost livest and reignest one God.

Charles Henry Brent, 1862–1929

1103 Blessed be thou, Almighty Father of our Lord Jesus Christ, for thy guiding power which has brought us here to serve thee in this church. Look upon us, we beseech thee, who are called by the name of thy dear Son, and grant that we may ever walk worthily of our Christian vocation. Unite us all in mutual love and forbearance; put far from us all selfish indifference to the needs of others; and give us grace gladly to bear our burdens and fulfil our duties as members of this church and citizens of this country, to the glory of thy name; through the same Jesus Christ, our Lord. Amen.

Church of Pakistan

1104 O Lord, you have called us to be your witnesses to all the nations. Have mercy on us who have known your will but failed to do it. Cleanse us from unbelief and sloth and fill us with hope and zeal, that we may do your will and bear your cross and bide your time and see your glory, who with the Father and the Holy Spirit are one God, world without end.

Church of South India

1105   Infinite Lord and eternal God,
        Rouse your Church in this land,
        Restore your people's sense of mission,
        And revive your work in holiness and strength.
        By your Spirit, teach us to give our energy,
        Our time, our money, our service and our prayer,
        That your kingdom may be advanced
        Here and in all the world;
        In the name of Jesus Christ our Lord.

        Church in Wales

Lord of light – shine on us;   *1106*
Lord of peace – dwell in us;
Lord of might – succour us;
Lord of love – enfold us;
Lord of wisdom – enlighten us.
Then, Lord, let us go out as your witnesses, in obedience to your command; to share the good news of your mighty love for us in the gift of your Son, our Saviour, Jesus Christ.

Church in Wales

Give to your Church, O God, a bold vision and a daring charity, a *1107*
refreshed wisdom and a courteous understanding, that the eternal message of your Son may be acclaimed as the good news of the age; through him who makes all things new, even Jesus Christ our Lord.

The Daily Office

Jesus Christ, Son of God, make yourself known through me. Jesus *1108*
Christ, Son of the living God, speak through me to others.

Episcopal Church of the United States of America

O Lord, our heavenly Father, whose blessed Son came not to be *1109*
ministered unto but to minister: we beseech thee to bless all those who follow in his steps and give themselves to the service of their fellowmen. Endue them with wisdom, patience, and courage, to strengthen the weak and raise up those who fall; that being inspired by thy love, they may worthily minister in thy name to the suffering, the friendless, and the needy; for the sake of him who laid down his life for us, the same thy Son, our saviour Jesus Christ.

Episcopal Church of the United States of America. Book of Common Prayer

Give to your Church, O God, the grace to follow in the steps of Jesus, *1110*
who came among us as one who serves. May it be ready in all the world to spend and be spent in the service of the poor and the hungry, the sick and the ignorant. May it work with strength and suffer with courage for the liberation of the oppressed and the restoration to all of the dignity and freedom of those created in your image: grant this, O Father, for the sake of the same Jesus Christ our Lord.

John Kingsnorth (USPG)

1111   O thou, who art the author of all good things in thy holy Church, work mightily in all thy servants, that they may be profitable to all men, and vessels of thy mercy and grace. Control us all, and so govern our thoughts and deeds, that we may serve thee in righteousness and true holiness; and sanctify us all unto that eternal life, which we, with all thy creatures, groaning and travailing together, wait for and expect; through Jesus Christ our Lord.

Philip Melanchthon, 1497–1560

1112   Father, we bring to you in prayer the hopes and the needs of the world. Each person you have made bears your image: but in each that image is assaulted by many enemies. Hunger and homelessness, violence and the fear of violence, greed, jealousy, boredom – all these threaten the humanity of men and women which is your breath within them.

May your Church everywhere be a force for peace with justice. May the gospel of Jesus awaken everywhere such a vision of our real destiny that evil may be overcome, not with other evil but with good.

And upon all who strive for the fulfilment of your reign on earth, may there come such a spirit of trust and hope that nothing may seem too hard to do in the name of your Son, Jesus Christ our Lord.

Caryl Micklem

1113   Most merciful Father, you have called us to be a caring Church, reflecting in our lives your infinite care for us your children.

Help us to fulfil our calling and to care for one another in an unselfish fellowship of love; and to care for the world around us in sharing with it the good news of your love and serving those who suffer from poverty, hunger and disease.

We ask it in the name of Christ our Lord.

Michael Ramsey

Heavenly Father, fill us with your Holy Spirit, that through us your *1114*
Word may be spread throughout the nations. Use us to speak the
truth about yourself, and give us confidence and courage to speak the
words that give you honour.
> For those who are weak in faith,
> Give them courage.
> For those who search for you,
> Give them courage.
> For those who long to speak of you,
> Give them courage.

May the Lord bless us and keep us,
May Christ smile upon us and give us his grace,
May he unveil his face to us and give us peace.
In his name we ask.

Scottish Episcopal Church

O God, who hast made man's mouth and canst cause even the dumb *1115*
to speak, open our lips, we beseech thee, that we may show forth thy
praise. Forgive us for our slow and stammering speech. Cause the
fires to burn in our hearts until we can no longer hold our peace.
Grant that, through our humble testimony to thy Son Jesus Christ,
our friends and neighbours may turn to him as their Saviour and
Lord, and magnify him with us, in the fellowship of his Church, for
the greater glory of his name.

John R. W. Stott

O God the Father of all, you ask every one of us to spread love where *1116*
the poor are humiliated, joy where the Church is brought low, and
reconciliation where people are divided, father against son, mother
against daughter, husband against wife, believers against those who
cannot believe, Christians against their unloved fellow Christians.
You open this way for us, so that the wounded body of Jesus Christ,
your Church, may be leaven of communion for the poor of the earth
and in the whole human family.

(Mother) Teresa of Calcutta

1117 Grant, O Lord, that this mind may be in us, which was also in Christ Jesus, who left the heaven of thy holiness and of thy glory that he might take upon him our sins and our sorrows, and seek and save that which was lost. Stir the hearts of thy people that they may multiply their labours in the cause of charity and love, that they may minister to the wants of others, and by their good works lead many to glorify our Father who is in heaven; through the same Jesus Christ our Lord.

Charles John Vaughan, 1816–97

1118 O almighty and most merciful Father, who didst send thy beloved Son to die for the sins of the whole world, look down, we beseech thee, upon all nations who have not known his name, and in thine own good time lead them to his cross. Strengthen with the comfort of thy Spirit all who bear abroad the message of the gospel. Raise up among us a lively sympathy for their labours. Take away from those who hear all hardness of heart, and pride, and impenitence; and so move them, blessed Lord, with infinite love, that the day may speedily come when all the ends of the world shall be turned unto thee, and there shall be one flock and one shepherd; we ask all for the sake of Jesus Christ our Lord.

Brooke Foss Westcott, 1825–1901

1119 O God we thank you
for the wholeness of the human family:
for people of other faiths and of none, especially those who are our
friends and neighbours;
for the rich variety of human experience and the gifts we bring to one
another when we meet in a spirit of acceptance and love;
for dialogue in community, and for mutual enrichment and growing
understanding;
for movements to establish and sustain the legitimate rights of
persons of every religious conviction.
And we pray to you
that people of all faiths may enjoy the freedom to set forth their
conviction with integrity and listen to one another in humility;
that the Church may perform a reconciling ministry in a world
divided by suspicion and misunderstanding,
and bring healing to those places where religious intolerance
fractures human community;

that the Church may bear a true and loving witness to the one it calls
Lord, in whose name we pray.

World Council of Churches

CHURCH UNITY

O God, the Father of our Lord Jesus Christ, our only Saviour, the   *1120*
Prince of Peace: give us grace seriously to lay to heart the great dangers we are in by our unhappy division. Take away all hatred and prejudice, and whatsoever else may hinder us from godly union and concord; that, as there is but one Body, and one Spirit, and one hope of
our calling, one Lord, one faith, one baptism, one God and Father of
us all, so we may henceforth be all of one heart and of one soul, united
in one holy bond of truth and peace, of faith and charity, and may
with one mind and one mouth glorify thee; through Jesus Christ our
Lord.

Church of England. Accession Service, 1714

Father, we pray for your Church throughout the world, that it may   *1121*
share to the full in the work of your Son, revealing you to men and
reconciling men to you and to one another; that Christians may learn
to love one another and their neighbours, as you have loved us; that
your Church may more and more reflect the unity which is your will
and your gift; we pray through Jesus Christ our Lord.

Coventry Cathedral (Prayer from the Chapel of Unity)

1122 O God, whose will it is that all your children should be one in Christ; we pray for the unity of your Church. Pardon all our pride and our lack of faith, of understanding and of charity, which are the causes of our divisions. Deliver us from narrow-mindedness, from our bitterness, from our prejudices. Save us from considering as normal that which is a scandal to the world and an offence to your love. Teach us to recognize the gifts of grace among all those who call upon you and confess the faith of Jesus Christ our Lord.

French Reformed Church Liturgy

1123 O God who has called men and women in every land to be a holy nation, a royal priesthood, the Church of your dear Son; unite us in mutual love across the barriers of race and culture, and strengthen us in our common task of being Christ and showing Christ to the world he came to save.

John Kingsnorth (USPG)

1124 O God the Father, origin of divinity, good beyond all that is good, fair beyond all that is fair, in whom is calmness, peace, and concord; do thou make up the dissensions which divide us from each other, and bring us back into a unity of love, which may bear some likeness to thy divine nature. And as thou art above all things, make us one by the unanimity of a good mind, that through the embrace of charity and the bonds of affection, we may be spiritually one, as well in ourselves as in each other; through that peace of thine which maketh all things peaceful, and through the grace, mercy, and tenderness of thy Son, Jesus Christ.

Liturgy of St Dionysius, 9th century

1125 O Sovereign and almighty Lord, bless all thy people, and all thy flock. Give thy peace,thy help, thy love unto us thy servants, the sheep of thy fold, that we may be united in the bond of peace and love, one body and one spirit, in one hope of our calling, in thy divine and boundless love.

Liturgy of St Mark, 2nd century

Creator of rainbows, 1126
come through the closed doors
    of our emotions, mind and imagination;
come alongside us as we walk,
come to us at work and worship,
come to our meetings and councils,
come and call us by name,
call us to pilgrimage.

Wounded healer,
out of our dis-unity
may we be re-membered,
out of the pain of our division
may we see your glory.
Call us from present
pre-occupation
to future community.

Spirit of Unity,
challenge our preconceptions,
enable us to grow in love and understanding,
accompany us on our journey together,
that we may go out with confidence
into your world as a new creation –
one body in you,
that the world may believe.

Kate McIlhagga

1127   O God, we are one with you.
You have made us one with you.
You have taught us that if we are open to one another, you dwell in
    us.
Help us to preserve this openness and to fight for it with all our
    hearts.
Help us to realize that there can be no understanding where there is
    mutual rejection.
O God, in accepting one another wholeheartedly, fully, completely,
we accept you, and we thank you, and we adore you;
and we love you with our whole being,
    because out being is in your being,
    our spirit is rooted in your Spirit.
Fill us then with love,
and let us be bound together with love as we go our diverse ways,
united in this one Spirit which makes you present to the world,
and which makes you witness to the ultimate reality that is love.
Love has overcome.
Love is victorious.

Thomas Merton

1128   Holy Father, whose blessed Son prayed not only for his chosen twelve, but for them also who were to believe on him through their word, that they all might be one; grant that as thou, Father, art in him and he in thee, they also may be perfected into one, that the world may know that thou dost love thy Church as thou dost love thy Son; who now liveth and reigneth with thee and the Holy Ghost, ever one God, world without end.

John Neale

1129   O Lord Jesus Christ, who didst say to thine apostles, 'Peace I leave with you, my peace I give unto you': regard not our sins, but the faith of thy Church, and grant it that peace and unity which is agreeable to thy will; who livest and reignest with the Father and the Holy Spirit, one God, world without end.

Roman Missal

O Lord Jesus Christ, who prayed for thy disciples that they might be *1130*
one, even as thou art one with the Father: draw us to thyself, that in
common love and obedience to thee we may be united to one another,
in the fellowship of the one Spirit, that the world may believe that
thou art Lord, to the glory of God the Father.

William Temple, 1881–1944

Be with thy Church everywhere. May she walk warily in times of *1131*
peace and quietness, and boldly in times of trouble. Do thou remove
all harshness and bitterness from amongst us, towards those who
walk not in all things with us, but who worship our Lord in sincerity
and truth.
   And all this we ask for the sake of thy dear Son.

Helen Waddell, 1889–1965

O God, bless and preserve thy Church dispersed over the face of the *1132*
earth. Restore to it unity and concord, in the acknowledgement of the
Truth and the practice of righteousness. Remove out of it all errors
and dissensions, that they who profess the same faith may no longer
persecute and destroy one another, but be kind and tender-hearted
one towards another, as it becomes brethren and those that are heirs
of the same common salvation.

(King) William III, 1650–1702

CHURCH LEADERS
AND WORKERS

1133 O Lord, who for our sake became poor, that we through your poverty might become rich; strengthen all those who, at your call and after your example, have left possessions, parents, hope of family, and their own wills, that they might take up the cross and follow you in the threefold way of poverty, chastity and obedience. Through the consecration of their lives and the power of their prayers may your Church be strengthened to be the more perfectly conformed to your image; for you are alive and reign with the Father and the Spirit, one God, now and for ever.

A Book of Common Prayer, South Africa

1134 O Lord, grant all who contend for the faith, never to injure it by clamour and impatience; but, speaking thy precious truth in love, so to present it that it may be loved, and that men may see in it thy goodness and beauty.

William Bright, 1824–1901

1135 Lord, still me.
Let my mind be inquiring, searching.
Let my heart be open.
Save me from mental rust.
Deliver me from spiritual decay.
Keep me *alive* and alert.
Teach me, that I may teach them.

Donald Coggan

O Lord Jesus Christ, who at thy first coming didst send thy messenger   *1136*
to prepare thy way before thee: grant that the ministers and stewards
of thy mysteries may likewise so prepare and make ready thy way, by
turning the hearts of the disobedient to the wisdom of the just, that at
thy second coming to judge the world we may be found an acceptable
people in thy sight; who livest and reignest with the Father and the
Holy Spirit, ever one God, world without end.

John Cosin, 1595–1672

O God our Saviour, who willest that all men should be saved and   *1137*
come to the knowledge of the truth, prosper, we pray thee, our brethren who labour in distant lands. Protect them in all perils by land and
sea, support them in loneliness and in the hour of trial; give them
grace to bear faithful witness unto thee, and endue them with burning
zeal and love, that they may turn many to righteousness and finally
obtain a crown of glory; through Jesus Christ.

Episcopal Church of Scotland. The Scottish Book of Common Prayer

O Lord Jesus Christ   *1138*
Who called people from their daily work
Saying to them 'Come ye after me',
May your children today hear your voice
    And gladly answer your call
    To give their lives to you
    To serve your Church
    To offer their gifts
    And give away their hearts
    To you only.

    Bless their hopes
The first tiny stirrings of desire
The little resolve to go forward.
The small vision of what might be.

    Deal gently with their fears
The hesitation of uncertainty
The darkness of the unknown
The lack of confidence in their own capacity
    And turn it all to trust in you.

Gabrielle Hadingham (USPG)

1139   Lord, nothing has worked out the way I thought it would.

People in your Church disappoint me. I've wondered many times if I shouldn't give them up and come to terms with you alone. Their shortcomings hurt and upset me. This failure to live what they preach offends me, especially since they claim to represent what is right. This self-assurance also . . . When you hear some of them, you might conclude that you personally exemplify the truth of their every word. Even when they speak of things they don't know anything about.

I wish they were more saintly. I wish they were more humble. Quite frankly, Lord, they make me angry at times. I think that you were almost bordering on carelessness when you said to the disciples: 'He who hears you hears me' (Luke 10.16).

And yet, Lord, I mustn't turn my back on your Church. I mustn't separate myself from the whole under the pretence that I would find you more easily then. I want to stay among your own, where you are.

When all is said and done, you have supported and upheld us all. I must learn to love. Not a sentimental love. That's not what you ask for. What you want is love which knows no aversions. Lord, I should like to pledge to you my effort to love. But I need your help.

Make me understand that my brothers and sisters are human. Like me, no worse and no better. How else could you have revealed yourself to man except through man?

What did I expect? That your people would be perfect? Did I forget the history and nature of man, and what salvation is all about, when I dreamed of a Church free from misery, human ambitions, and failure?

I had built my own dream Church . . . a Church that was not human, didn't even exist. Is your Church responsible for my dreams? Can it be blamed for my expectations? Lord, let me not forget the human condition.

Lord, guard me against my optimism as well as my pessimism. Teach me to be just, which is something quite different – and infinitely more difficult.

Paul Geres

O Jesus, Son of the living God, who became man and made the sup-   *1140*
reme sacrifice of yourself in order to reveal the mystery of the Father's
love and his plan of mercy and salvation for all peoples, we adore you
and praise you, because you have enlightened and redeemed us.

O Jesus, you who sent out your apostles to gather in the harvest
from all the fields of the world and did promise to draw all men to
yourself on the cross, we thank you for having sent to us those who
have taught us the truth and made us sharers in your grace.

(Pope) John XXIII, 1881–1963

Eternal Father, it is your joy to call men and women to serve you   *1141*
    across the barriers of race and language and culture:
Give them strength and courage,
and satisfy their longing to make known the good news of Christ.
Bless those who are called along the humble road,
to serve and support but not to lead.
    When they face danger, save them from fear;
    When they are disheartened, be their friend;
    When they think they have failed, show them the cross.
Give them peace in their hearts,
    and peace in their homes,
and the joy of acceptance by those whom they serve.
For Jesus Christ's sake.

John Kingsnorth (USPG)

Grant, O God, we beseech thee, that the same mind may be in all the   *1142*
ministers of thy Church that was in Christ Jesus:
    his self-forgetting humility;
    his interest in common things;
    his love for common people;
    his compassion for the fallen;
    his tolerance with the mistaken;
    his patience with the slow;
    and in all their work and converse make them continually sensitive
to thy guidance and ready for thy will; through Jesus Christ our Lord.

Methodist Church. Book of Offices

1143   O blessed Jesus, Lord of the harvest, we pray thee send forth labourers into thy harvest; and by thy Holy Spirit stir the hearts of many that they may be ready to spend and be spent in thy service, and if it please thee, so to lose their life in this world, that they may gather fruit unto life eternal, O Lord, thou lover of souls.

Henry Hart Milman, 1791–1868

1144   O Father, guide thou our guides, and keep them worthy of the place whereunto thou hast called them. Keep them lowly and true, as followers of Christ Jesus, that by life, word, and example they may lead souls nearer to him whom here they serve.

Lauchlan MacLean Watt, 1867–1957

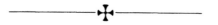

BLESSINGS AND

DOXOLOGIES

Amen! Blessing and glory and wisdom
and thanksgiving and honour and power
and might be to our God for ever and ever!

Amen.

Revelation 7.12

BLESSINGS

May the God of hope fill you with all joy and peace as you trust in   *1145*
him, so that you may overflow with hope by the power of the Holy
Spirit.

Romans 15.13 (New International Version)

May grace and eternal life be with all those who love our Lord Jesus   *1146*
Christ.

Ephesians 6.24 (Jerusalem Bible)

May the God of peace make you perfect and holy; and may you be   *1147*
kept safe and blameless, spirit, soul and body, for the coming of our
Lord Jesus Christ. God has called you and he will not fail you.

1 Thessalonians 5.23–4 (Jerusalem Bible)

May our Lord Jesus Christ and God our Father, who loved us and in   *1148*
his grace gave us unfailing courage and a firm hope, encourage you
and strengthen you to always do and say what is good.

2 Thessalonians 2.16–17 (Good News Bible)

May the Lord himself, who is our source of peace, give you peace at   *1149*
all times and in every way. The Lord be with you all.

2 Thessalonians 3.16 (Good News Bible)

Now the God of peace, that brought again from the dead our Lord   *1150*
Jesus Christ, that great shepherd of the sheep, through the blood of
the everlasting covenant, make you perfect in every good work to do
his will, working in you that which is well-pleasing in his sight; to
whom be glory for ever and ever.

Hebrews 13.20–21 (Authorized Version)

1151 God bless you.

James 2.16 (Good News Bible)

1152 The God of all grace, who has called you to his eternal glory in Christ
. . . support, strengthen and establish you. To him be the power for
ever and ever.

1 Peter 5.10–11 (New Revised Standard Version)

1153 May God the Father and Jesus Christ, the Father's Son, give us grace,
mercy, and peace; may they be ours in truth and love.

2 John 3 (Good News Bible)

1154 Peace be with you.

3 John 15

1155 Grace be to you and peace, from him who is, who was, and who is to
come, from the seven spirits before his throne, and from Jesus Christ,
the faithful witness, the first-born from the dead.

Revelation 1.4–5 (Revised English Bible)

1156
>Do thou, O God, bless unto me
>   Each thing mine eye doth see;
>Do thou, O God, bless unto me
>   Each sound that comes to me;
>Do thou, O God, bless unto me
>   Each savour that I smell;
>Do thou, O God, bless unto me
>   Each taste in mouth doth dwell;
>Each sound that goes unto my song,
>   Each ray that guides my way,
>Each thing that I pursue along,
>   Each lure that tempts to stray,
>The zeal that seeks my living soul,
>The Three that seek my heart and whole,
>   The zeal that seeks my living soul,
>   The Three that seek my heart and whole.

Source unknown (Early Scottish)

Deep peace of the running wave to you,   *1157*
Deep peace of the flowing air to you,
Deep peace of the quiet earth to you,
Deep peace of the shining stars to you,
Deep peace of the Son of Peace to you, for ever.

Source unknown (Early Scottish)

Go in peace: the wisdom of the Wonderful Counsellor guide you, the   *1158*
strength of the Mighty God defend you, the love of the Everlasting
Father enfold you, the peace of the Prince of Peace be upon you. And
the blessing of God Almighty, Father, Son, and Holy Spirit be upon
you all this night and for evermore.

Source unknown

Keep us in peace, O Christ our God, under the protection of your   *1159*
holy and venerable cross; save us from our enemies, visible and invisible, and count us worthy to glorify you with thanksgiving, with the
Father and the Holy Spirit, now and for ever, world without end.

Source unknown (Armenian Orthodox dismissal)

May God give us light to guide us, courage to support us, and love to   *1160*
unite us, now and evermore.

Source unknown

May the Lord bless you and protect you.   *1161*
May the Lord smile on you and show you his favour.
May the Lord befriend you and prosper you.

Source unknown

May the love of the Father enfold us, the wisdom of the Son enlighten   *1162*
us, the fire of the Spirit inflame us; and may the blessing of the triune
God rest upon us, and abide with us, now and evermore.

Source unknown

1163   May the road rise to meet you,
May the wind be always at your back,
May the sun shine warm upon your face,
May the rains fall softly upon your fields.
Until we meet again,
May God hold you in the hollow of his hand.

Source unknown (Celtic)

1164   Our Lord Jesus Christ be near thee to defend thee,
within thee to refresh thee,
around thee to preserve thee,
before thee to guide thee,
behind thee to justify thee,
above thee to bless thee,
who liveth and reigneth with the Father and the Holy Ghost,
    God for evermore.

Source unknown

1165   The benison of God be to thee,
The benison of Christ be to thee,
The benison of Spirit be to thee,
And to thy children,
To thee and to thy children.

The peace of God be to thee,
The peace of Christ be to thee,
The peace of the Spirit be to thee,
During all thy life,
All the days of thy life.

Source unknown (Early Scottish)

1166   The palmful of the God of Life
The palmful of the Christ of Love
The palmful of the Spirit of Peace
    Triune
    Of grace.

Source unknown (Early Scottish)

The circle of Jesus keep you from sorrow
The circle of Jesus today and tomorrow
The circle of Jesus your foes confound
The circle of Jesus your life surround

The Father on you his blessing bestow
The Son his love towards you flow
The Spirit his presence to you show
On you and all the folk you know
On you and all who around you go
The Threefold blessing may you know

The joy of this day be yours
The joy of this week be yours
The joy of this year be yours
The joy of the Father be yours
The joy of the Spirit be yours
The joy of the Son be yours
Joy for ever and ever be yours

The hands of the Father uphold you
The hands of the Saviour enfold you
The hands of the Spirit surround you
And the blessing of God Almighty
Father, Son and Holy Spirit
Uphold you evermore.

David Adam

May God the Father bless us; may Christ take care of us; the Holy
Ghost enlighten us all the days of our life. The Lord be our defender
and keeper of body and soul, both now and for ever, to the ages of
ages.

Æthelwold, c.908–984

1167

1168

1169
Thou knowest my heart, Lord,
that whatsoever thou hast given to thy servant,
I desire to spend wholly on your people
and to consume it all in their service.
Grant unto me then, O Lord my God,
that thine eyes may be opened upon them day and night.
Tenderly spread thy care to protect them.
Stretch forth thy holy right hand to bless them.
Pour into their hearts thy Holy Spirit
who may abide with them while they pray,
to refresh them with devotion and penitence,
to stimulate them with hope,
to make them humble with fear,
and to inflame them with charity.
May he, the kind Consoler,
succour them in temptation
and strengthen them in all the tribulations of this life.

Aelred, 1109–1167

1170
God be your comfort, your strength;
God be your hope and support;
God be your light and your way;
and the blessing of God, Creator, Redeemer and Giver of life,
remain with you now and for ever.

Anglican Church in Aotearoa, New Zealand and Polynesia.
A New Zealand Prayer Book

1171 May God the Father bless us;
May Christ take care of us;
The Holy Spirit enlighten us all the days of our life.
The Lord be our Defender and Keeper of body and soul, both now
and for ever, to the ages of ages.

The Book of Cerne, 10th century

The peace of God, which passeth all understanding, keep your hearts 1172
and minds in the knowledge and love of God, and of his Son Jesus
Christ our Lord: and the blessing of God Almighty, the Father, the
Son, and the Holy Ghost, be amongst you and remain with you
always.
Church of England. Book of Common Prayer

The grace of our Lord Jesus Christ, and the love of God, and 1173
the fellowship of the Holy Ghost, be with us all evermore.
Church of England. Book of Common Prayer (based on 2 Corinthians 13.13)

Go forth into the world in peace; be of good courage; hold fast that 1174
which is good; render to no man evil for evil; strengthen the faint-
hearted; support the weak; help the afflicted; honour all men; love
and serve the Lord, rejoicing in the power of the Holy Spirit.
   And the blessing of God Almighty, the Father, the Son, and the
Holy Ghost, be upon you, and remain with you for ever.
*Church of England. Book of Common Prayer (with the Additions and Deviations
Proposed in 1928)*

May the cross of the Son of God, which is mightier than all the hosts 1175
of Satan and more glorious than all the hosts of heaven, abide with
you in your going out and your coming in. By day and night, at morning and at evening, at all times and in all places may it protect and
defend you. From the wrath of evildoers, from the assaults of evil
spirits, from foes visible and invisible, from the snares of the devil,
from all passions that beguile the soul and body: may it guard, protect and deliver you.
Church of India, Pakistan, Burma and Ceylon. Book of Common Prayer

The everlasting Father bless us with his blessing everlasting. 1176
Thomas Cranmer, Prymer, 1559

The Lord bless us, and preserve us from all evil, and keep us in eternal 1177
life.
The Daily Office

1178
I lay me down with thee, O Jesus
And mayest thou be about my bed,
The oil of Christ be upon my soul,
The Apostles' Creed be above my head.
O Father who wrought me
O Son who bought me
O Spirit who sought me
Let me be thine.

Esther de Waal

1179 May the grace of the Lord Jesus sanctify us and keep us from all evil; may he drive far from us all hurtful things, and purify both our souls and bodies; may he bind us to himself by the bond of love, and may his peace abound in our hearts.

Gregorian Sacramentary, 6th century

1180 The almighty God bless us with his grace: Christ give us the joys of everlasting life; and unto the fellowship of the citizens above may the King of angels bring us all.

King's College, Cambridge

1181 Christ our God, who art thyself the fulfilment of the law and the prophets, and didst fulfil all the ordered purpose of the Father, always fill our hearts with joy and gladness, now and for ever, world without end.

Liturgy of John Chrysostom and Basil the Great

1182 The blessing of the Lord rest and remain upon all his people, in every
      land and of every tongue;
The Lord meet in mercy all who seek him;
The Lord comfort all who suffer and mourn;
The Lord hasten his coming, and give us his people peace by all
      means.

Handley C. G. Moule, 1841–1920

May the infinite and glorious Trinity, the Father, the Son, and the 1183
Holy Spirit, direct our life in good works, and after our journey
through this world, grant us eternal rest with the saints.

Mozarabic Liturgy, 7th century

In thy journeys to and fro 1184
  God direct thee;
In thy happiness and pleasure
  God bless thee;
In care, anxiety, or trouble
  God sustain thee;
In peril and in danger
  God protect thee.

Timothy Olufosoye

The Lord bless us, and preserve us from all evil, and bring us to ever- 1185
lasting life; and may the souls of the faithful, through the mercy of
God, rest in peace.

Sarum Primer

Go, and know that the Lord goes with you: let him lead you each day 1186
into the quiet place of your heart, where he will speak with you;
know that he loves you and watches over you – that he listens to you
in gentle understanding, that he is with you always, wherever you are
and however you may feel: and the blessing of God – Father, Son and
Holy Spirit – be yours for ever.

Still Waters, Deep Waters

May the love of the Lord Jesus draw us to himself; 1187
may the power of the Lord Jesus strengthen us in his service;
may the joy of the Lord Jesus fill our souls;
and may the blessing of God Almighty, the Father, the Son and the
Holy Ghost, be with you and abide with you always.

William Temple, 1881–1944

1188   Trust in God
      Let nothing disturb you,
      let nothing frighten you;
      All things pass:
      God never changes.
      Patience achieves
      all it strives for.
      He who has God
      finds he lacks nothing,
      God alone suffices.

Teresa of Avila, 1515–82 (her bookmark)

1189   Bless us, O God the Father, who hast created us,
      Bless us, O God the Son, who hast redeemed us,
      Bless us, O God the Holy Ghost, who sanctifieth us.
      O Blessed Trinity, keep us in body, soul, and spirit unto everlasting life.

Weimarisches Gesangbuch, 1873

DOXOLOGIES

1190   My soul magnifies the Lord, and my spirit rejoices in God my
      Saviour.

Luke 1.46–47 (New Revised Standard Version)

Oh, the depth of the riches of the wisdom and knowledge of God!   *1191*
 How unsearchable his judgments,
  and his paths beyond tracing out!
'Who has known the mind of the Lord?
 Or who has been his counsellor?'
'Who has ever given to God,
  that God should repay him?'
For from him and through him and to him are all things.
 To him be the glory for ever!

Romans 11:33–36 (New International Version)

To the King eternal, immortal, invisible, the only God, be honour and   *1192*
glory for ever and ever.

1 Timothy 1.17 (Revised English Bible)

Unto him who is the blessed and only potentate, the King of kings and   *1193*
Lord of lords; who only hath immortality, dwelling in the light which
no man can approach unto; whom no man hath seen, nor can see: be
honour and power everlasting.

1 Timothy 6.15–16 (Authorized Version, adapted)

Now unto him that is able to keep you from falling, and to present   *1194*
you faultless before the presence of his glory with exceeding joy, to
the only wise God our Saviour, be glory and majesty, dominion and
power, both now and ever.

Jude 24–25 (Authorized Version)

To him who loves us and has set us free from our sins with his blood,   *1195*
who has made us a royal house to serve as the priests of his God and
Father – to him be glory and dominion for ever!

Revelation 1.5, 6 (Revised English Bible)

Holy, holy, holy is the Lord God Almighty, who was, who is, and   *1196*
who is to come.

Revelation 4.8

1197 You are worthy, our Lord and God, to receive glory and honour and power, for you created all things, and by your will they were created and have their being.

Revelation 4.11 (New International Version)

1198 Blessing and glory and wisdom and thanksgiving and honour and power and might be to our God for ever and ever!

Revelation 7.12 (New Revised Standard Version)

1199 Glory be to the Father and to the Son and to the Holy Spirit. As it was in the beginning is now and ever shall be, world without end.

Source unknown

1200
  May none of God's wonderful works
   Keep silence, night or morning.
  Bright stars, high mountains, the depths of the seas,
   Sources of rushing rivers:
  may all these break into song as we sing
   to Father, Son and Holy Spirit.
  May all the angels in the heavens reply:
   Amen! Amen! Amen!
  Power, praise, honour, eternal glory
   to God, the only giver of grace.
   Amen! Amen! Amen!

Source unknown, 3rd century (Egypt)

1201 Glory be to thee, O Lord, glory to thee, O holy One, glory to thee, O King!

John Chrysostom, c.347–407

1202 Glory to God, Source of all being, Eternal Word and Holy Spirit: as it was in the beginning, is now, and shall be for ever.

The Daily Office

The God and Father of our Lord Jesus Christ open all our eyes, that *1203* we may see that blessed hope to which we are called; that we may altogether glorify the only true God and Jesus Christ, whom he hath sent down to us from heaven; to whom with the Father and the Holy Spirit be rendered all honour and glory to all eternity.

John Jewel, 1522–71

Blessing and honour and thanksgiving and praise, more than we can *1204* utter, more than we can conceive, be unto thee, O holy and glorious Trinity, Father, Son, and Holy Ghost, by all angels, by all men, all creatures, for ever and ever.

Thomas Ken, 1637–1711

To God the Father, who first loved us, and made us accepted in the *1205* beloved:

To God the Son, who loved us, and washed us from our sins in his own blood:

To God the Holy Ghost, who sheds the love of God abroad in our hearts:

Be all love and all glory, for all time and for eternity.

Thomas Ken, 1637–1711

And now to him who is able to keep us from falling, and lift us from *1206* the dark valley of despair to the bright mountain of hope, from the midnight of desperation to the daybreak of joy; to him be power and authority, for ever and ever.

Martin Luther King (Blessing spoken to his congregation in Montgomery as he left them to devote all his time to political action)

Glory be to thee, O God, the Father, the Maker of the world: *1207*
Glory be to thee, O God, the Son, the Redeemer of mankind:
Glory to be thee, O God, the Holy Ghost, the Sanctifier of thy people.

Brooke Foss Westcott, 1825–1901

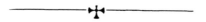

INDEXES

Search, and you will find.

Matthew 7.7

INDEX OF AUTHORS
AND SOURCES

INDEX OF SUBJECTS

ACKNOWLEDGEMENTS

The publishers are grateful to the following authors and publishers for permission to reproduce copyright material.

Abingdon Press: From *Sister Images* by Mary Zimmer. Copyright © 1993 by Abingdon Press. Used by permission.
American Bible Society: Scriptures quoted from the *Good News Bible* published by The Bible Societies/HarperCollins Publishers Ltd UK © American Bible Society, 1966, 1971, 1976, 1992.
Lesley Anderson.
Andrews & McMeel: *Prayers of Life* by Michel Quoist.
The Anglican Church in Aotearoa, New Zealand and Polynesia: This copyright material is taken from *A New Zealand Prayer Book – He Karakia Mihinare o Aotearoa* (1989) and is used with permission.
The Anglican Church of Canada: Prayers from the *Alternative Service Book*.
Arthur James: *Seven Whole Days* by Howard Booth; *A Day at a Time* by Denis Duncan; *The Pain that Heals* by Martin Israel; *Healing Prayer* by William Portsmouth.
Augsburg Fortress Publishers: Reprinted from *Prayers for Impossible Days* by Paul Geres, copyright © 1976 Fortress Press. Used by permission of Augsburg Fortress.
Ave Maria Press: Excerpt from *Praying Our Goodbyes* by Joyce Rupp. Copyright © 1988 by Ave Maria Press, Notre Dame, IN 46556. All rights reserved. Used with permission of the publisher.
Halcyon Backhouse.
BBC Worldwide: Reproduced from *New Every Morning* with the permission of BBC Worldwide Limited.
Jan Berry.
Bloodaxe Books: Reprinted by permission of Bloodaxe Books Ltd from: *Mass for Hard Times* by R. S. Thomas (Bloodaxe Books, 1992).
Michael Botting.
Francis Brienen.
Anna Briggs.
Ian Bunting.
Burns & Oates: *Elected Silence* by Thomas Merton; *Prayers for Meditation* by Karl Rahner (trans. R. Brennan).
Cairns Publications: *By Stony Paths*, *Prayer at Night*, and *Through Desert Places* by Jim Cotter; *Desert Flowers* by Mary Robins.
Cambridge University Press: Extracts from

The Book of Common Prayer, the rights in which are vested in the Crown, are reproduced by permission of the Crown's Patentee, Cambridge University Press. The text of the Authorized Version of the Bible is the property of the Crown in perpetuity.
Cassell plc: *The Daily Office*; *Prayers for Today* by Norman Goodacre; *The Prayer Manual* by F. B. Macnutt; *Songs and Prayers from Taizé*; *The Promise of His Glory*.
Catholic Supplies (NZ) Ltd: *Aotearoa Psalms* by Joy Cowley.
Christian Aid: Prayers from *Companions of God* by Janet Morley; prayers from *Bread of Tomorrow* edited by Janet Morley (Christian Aid/SPCK); *Thank God for Life before Death* by Barbara Vellacott.
Christian Conference of Asia: Prayer from *Intercessions for Asia Sunday, 3 June 1984*.
Church of England Central Board of Finance: *Alternative Service Book, 1980* is copyright © The Central Board of Finance of the Church of England. Extracts are reproduced with the permission of the copyright owner. Material adapted from the Book of Common Prayer, the rights in which are vested in the Crown in the United Kingdom, is included by permission of the Crown's patentee, Cambridge University Press.
Church Hymnal Corporation: *The Book of Common Prayer*.
Church of Ireland: Prayer nos 241, 305, 608, 934 reproduced with permission from the Church of Ireland *Book of Common Prayer*, copyright © 1960, The General Synod of the Church of Ireland, published by APCK/Oxford University Press.
Church of Scotland: Prayers from the *Book of Common Order*.
Donald Coggan.
Collins & Collins: *A Private House of Prayer* by Leslie D Weatherhead.
Collins Dove: *Woman Wisdom: A Feminist Lectionary and Psalter: Women of the Hebrew Scriptures: Part One* by Miriam Therese Winter.
Church of the Province of Southern Africa Provincial Trustees: Prayers from *A Book of Common Prayer*.
Crossroad Publishing Co.: *Prayers of our Hearts: In Word and Action* by Vienna Cobb

Anderson. Copyright © by Vienna Cobb Anderson. Reprinted by permission of The Crossroad Publishing Co., New York; *Birthings and Blessings: Liberating Worship Services for the Inclusive Church* by Rosemary Catalano Mitchell and Gail Anderson Ricciuti. Copyright © 1991 by Rosemary Catalano Mitchell and Gail Anderson Ricciuti. Reprinted by permission of The Crossroad Publishing Co., New York; *Blessings II: More Liberating Worship Services for the Inclusive Church* by Rosemary Catalano Mitchell and Gail Anderson Ricciuti. Copyright © 1993 by Rosemary Catalano Mitchell and Gail Anderson Ricciuti. Reprinted by permission of The Crossroad Publishing Co., New York; *More than Words: Prayer and Ritual for Inclusive Communities* by Janet Schaffran and Pat Kozak. First edition copyright © 1986 by Pat Kozak, CSJ and Janet Schaffran, CDP; second revised edition copyright © 1986 by Pat Kozak, CSJ and Janet Schaffran, CDP. Reprinted by permission of The Crossroad Publishing Co., New York; *Woman Wisdom: A Feminist Lectionary and Psalter: Women of the Hebrew Scriptures: Part One* by Miriam Therese Winter. Copyright © 1991 by Medical Mission Sisters. Reprinted by permission of The Crossroad Publishing Co., New York.
Curtis Brown: Prayers by Thomas Merton.
Darton, Longman & Todd Ltd: From *The Jerusalem Bible* © 1966 by Darton, Longman & Todd Ltd and Doubleday and Co. Inc.; *The Catholic Prayer Book* by Anthony Bullen published by Darton, Longman and Todd Ltd (copyright © 1970) and used by permission of the publishers; *A Thousand Reasons for Living* by Helder Camara published by Darton, Longman and Todd Ltd (copyright © 1981) and used by permission of the publishers; *Good Friday People* by Sheila Cassidy published by Darton, Longman and Todd Ltd (copyright © 1991) and used by permission of the publishers; *Prayers for Pilgrims* by John Johansen-Berg published by Darton, Longman and Todd Ltd (copyright © 1993) and used by permission of the publishers; *Aids: Sharing the Pain* by Bill Kirkpatrick published by Darton, Longman and Todd Ltd (copyright © 1988) and used by permission of the publishers; *The Fire of Your Life: A Solitude Shared* by Maggie Ross published by Darton, Longman and Todd Ltd (copyright © 1992) and used by permission of the publishers; *Becoming What I Am* by Harry Williams published by Darton, Longman and Todd Ltd (copyright © 1991) and used by permission of the publishers.
Hugh Dickinson.
Dohnavur Fellowship: Prayers by Amy Carmichael.
Doubleday Books: *Seeds of Hope* by Henri Nouwen.
Timothy Dudley-Smith.
Eagle Books: *Prayers for Healing* by John Gunstone.
Robert Eames.

Epworth Press: *Prayers of the Way* by John Johansen-Berg.
Faber & Faber Ltd: *The Collected Poems 1909–1962* by T. S. Eliot; *The Complete Poems* by Randall Jarrell.
Farrar, Straus & Giroux Inc: *The Complete Poems* by Randall Jarrell.
Friends of Christ Church Moss Side: *Some Daily Prayers for Church of England People.*
Friendship Press: From *The Cross is Lifted* by Chandran Devanesan. Copyright 1954 by Friendship Press, Inc. Used by permission.
Monica Furlong.
Gill & Macmillan: The poem *Before you, Lord* from Michel Quoist's *Prayers of Life* is reproduced with the permission of the publishers, Gill & Macmillan, Dublin.
Harcourt Brace & Co: Prayer by T. S. Eliot in *Collected Poems 1909–1962.*
Harold Shaw Publishers: Reprinted from the *Weather of the Heart,* by Madeleine L'Engle, © 1978 by Crosswicks. Used by permission of Harold Shaw Publishers, Wheaton, IL.
Harper and Row: *Prayers for Young People* by William Barclay.
HarperCollins Publishers Ltd (New York): *The Fire of Your Life: A Solitude Shared* by Maggie Ross.
HarperCollins Publishers Ltd (UK): *A Plain Man's Book of Prayers* by William Barclay; *Collected Poems* by C. S. Lewis; *Heaven on Earth* by Brother Ramon; *A Woman's Book of Prayers* by Rita Snowden; *A World Made Whole* by Esther de Waal.
Richard Harries.
William Heinemann Ltd: *Are You Running with me, Jesus?* by Malcolm Boyd.
Highland Books: *Prayers for Healing* by John Gunstone.
Hodder Headline plc: *Contemporary Parish Prayers* by Frank Colquhoun; prayer by Sue Ryder and Leonard Cheshire in *Blessings* by Mary Craig; *Diary of Prayer* by Elizabeth Goudge; *God of Our Fathers* by Marjorie Holmes; *A Healing House of Prayer* by Morris Maddocks; *Your Confirmation* by John R. W. Stott.
Holt, Rinehart and Winston Inc.: *Are You Running With Me, Jesus?* by Malcolm Boyd.
Joyce Huggett.
Basil Hume.
International Bible Society: Reprinted from the *New International Version,* copyright © 1973, 1978, 1984 by the International Bible Society. Published by Hodder & Stoughton.
James Clarke / Lutterworth Press: *Prayers at Breakfast* by Beryl Bye.
Joint Board of Christian Education: *Echoes of Our Journey* by Dorothy McCrae-McMahon.
Kevin Mayhew: © 1994 Kevin Mayhew Ltd. Reproduced by permission from *Fasts and Festivals* by Michael Forster, Licence number 594072.
Kingsway Publications Ltd: *Each New Day* by Corrie ten Boom; *Prayers for Today's Church* edited by Dick Williams.

ACKNOWLEDGEMENTS

Alfred A. Knopf Inc: From *Markings* by Dag
Hammarskjold, trans. W. H. Auden and Leif
Sjoberg. Translation copyright © 1964 by
Alfred A. Knopf Inc. and Faber & Faber Ltd.
Reprinted by permission of Alfred A. Knopf
Inc.
Christopher Lamb.
Lion Publishing plc: Prayers by Mary Batchelor
reprinted from *The Lion Prayer Collection*
edited by Mary Batchelor. Reproduced with
permission by Lion Publishing Plc.
Liveright Publishing Corp.: *Complete Poems*
by E. E. Cummings (ed. G. J. Firmage).
Trevor Lloyd.
Peter Lockwood: Prayer first published in
Healing and Wholeness and is reproduced with
their permission.
LuraMedia Inc.: Excerpted from the book,
*Wrestling the Light: Ache and Awe in the
Human-Divine Struggle* by Ted Loder.
Copyright © 1991 by LuraMedia. Reprinted
by permission of LuraMedia, Inc., San Diego,
CA.
Lutterworth Press: *Lord of Time* by Frank
Topping.
McCrimmon Publishing: *It's Me O Lord* and
The One Who Listens by Michael Hollings and
Etta Gullick.
James MacGibbon: Reprinted from *The
Collected Poems of Stevie Smith* (Penguin 20th
Century Classics). Reproduced by permission
of James MacGibbon.
Kate McIlhagga.
Malling Abbey: Prayer by Elizabeth Bassett in
Interpreted by Love (DLT).
Methodist Publishing House: Prayers from the
Book of Offices. Used by kind permission of
the Methodist Publishing House.
Jean Mortimer: *Exceeding our Limits* (URC
1991).
The Mothers' Union: *Mothers' Union Prayer
Book; Mothers' Union Service Book*; prayer by
Eunice Davies in *Women at Prayer* edited by R.
Stowe; prayer by Joy Edwards in *Women at
Prayer* edited by R. Stowe.
**The National Council of the Churches of
Christ:** Reprinted from *The New Revised
Standard Version of the Bible* © 1989.
New Directions Publisher: Reprinted from *The
Collected Poems of Stevie Smith* (Penguin 20th
Century Classics).
W. W. Norton: 'i thank You God for most this
amazing' is reprinted from *Complete Poems
1904–1962*, by E. E. Cummings, edited by
George J. Firmage by permission of W. W.
Norton & Company Ltd. Copyright © 1950,
1978, 1979, 1991 by the Trustees for the E. E.
Cummings Trust and George J. Firmage.
Peter Nott.
Janet Orchard.
Stephen Orchard.
Oxford University Press (UK): Reprinted from
The Revised English Bible © 1989 Oxford and
Cambridge University Presses; reprinted from
A Diary of Prayer by John Baillie (1936) by
permission of Oxford University Press;

reprinted from *Prayer for People in Hospital* by
Neville Smith (1994) by permission of Oxford
University Press.
Oxford University Press (USA): Reprinted
from *The Pastor's Prayerbook* by R. N.
Rodenmayer (1960) by permission of Oxford
University Press.
Paulist Press: Reprinted from *A Counselor's
Prayer Book* by Kathleen Fischer & Thomas
Hart © 1994 by Kathleen Fischer & Thomas
Hart. Used by permission of Paulist Press;
reprinted from *Your Word is Near* by Huub
Oosterhuis © 1968 by The Missionary Society
of St. Paul the Apostle in the State of New
York. Used by permission of Paulist Press.
Penguin Books Ltd: *The Prayers and
Meditations of St Anselm* (pp 232, 239–240,
243, 244, 266) translated and edited by Sister
Benedicta Ward, SLG (Penguin Classics,
1973). Copyright © Benedicta Ward, 1973.
Reproduced by permission of Penguin Books
Ltd.
Michael Perham.
Robert Runcie.
St Andrew Press: *Worship Now* edited by
Christohper Idle.
Saint George's Church Oakdale: Prayer by
Michael Perham.
Michael Saward.
SCM Press: *Letters and Papers from Prison* by
Dietrich Bonhoeffer (SCM Press 1971); *A Kind
of Praying* by Rex Chapman (SCM Press
1970); *Contemporary Prayers* edited by Caryl
Micklem (SCM Press 1993); *Contemporary
Prayers for Church and School* edited by Caryl
Micklem (SCM Press 1975); *Contemporary
Prayers for Public Worship* edited by Caryl
Micklem (SCM Press 1967).
Sheed & Ward: *A Calendar of Prayer* by
Michel Quoist.
David Silk.
Simon & Schuster: *Letters and Papers from
Prison* by Dietrich Bonhoeffer.
SLG Press: *The Face of Love* by Gilbert Shaw.
Stephen Smalley.
SPCK: *Border Lands: The Best of David Adam*
by David Adam; *Jerusalem Prayers for the
World Today* by George Appleton; *One Man's
Prayers* by George Appleton; *Paths of the
Heart: Prayers of Medieval Christians* edited
by John Blakesley; *Hildegard of Bingen: An
Anthology* edited by Fiona Bowie & Oliver
Davies; *Praying with Saint Francis* translated
by R. J. Armstrong & Ignatius C. Brady;
Learning of God by Amy Carmichael; *Praying
with Saint Augustine* translated by Paula
Clifford; *Praying with Saint Teresa* translated
by Paula Clifford; *Family Prayers* by Frank
Colquhoun; *My God and King: Prayers of
Christian Devotion* by Frank Colquhoun;
Prayers for Everyone by Frank Colquhoun;
Prayers for Today by Frank Colquhoun;
*Between Two Eternities: A Helen Waddell
Anthology* edited by Dame Felicitas Corrigan
OSB reproduced by permission of Mary M.
Martin; *A Little Book of Prayers* by Lilian

Cox; *Celtic Christian Spirituality* by Oliver Davies; *Just as I am: Personal Prayers for Every Day* by Ruth Etchells; *Love Burning Deep* by Kathy Galloway; *Talking to the Bones* by Kathy Galloway; *Seven for a Secret that's Never Been Told* by Tracy Hansen; *The One Genius: Readings through the Year with Austin Farrer* edited by Richard Harries; *Praying with the New Testament* edited by Philip Law; *Hearts Aflame: The Prayers of Susanna, John & Charles Wesley* edited by Michael McMullen; *My God, My Glory* by Eric Milner-White; *A Procession of Passion Prayers* by Eric Milner-White; *All Desires Known* by Janet Morley; *Bread of Tomorrow: Praying with the World's Poor* edited by Janet Morley; *A Manual of Eastern Orthodox Prayers* edited by Metropolitan Philaret of Moscow; *A St Francis Prayer Book* by M. L. Playfoot; *God in our Midst: Prayers and Devotions from the Celtic Tradition* by Martin Reith; *Prayers for Peace* edited by Robert Runcie and Basil Hume; *Women Included* by the St Hilda Community; *Life After Life: Readings & Prayers to Comfort the Bereaved* by Frazer Smith; *In the Silence of the Heart* by Mother Teresa, edited by Kathryn Spink.
John Shelby Spong.
David Stancliffe.
Siân Swain Taylor.
Lesley Taylor.
Bernard Thorogood.

United Reformed Church: Prayers by Francis Brienen and Bernard Thorogood in *A Restless Hope*; prayers by Kate McIlhagga in *Encompassing Presence*; prayers by Jean Mortimer in *Exceeding our Limits*; prayers by Stephen Orchard in *All the Glorious Names*.
United Society for the Propagation of the Gospel: *Prayer is My Life: A Study Guide for Christian Groups* by Margaret Dewey; prayer by John Kingsnorth in *A Still Place of Light: A Book of Prayers for Sharing in God's Mission Today* compiled by Robin Green and edited by Wendy S Robins; prayers by John Kingsnorth in *Prayers for Mission: For Public Use* edited by Canon John Kingsnorth.
Michael Vasey.
Terry Waite.
Angela West.
Westminster John Knox Press: From *Justice and Mercy* by Reinhold Niebuhr edited by Ursula Niebuhr. © 1974 Ursula Niebuhr. Used by permission of Westminster John Knox Press.
Ian White Thomson.
Lala Winkley.
Wild Goose Publications: Prayers by John Bell; prayer by George F. Macleod (1895–1991) from *The Whole Earth Shall Cry Glory* (Wild Goose Publications, 1985) copyright Iona Community, Glasgow G51 3UU, Scotland.
Maurice Wood.
World Council of Churches: Prayers from *Jesus Christ the Life of the World: A Worship Book*.

Every effort has been made to trace and acknowledge copyright holders of all the prayers included in this anthology. We apologize for any errors or omissions that may remain, and would ask those concerned to contact the publishers, who will ensure that full acknowledgement is made in the future.